THE
ROSICRU
COUNTERCL_

"Ronnie Pontiac's *The Rosicrucian Counterculture* brings to 21st-century life the most famous secret society that never existed. Who were the Rosicrucians? Not even René Descartes could find out. But when the mysterious Rosicrucian Manifestos turned up in a sleepy German town shortly after the great Hermes Trismegistus lost his street cred, an esoteric treasure hunt began with participants who are still at work today. Join in: you may discover that you were a Rosicrucian and didn't know it."

GARY LACHMAN, AUTHOR OF *TOUCHED BY THE PRESENCE*,
THE RETURN OF HOLY RUSSIA, AND *MAURICE NICOLL*

"Ronnie Pontiac vividly places the Rosicrucian phenomenon in the rich historical tapestry from which it emerged and traces its multiple reverberations up to modern times. The book covers a broad panorama with a lively and engaging style."

CHRISTOPHER MCINTOSH, AUTHOR OF *OCCULT RUSSIA*,
OCCULT GERMANY, AND *THE CALL OF THE OLD GODS*

"Ronnie Pontiac's history of the Rosicrucian movement is learned, engaging, and remarkably breezy reading. He has done an enormous service in sifting what can be known about the Rosicrucians from speculation and fancy."

RICHARD SMOLEY, AUTHOR OF *A THEOLOGY OF LOVE*
AND *FORBIDDEN FAITH*

"Ronnie Pontiac's remarkable talent for researching hidden history and esoteric secrets, combined with his passion for storytelling, really shines through in this masterwork! He takes us on a captivating journey through time, brilliantly demonstrating how Rosicrucian countercultural ideals have shaped civilizations for centuries and continue to influence contemporary culture today. This is a must-read that revolutionizes our understanding of our modern world by illuminating the invisible threads that connect our past and present."

"This work is simply dazzling. It follows a single Rosicrucian thread to unfold a vast historical tapestry of people and events made real through a prose that sings with life. Ronnie Pontiac describes himself as a storyteller, and it is with this special gift that he invites the reader to step from the past into the present, bearing the blessings of the phoenix: counterculture itself."

"Ronnie Pontiac's *The Rosicrucian Counterculture* traces the deep and often overlooked roots of Rosicrucianism, following its flowering within the heart of the European intellectual tradition in the 16th and 17th centuries and its eventual diffusion across the Atlantic into early American culture. In doing so, he reveals how this esoteric current helped shape the often-hidden spiritual, artistic, and philosophical undercurrents that continue to resonate today. With both scholarly rigor and evocative storytelling, Pontiac illuminates the enduring legacy of a visionary tradition that is too often overlooked within European culture and its transatlantic inheritors."

THE ROSICRUCIAN COUNTERCULTURE

The Origins
and Influence of
the Invisible Society

RONNIE PONTIAC

INNER TRADITIONS
ROCHESTER, VERMONT

Inner Traditions
One Park Street
Rochester, Vermont 05767
www.InnerTraditions.com

Cataloging-in-Publication Data for this title is available from the Library of Congress

ISBN 979-8-88850-035-4 (print)
ISBN 979-8-88850-036-1 (ebook)

Printed and bound in the United States by Lake Book Manufacturing, LLC

10 9 8 7 6 5 4 3 2 1

Text design by Priscilla Harris Baker and layout by Alfonso Reyes G.
This book was typeset in Garamond Premier Pro with Adobe Jensen Pro, Adobe Wood Type Ornaments, The Bartender, and Optima used as display typefaces

To send correspondence to the author of this book, mail a first-class letter to the author c/o Inner Traditions, One Park Street, Rochester, VT 05767, and we will forward the communication.

Scan the QR code and save 25% at InnerTraditions.com. Browse over 2,000 titles on spirituality, the occult, ancient mysteries, new science, holistic health, and natural medicine.

This book is dedicated to Tamra.

*"Blessed Aurora will from now on begin to appear
(after the passing away of the dark
Night of Saturn)—"*

FAMA FRATERNITATIS

*Thank you Manly Palmer Hall, Tod Davies,
Sasha Chaitow, Ian H. Gladwin, Sam Robinson,
Juan Ayala, Kimberly Cooper Nichols,
and Newtopia Magazine.*

Contents

What Is a Rosicrucian?

*A scattered dynasty of solitary men has changed the face of
the world. Their task continues.*

JORGE LUIS BORGES

The many years of research that led to this book began when Manly
Palmer Hall generously gave me his own copy of A. E. Waite's
The Brotherhood of the Rosy Cross. Reading it while working at the
Philosophical Research Society meant I had access to artifacts of the history Waite wrote about. After I read his chapters on the Rosicrucian manifestos, in the PRS library vault I held in my hands the earliest editions.
When Waite wrote about the alchemist Bacstrom, whose ocean voyages
spanned the globe from Iceland to South Africa, I read Bacstrom's handwritten journals, and studied his own copy of his Rosicrucian diploma.
When Waite wrote about Robert Fludd, I gazed at the famous drawing
of Fludd's monochord in a book by him published during his lifetime. I
was moved by the courage and creativity of these independent thinkers.

I'm not a PhD, I'm a storyteller. The stories in this book have been
gathered from scholarly sources spanning the centuries, but especially from
academic works from the last twenty years because they have revised our
understanding of the Rosicrucian counterculture. After the publication of
the Rosicrucian manifestos in the early seventeenth century, Europe trem-
bled with anticipation but also fear at the possibility of a hermetic Holy

1

Roman emperor and a universal reformation. A new mythology was born then that continues to influence Western culture, showing up in unexpected places even in the twentieth and twenty-first centuries.

In his classic shtick "Father Flotski's Triumph" (1960), comedian Lenny Bruce has Dutch, his convict character, dismiss Flotski by accusing him of trying "to give me all that Rosicrucian jazz and all that other non-scheduled theologies there."

The hit comedy show *Second City Television* (SCTV) in 1985 aired an episode of the old black-and-white western series *The Cisco Kid*. The comedians dubbed their own voices over the original dialogue. In one scene Cisco and his sidekick Pancho earnestly debated Rosicrucian ideas about the individuality of the soul.

In 2015, James Ellis wrote an article called "Shadows in the Shadows: The Rosicrucians, a Fake Secret Society, Had a Real Impact on the World" for the *Newsweek* special edition he curated: "Secret Societies: Infiltrating the Inner Circle" (Ellis 2015).

In her book *Provocations: Collected Essays on Art, Feminism, Politics, Sex, and Education,* Camille Paglia offered this definition: "The Rosicrucians, called Illuminati, claimed their esoteric order was founded in ancient Egypt and was brought to Europe by knightly crusaders; however, it probably dates from the seventeenth century. Its cabalistic and Hermetic imagery includes the Rose" (Paglia 2019, 450).

What does the rose cross symbolize? A question with many answers. Some scholars have written that the rosy color is the blood of Christ. Others that Jesus is the Rose of Sharon. Some have pointed out that the Rose of Sharon is the congregation, together and individually, tended by the Lord like roses in a garden. Another perspective tells us that the alchemists wrote about collecting a mysterious substance they used the Latin word *ros* (dew) to describe. Some called it celestial sweat, and the first matter, a distillation of cosmic energy. The purifying and healing power of the first matter was said to be the key to the philosopher's stone. Others say it is the symbol of the purity every alchemist must attain before achieving the Great Work. The New Age interpretation equated the rose on the cross with the Hindu symbol of the jewel in the lotus. The rose and the jewel represent the soul; the cross and the lotus represent the body. It has been suggested more recently that the *ros*-gathering Rosicrucians were practicing what might be called a tantric sexual discipline.

Rosicrucian is one of the most romanticized proper nouns in the esoteric world. A sometimes specifically defined creature but also a mirror in which many different reactions have been revealed—from the widespread panic of the French when they found posters put up overnight declaring the arrival of the Rosicrucians (probably a prank) to the admiration of English and colonial intellectuals, such as the celestial intelligencers of the seventeenth century, among whom the Rosicrucian ideal was synonymous with free medicine, protection of the oppressed, alchemy, early science, and a dedication to the betterment of society. Inspired by the Rosicrucians, people here and there lived exceptional lives; for example, John Winthrop the Younger, the alchemist who was a founding father of Connecticut.

The Rosicrucians have been described as Protestant Jesuits, but also the devil's Jesuits, and even a trick of the Jesuits. They've also been revered as the ultimate example of Christian spiritual evolution. They have been blamed for throwing fuel on the fires that started the bloody Thirty Years' War between Protestants and Catholics. That war, along with the plague and starvation it caused, killed roughly one out of ten Europeans. Some areas lost half their population. But what does any of that have to do with the relatively more recent public Rosicrucian groups that, alongside their esoteric studies, have practiced good citizenship through public service?

Our subject is complex. We'll explore many lives and events before we are able to gain some understanding of context. Our protagonists will appear, disappear, and appear again, each time revealing more about themselves and history. We will move forward and backward in time, tracing the intricate patterns of many tributaries as though we were viewing them all from above and glancing where our curiosity leads us.

Inspired by recent research, the result of a significant evolution in esoteric studies in academia, the intent of this book is to provide historical context for the emergence of the Rosicrucians. Where did it happen? Who is most likely to have been behind it? What events inspired them to take such a radical stance? We will let them define themselves, and we will see how others defined them. More questions will be raised than answered.

This book is the third of a trilogy on counterculture. The first, *American Metaphysical Religion: Esoteric and Mystical Traditions of the New World*, presented a neglected lineage of spiritual pioneers, some fraudulent, some sincere, but frequently a combination of both—an important and constant influence on four hundred years of American history.

The second in the counterculture trilogy, *The Magic of the Orphic Hymns: A New Translation for the Modern Mystic*, coauthored with Tamra Lucid, examines a uniquely important source for not only esoteric but also literary, musical, and artistic countercultures throughout Western history, including connections with Rosicrucianism.

This, the third book in the series, explores the lives of three of the most influential people of their time: Holy Roman emperor, art collector, and occultist Rudolf II (1552–1612) and the often-romanticized royal couple Frederick V (1596–1632) , Elector Palatine, and his wife, Elizabeth Stuart (1596–1662), briefly the king and queen of Bohemia. She was also known as the Queen of Hearts. Many books have been written about her, but almost every author copied sources that were little more than propaganda, not to mention the sins of omission of generations of scholars who considered the letters of women unworthy of study or publication.

Beginning the research that became this book, I expected to share a romance between two esotericists who happened to be monarchs. I imagined them fostering the Rosicrucian movement. Twenty years of scholarship by Nadine Akkerman provides a richly detailed new vision of Elizabeth that contradicts the romantic ideal exemplified in a wonderful but sometimes inaccurate book by Frances Yates, *The Rosicrucian Enlightenment*.

Yates argued that it's unlikely that either Father CRC (Christian Rosy Cross) or his secret Rosicrucian society ever existed. Instead, the movement was born from a loose-knit group of esotericists who were also social critics. But Yates sometimes proposed connections and organizations where they have not been found. A colleague of hers said she squared every circle. Yates did not have the benefit of the letters and other papers associated with Elizabeth that we now have thanks to the scholarship of Dr. Akkerman.

Some of the visions of the Rosicrucians have been realized. For example, the Invisible College—their ideal school that could be anywhere at any time without being physically present—has been achieved somewhat online. When all the knowledge in the world is online, we will have the realization of the Rosicrucian book *M*, which holds the keys of the world; M for *mundi*, Latin for "of the universe." *The Book of the Universe* was found with other secret holy books in the vault where the founder of Rosicrucianism's body was supposed to have been discovered perfectly preserved. Every aspect of the vault including its measurements symbolized cosmic harmony and truth.

The vault holds another secret, one that points to Arabic influence on the author of the *Fama* by way of a book the Holy Roman Emperor Rudolf II was also familiar with, as we shall see. Referring to an Islamic text that describes a vault, Christopher McIntosh wrote: "That is strikingly similar to the description of the vault in the *Fama*. The passage comes from a book called *The Aim of the Sage*, which was circulated among a Sufi sect called the Pure Brethren, who would have been active around the time that Christian Rosenkreutz was supposed to have made his journey to the Middle East. *The Aim of the Sage* was translated into Latin and printed as a book entitled *Picatrix*, which Andreae is very likely to have known about and may even have been influenced by when he wrote the *Fama*" (White 1999, 253).

The vault of Father CRC is itself a dreamlike symbol of counterculture. The vault, esoterically informed in every detail, exists underground where it preserves the knowledge lost by the worldly. Within this cultural cocoon masters of the mystical and of the arts incubate until called to change an era.

We will meet Rudolf II, ever eager to avoid imperial bureaucracy, disappearing into his castle to admire art, practice early astronomy and other esoteric pursuits, and enjoy numerous romantic dalliances. His favorite pet was a lion, which roamed freely in his castle, often napping at Rudolf's feet. Sometimes Rudolf had to buy the silence of visitors the lion nipped. Rudolf collected masterpieces by Hieronymus Bosch, Titian, Leonardo da Vinci, Albrecht Dürer, Antonio da Correggio, Hans Holbein, and Paolo Veronese. He also had a collection of famous alchemists and astronomers for whom he provided laboratories, the materials needed to make gold, and some of the first telescopes ever assembled. Whenever threatened by what he considered the psychic attacks of his enemies, especially those in the Roman Catholic Church, Rudolf would sip from what he believed was the Holy Grail. The Holy Roman Empire was scandalized when the news got out that he had refused the last rites.

We will also meet Frederick and Elizabeth, who lived a tragic yet romantic love. Her motto was "I esteem only honor." Their idealism was their downfall, and it ultimately led to the destruction of the people and the places they loved. The support they expected to get from her English and his German relatives evaporated in a series of political fiascos that left them abandoned to the horrors of war. As we will see, they survived, and among their many children can be found Princess Elisabeth, a brilliant but lonely daughter. Her exchange of letters with Descartes helped him develop his philosophy. He famously wrote "I think therefore I am." Frederick and Elizabeth's son, the dashing Prince Rupert, was a prince and a pirate who helped establish the earliest English colony in North America.

We will meet many unforgettable characters: some well known, like John Dee, others who fell into obscurity, and still others whose bravery and desire to acquire and share knowledge led to a revolution. While the Rosicrucians have been characterized for centuries as what modern occultists call ascended masters, from the vantage provided by modern scholarship, we see among the likely originators of the Order of the Rosy Cross some who could be described as cultural provocateurs and college pranksters.

Societies that seek to dominate continents, to impose a dreary existence of censorship and conformity, have reappeared throughout history. By definition, countercultures are reactions against these regimes that smother the joy and beauty of life with deflection and repression. But we should keep in mind, as Wouter Hanegraaff notes in his article "Beyond the Yates Paradigm" (2001, 8): "'counterculturalism' as understood here and throughout this article is not linked to any specific political orientation. While the counterculture of the 1960s with its antibourgeois sentiments tended to be left wing, Eranos participants tended to be politically conservative." We must be all the more careful when considering political affiliations of seventeenth-century Europe. It can be too easy to project our modern perspectives and preferences onto people who lived in very different times.

The myths countercultures create are more inspiring and admirable than the human details of most movements that are borne against the grain. Idealized heroes replace the messy facts of human lives. Countercultures can be suppressed, co-opted, infiltrated, and degraded, but the daybreak flood of light they represent communicates itself inevitably to those who long for more from life. For Western culture, the dawn of Rosicrucianism, as brief and ill-fated a golden age as it was, changed the world in ways that we are only beginning to understand.

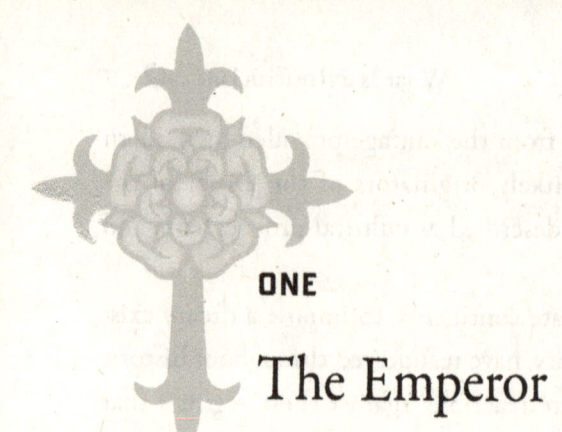

ONE

The Emperor of All Bohemians

In English, calling someone bohemian can be a way of dismissing them, accusing them of being not just artistic but also odd and out of the ordinary and probably devoted to underground arts—tinkering with intoxicants and deviant carnal and spiritual pursuits. In some circles the word has a cool cachet, but others consider it an offensive caricature and an appropriated racial slur. Many don't know that Bohemia was a country in Central Europe. How did the name of the people of what we now call the Czech Republic become a synonym for counterculture?

Today's progressives and conservatives alike share a fear of a future surveillance state: a society where nothing is private, where everything happening everywhere is known by authorities, who govern all aspects of life. It's a world depicted in Aldous Huxley's novel *Brave New World* and in another seminal work, *1984* by George Orwell. Perhaps this fear of the future is based on a vaguely remembered fear of the past. The surveillance state existed in the Dark Ages thanks to the confessional. The Catholic sacrament of confession allowed Roman Catholic authorities access to information from the lowest to the highest levels of society. The pope didn't need the internet or cameras; he had the confessions of all Catholics in all Europe. Whoever refused to confess gambled with an eternity in hell.

Then the Renaissance broke like dawn over the Dark Ages, bringing with it renewed interest in the pagan wisdom of Plato, Hermes

Trismegistus, Plotinus, and the mysteries of Orpheus, all made available by the philosopher Marsilio Ficino and his circle of Platonists in Florence, Italy. Religious freedom seemed possible again. Why must we turn to priests for forgiveness and a relationship with the divine, Ficino seemed to ask, when the pagan mysteries promised a direct revelation?

In 1517, Martin Luther reduced the individualizing ideals of the Renaissance to the ninety-five theses he nailed on a church door, challenging the Catholic Church's teachings. His basic objection to the church—that it was not a necessary intermediary between the people and God—spelled the end of monolithic Catholic domination of the political and religious life of Europe. Protestant beliefs flourished in the Netherlands, England, Germany, and within the borders of Spain, France, Austria—and even Italy itself, so near the pope's throne.

The year 1555 began the longest peacetime in German history, when the powers of Europe ended their endless war by agreeing that religious differences would be recognized by territory. If a priest decided to become Protestant, that was all right with Mother Church, no inquisition or burning would be necessary, but all their lands and all their resources would always belong to the Vatican. Besides, the pope had a new order of priests working on long-range plans. Born in 1534, the Society of Jesus is better known as the Jesuits.

Though it produced peace, no one was happy with this arrangement. The Jesuits wanted to win back Europe for the true faith and stamp out dangerous heresies in Germany and England. They would force all Europeans, from enslaved people to royals, back into the confessionals. The new Protestant merchant class, the ancestors of today's businessmen, were impatient with their lower legal status, which created all sorts of complications when going before the courts. And true reformers of the new faiths were angry that the pope would not give them formal recognition; they, in fact, believed their own forms of Christianity superior to Catholicism, which they considered tainted by paganism, idolatry, and wealth.

For centuries the church relied on one family, the Habsburgs, to provide successors to the throne of Charlemagne, the first Holy Roman emperor, whose reign began on Christmas in the year 800. But the Habsburgs had their own priorities and ambitions. Emperor Rudolf II's father and grandfather may have been Holy Roman emperors, but the Habsburgs of Austria controlled much less than their cousins, whose kingdom included Spain and key possessions in Germany, Italy, and the New World. The most powerful man in Europe was Philip II, King of Spain.

Drawing wealth from the New World, confident that it had been divinely granted for the saving of souls, Spain and the Vatican felt as ready to conquer the Protestant heretics as they were to conquer the indigenous tribes of the Americas. After all, Catholic bishops wielded power from Germany to Mexico and even China, where the Italian Franciscan priest John of Montecorvino arrived in 1294. He built a church five years later in what would become Beijing.

But the Catholics did not comprehend an important new development. A third religion, metaphysical religion, was in the mix; a religion so pervasive even Catholics and Protestants were reading its texts and experimenting with its practices. This third religion was the catalyst for changes so radical it could be the beginning of the modern world.

European metaphysical religion blended folk traditions, astrology, Neoplatonism, the writings attributed to Hermes, Kabbalah, and more. Alchemy's popularity reached even the church. Intellectual Catholic clergy tinkered with matter in alembics, pored over the mysterious symbols in alchemical emblem books, and cherished opportunities to peruse treasures, like unpublished manuscripts by Paracelsus (1493–1541), the Swiss physician, alchemist, and philosopher.

The best-educated minds debated the techniques and theories of transmutation. Anyone with enough money invested in changing a storage room into a lab filled with equipment. The poor dreamed of turning lead into gold, or at least convincing a king they could, and children at play pretended to be alchemists. "Only fools and lawyers hate alchemy," was a popular saying of the time. Even Philip II kept an ever-changing collection of alchemists and a well-stocked alchemical laboratory in his castle in Spain. Natural magic was synonymous with science. If you experimented to gain a greater understanding of the world, you weren't a scientist; you were a natural magician. For all the greatest masters of these arts, and all arts, one destination was more attractive than any other: Emperor Rudolf's Prague.

Rudolph's older brother sickened and died so near Rudolph's birth that their mother could never show anything but cold courtesy to her second son. Maria of Spain was sister to King Philip II. She was a traditional Spanish royal, strictly Catholic, eager to report to the pope and to work on his behalf and her brother's, to influence her husband and sons. It's hard to believe she got along with Rudolf's father, but they had seventeen children together.

Rudolf's father, the Holy Roman Emperor Maximilian II (1527–1576), was the kind of ruler who gives emperors a good name. He was amiable and decent. He braved not only the endless river of paperwork that is an empire, but also the difficult relationships of rulership, and he was a master at resolving the constant contradictions of opposing demands. He disapproved of how his brother-in-law Philip ran the Spanish Empire. Maximilian was famous for being so charming that opponents often wound up agreeing with him even though they had been bitterly opposed. He was an art collector, an avid lover of flowers, and had a great interest in the esoteric. He even had the famous Nostradamus himself calculate his son Rudolf's astrological chart.

Maximilian shared with his father, Ferdinand I, and his son Philip the love of collecting. He built a zoo to house all the exotic creatures ambassadors from far-off lands brought him, including tigers and what they called Indian crows but we call parrots. Maximilian loved to put on allegorical spectacles, including a sparking and smoking artificial volcano, or a real elephant with a symbolic king of India riding atop. Maximilian was a tolerant emperor: he allowed men of all beliefs in his court, where Catholics, astrologers, Calvinists, and even atheists coexisted. Believing the Catholic Church was in serious need of reform, Maximilian tried in vain to convince the pope to allow priests to marry.

Emperor Maximilian II waged wars but without real victories. He once declared that "religious questions cannot be resolved by the sword." He had to pay tribute to the Turks, who were still in Hungary despite his best efforts to expel them. Typhus fever decimated the imperial army, and from there the scourge spread all over Europe.

Maria and her brother King Philip II pressured Maximilian to send Rudolf to Madrid for a few years to experience life with the other side of the family. To prepare his son for ruling an empire, and perhaps to get him better acquainted with the competition, Maximilian agreed.

Though only eleven years old, Rudolf was asked to observe the court proceedings when Philip served as both judge and chief prosecutor against his enemies. And then there was the mandatory attendance at the burning of heretics at the stake. Philip's father had set up the Spanish Inquisition, and Philip not only relied on it, he also gave it more power.

Philip read every document that passed under the royal seal. He personally met with petitioners and devoted himself to all the meticulous details of running an enterprise as enormous as the kingdom of Spain. He was ruthless against enemies at home and abroad. What remained of the Muslims of Moorish Spain suffered his wrath, as did the Protestants who lived in the north of his domains, and it wasn't a happy time for the Jews of Spain. But during his long reign of five decades, he eventually became a more tolerant ruler.

Philip's creepy Spanish royal household was a horror movie enthusiast's dream come true. The royal castle was a former monastery. Joanna of Castile may have once been queen of Spain, Sicily, Naples, and the Americas, but a decade after her death, she was known as Juana la Loca, or Crazy Joan. She had been locked up in a nunnery, where she couldn't sleep because she was afraid the nuns were trying to kill her. The court gossiped about what could have happened to the once highly intelligent and well-educated princess who spoke several languages, loved playing musical instruments, and enjoyed hunting. Some whispered that she wasn't crazy at all. She was confined until death by her son to consolidate his power. He claimed she could no longer sleep, and needed help to bathe, to change her clothes, even to eat. She was not allowed visitors other than her caretakers. Children frightened one another with stories about her and the rooms where her ghost might appear.

Even scarier was Philip's son Don Carlos. Born with an abnormal curvature of the upper spine, he appears to have also suffered mental impairment, and he had a cruel streak. He enjoyed roasting living animals; their cries of agony delighted him. The court tolerated his cruelty. As the firstborn son, Don Carlos was the heir apparent to the throne of Spain and perhaps the Holy Roman Empire, but when word got out that Don Carlos was a madman, the succession changed. Philip may have wanted to spend a few years with Rudolf because he knew his nephew would be the next Holy Roman emperor.

Philip was a great collector of art, and among his paintings were several masterpieces by Hieronymus Bosch, including *The Garden of Earthly Delights*. In fact, without Philip's avid collecting of Bosch paintings, it's doubtful his art would have survived. Rudolf would stare at those paintings for hours. He had grown up around a great legacy of art, collected by family members over the generations, with many masterpieces to see, but nothing like the macabre art and society he encountered in Spain. Philip's collection included a handkerchief said to have caught the tears of Mary the mother of Jesus, a nail from the cross, and, of course, bones of saints. Philip would compel his children, and Rudolf, to kiss them.

Formerly betrothed to Don Carlos, Elisabeth of Valois, daughter of Henry II, king of France, and Catherine de' Medici, wed Philip instead, and then became pregnant with what everyone hoped would be the new heir. Elisabeth was the one person to whom Don Carlos showed only kindness. After the wedding, he became more deranged. He heaved a servant out a window to his death and threatened a noble with a knife. Philip realized his son would have to go the way of Juana la Loca.

Into a room with walled-up windows he went, where he starved himself to death at age twenty-three.

Elisabeth, queen of Spain, was Rudolf's only friend at the Spanish court. She had been the childhood roommate of Mary, Queen of Scots. She was an aspiring portrait painter. Philip appointed Sofonisba Anguissola, a court painter, as an art teacher and lady-in-waiting to the teenage queen. They became good friends.

Philip was so enamored of his fourteen-year-old bride he became a doting husband, even staying by her side when she almost died of smallpox. She miscarried her first pregnancy, female twins. She later bore him two daughters. Tragically, at age twenty-three, she died giving birth to a son who lived only a few minutes.

Heartbroken, Sofonisba left the Spanish court. But Philip looked after her, settling a fortune on her and marrying her to a Sicilian nobleman. Sofonisba became famous as she innovated new dimensions in mannerism and the art of portraiture. Women were not passive objects in her work, especially not in her self-portraits. She lived to be ninety-three. In her old age she lost her sight, so instead of painting she used her wealth to support worthy artists.

Elisabeth may have been an important influence on young Rudolf. He emulated her friendships with artists, and like her he would not be content observing: he would practice some of the arts he admired. He openly wept at her funeral. What must he have felt when, a year later, he heard that his own twenty-year-old sister, Anna of Austria, was to wed King Philip? But theirs would be a rare happy royal marriage. Philip was in love with Anna, and she with him. He had no mistresses during their marriage. Hers was a cheerful, vivacious presence. Even her blonde hair seemed to add warmth and light to Philip's somber court. Her favorite pastime was needlework. She bore him sons, including his heir, King Philip III of Spain. Their love lasted a decade, and then she died while giving birth to a daughter. Philip never remarried.

After Philip had become both Rudolf's uncle and his brother-in-law, the command Rudolf had been hoping for finally arrived: he was to return home to Vienna. His uncle's final words of wisdom to him included the ignored suggestion that he read only books provided by his confessor. But he also gave him this valuable advice: "Trust no one, listen to everyone, make decisions alone."

Rudolf spent eight years with Philip at that strange court. At the very least he had realized that even kings are subject to suffering and the ironies of fate. From his uncle he learned a deliberate and affected self-carriage that his Austrian subjects mistook for arrogance. They disliked his silence, his rigid posture, and his unfriendly expression. His unwillingness to include others in his decision-making seemed haughty, and it broke with the open-minded traditions of his father. Some feared he had returned a devout Catholic. His father pleaded with Rudolf to lighten up, but Spain had a lifelong influence on him. He always dressed in black. He preferred to use Spanish in formal conversation, and he always seemed to trust people with Spanish connections more than others. He even imitated Philip's way of making decisions, always waiting until the last moment and never allowing anyone to know beforehand which way he was leaning.

In 1575, Maximilian II was also crowned king of Poland, but a Polish prince with Catholic support chased him off the throne and out of the country. Maximilian's army was ready to invade again, but before he could reclaim the crown he died of sickness. The world was scandalized by the revelation that the Holy Roman emperor, as he lay dying, had refused the last rites of the Catholic faith.

Rudolf was twenty-four years old when the eight-hundred-year-old crown of Charlemagne was placed on his head as he sat upon the throne from which Charlemagne had ruled. The assembled princes, one by one, kissed his feet. Rudolf then toured his new lands while familiarizing himself with the archaic institutions of the Holy Roman Empire. His first public event was his father's funeral, which he made a splendid spectacle, complete with a new monument.

The first crisis of Rudolf's reign involved his twenty-year-old brother Matthias. Local nobles, ruined by the war between the Dutch Protestants and the Spanish Catholics, begged Matthias to represent them in an effort to make peace. Rudolf was furious that his little brother had not consulted him first before agreeing to try to help. He never forgave Matthias. Rudolf controlled and watched him, not realizing he was sealing his fate by creating a ruthless enemy in his own family. His first action was to force all his brothers to agree to a document of succession that gave Rudolf all power.

Rudolf soon decided to move the imperial capital from Vienna to Prague. The move took him seven years to complete. Why did he move the capital of the Holy Roman Empire away from the city that represented hundreds of years of Habsburg rule? Rudolf was not a man who enjoyed the company of family, nor did he care for the rigors of the court. When he harbored ambitions in his youth of being a second Augustus, he apparently did not realize that the first emperor of Rome built his success on meticulous accounting and daily reporting of activity across the empire. Rudolf didn't want to be bothered with accounting, or ceremony, or diplomatic meetings, or the nagging of his mother and other family members. He would become notorious for being late to events; often he would postpone them or claim that he had attended incognito. But flight from tradition and family weren't the only reasons he left Vienna. The Turkish army was only a hundred miles away, battling imperial forces in Hungary.

Then came the comet of 1577. Rudolf's appointed imperial astronomer, Tycho Brahe, and all the other astrologers of the day, didn't like the look of it, and the timing, at the beginning of Rudolf's reign, suggested an ill omen. Tycho pointed out that the comet was astrologically linked to Saturn, and its reddish color gave the quality of Mars, a disastrous combination.

Poor Rudolf didn't take the news well. He was soon bedridden with what was at first diagnosed as fish poisoning. But the stomach pains and exhaustion lingered for almost four years. Rudolf disappeared from the life of his court, and every day the empire awoke in fear of the news that he had died. Even after his health returned, his subjects thought of him as frail, though he reigned for over thirty years.

While Rudolf was sick, his mother schemed to gain more power for herself and her other children. Since he refused to see her, she wrote letters to him urging him to accept the guidance of his uncle Philip. She scolded him for being afraid that he would lose his throne and his people. Meanwhile, she married off his sisters to powerful princes. She convinced Philip to give his daughter Isabella Clara Eugenia, the Infanta herself (*infanta* meaning "princess" in Spanish), the daughter of Rudolf's friend Elisabeth, in marriage to Rudolf. She must have been elated by this coup, which gave Rudolf the right to reunite the Holy Roman Empire as king of Spain and ruler of the entire Catholic empire. Such an arrangement could not have been made without the approval of the pope.

At first Rudolf agreed. The marriage proposal seemed to help pull him from his sickbed. But soon he and his uncle were squabbling over details, and negotiations broke down. Isabella was only a child, after all, so they had plenty of time to work out an agreement.

What was it like to meet Rudolf II, Holy Roman emperor? The best advice anyone could give would be to find a rare and fine work of art, or a unique souvenir from a faraway place, and offer it as a gift to be personally presented. Even if it was something fabulous, Rudolf might decide he didn't really want to meet you, so you'd show up, wait around, and then be asked to leave your gift, brushed off with a promise of another appointment. This kind of treatment was especially likely if you were known to have a pressing Catholic, or for that matter Protestant, agenda. On the other hand, if alchemy, astrology, scientific instruments, clock making, pornography, or fine art collecting enhanced your reputation, you might actually meet Rudolf.

At just over five foot three, he was not an imposing figure. He was friendly, a charming man whose easy manner behind the scenes in no way diminished his dignity and obvious intelligence. Rudolf didn't like jokes, and he seldom laughed. He avoided noisy conversations, mostly listening. To control his heart palpitations, he carried crystals and amulets. Born under the sign of Cancer, Rudolf would have preferred to be a Capricorn, and he used the symbol of Capricorn as his seal on occasion, inspired by his favorite Capricorn, the self-proclaimed Capricorn Augustus.

At the height of Rudolf's reign, the population of Prague was about fifty thousand, much smaller than Imperial Rome's one million. Prague was 75 percent Protestant, but the 25 percent Catholic minority were backed up by the Catholic majority just across the border.

In Rome they whispered that one of his alchemists had bewitched Rudolf. But the people of Bohemia thought Rudolf's melancholy was a symptom of wisdom; his solitude suited a man deep in the study of the mysteries of the soul and the world. Most of them understood that by keeping both Catholic and Protestant extremists at bay, this disinterested monarch gave them peace and prosperity. Like his grandfather and his father, Rudolf was renowned for his love of flowers.

Rudolf had special stables built for his collection of three hundred of the most beautiful horses from all around the world; his favorites were his gray Andalusians. The gift of an especially fine horse was known to be one of the best ways to gain an audience with him. When pleased, his signature gift was a breeding pair of Andalusians.

In his heated hillside aviary, Rudolf had birds of paradise, parrots, and even a live dodo bird. In the nearby Lion's Court, tigers, bears, and other apex predators were housed. Rudolf's favorite lion, a cub he received as a gift from the sultan of Turkey, was allowed the run of the castle but was usually found napping beside the emperor like an overgrown house cat. Tycho Brahe was struck by the astrological connections between the charts of the lion and the emperor, and he declared their fates were entwined.

Among the curiosities included in Rudolf's collection of rare valuables were colorful corals from the tropics, exotic bird feathers, a ruby-studded rhino horn, various fossils, whale teeth, a six-foot-long unicorn horn (probably from a narwhal), two nails from Noah's Ark, and a grain of the earth from which Jehovah made Adam. Rudolf owned an agate bowl that at the time was widely considered to be the Holy Grail.

The court was full of fascinating inventions. The inventor of what he called a perspective lute claimed to capture the relationship between tones and colors. Perpetual motion machines were a constant fascination.

Rudolf encouraged the publication of lavish hand-colored herbals and bestiaries. He commissioned beautiful illustrated books, including *Museum of Rudolf II*, two volumes of painted vellum by leading artists depicting natural wonders from the imperial collection. He was a collector of clocks, including some of the first clocks to ever measure seconds. He had clocks that not only told time but also followed the positions of the planets.

But Rudolf wasn't just a collector of paintings; he had a collection of painters, as well. He liked to watch the process and would occasionally give a little word of advice, not wanting to intrude, just an imperial suggestion, what he liked to call his "impressions." Rudolf would arrive early every morning to see what work his artists had done since his last visit. He would offer advice on everything from the arrangement of subjects to the lighting. But not all his artists worked in the castle; others were sent to picturesque places or unknown frontiers to sketch or paint waterfalls, trees, and mountains.

Not content to collect, Rudolf learned to carve ivory, including a piece where one complex shape was carved inside another. He regularly visited his alchemy workshop, where he pursued his own experiments in addition to checking on the progress of his protégés.

His father's younger brother Archduke Ferdinand II had built in Prague a castle called the Letohrádej Hvezda (Star Villa or Star Summer Palace), in the shape of a six-pointed star. Called the Seal or Ring of Solomon by magicians, the shape is attributed to the signet ring of King Solomon in medieval occult tradition. The foundation stone had been laid according to the correct astrological day and hour. The sacred geometry of the castle inspired the great twentieth-century surrealist André Breton four centuries later to remark that it was "built with the Philosopher's Stone." Ferdinand also had a grand library and a passion for collecting that may have helped inspire Rudolf's own.

When Ferdinand died in 1595, Rudolf grieved the loss of his favorite uncle, but he was delighted to inherit the Star Summer Palace and his uncle's collections.

Rudolf's relations with women were always alienated, yet his court included Elizabeth Jane Weston, one of the few female poets of the era, especially notable for publishing under her own name. Even the woman with whom Rudolf had a relationship for most of his life, who bore him many children, received little intimacy and less legitimacy. He enjoyed regular deliveries of imperial courtesans, who traded their favors for jewels and other gifts. He had new prospects for empresses, too: Marie de Medici, Margaret of Savoy, and even his lovely cousin Anna of Tyrol were all potential wives. The Scottish writer John Barclay wrote acidly about Rudolf's "concubine troop," and the "virgins who greatly valued their chance to be deprived of that title" (Marshall 2006, 59). "Free love" was how he described the romantic philosophy of Rudolf with contempt.

The art of the high Renaissance was a celebration of classical antiquity. Ideals of perfection, the very Platonic ideas themselves, those original forms that give everything in the world its shape and identity, could be rendered by artists, providing a source of spiritual inspiration. Mannerism, the art of Rudolf's time, has been described as a reaction against the art of the high Renaissance and as the earliest beginning of surrealism. European magical realism might be a another name for it.

Mannerism wasn't a rejection of high Renaissance art. In fact, they shared many of the same inspirations, especially Neoplatonism. But mannerism was more interested in metaphor and symbol than revealing the Platonic ideal. Imperfections became more interesting than perfection. Perhaps the best example is the artist Giuseppe Arcimboldo, who besides being one of Rudolf's favorite painters also designed many fabulous costumes for imperial court masques and other official spectacles. Arcimboldo painted Rudolf's favorite portrait of himself. It portrayed him as Vertumnus, the Roman god of the seasons. The emperor is entirely composed of flowers, fruits, and vegetables.

Rudolf spent a fortune finding and acquiring the finest art in Europe, although it was said to be easier to get a promise of payment from the emperor than actual money. One painting was carried by four soldiers who had to carry the huge, framed canvas upright over the Alps through snow, never letting it touch ground.

Rudolf also had a collection of erotica to ogle. He commissioned paintings and sculptures in which old satyrs cavorted with naked nymphs. Minerva, the Roman goddess of wisdom, bare breasted and alluring, trampled an anonymous but muscular native who symbolized ignorance. On the back door to Rudolf's personal quarters in his castle in Prague was a carefully fashioned metal sculpture of a naked woman; the knocker was a penis that entered her mouth. Possibly the first knock-knock joke in history.

But Rudolf's favorite art, and therefore the great trend among artists of his time, was art as the revealer of mysteries, whether in engraved gems, esoteric diagrams, allegorical paintings, or in the study of the occult, alchemical experimentation, and the Kabbalah.

TWO

Dee, Kelley, and Rosicrucian Rumors

Rudolf was fascinated by Paracelsian medicine. Agrippa, Trithemius, Porta, and, above all, Paracelsus taught that only practical experience and experimentation could arrive at the truth about healing. He famously said that to read the book of nature you must walk its pages with your feet. He's been hailed as the father of pharmaceutical science. When his German disciples published his books in the 1560s and 1570s, the accepted theories and practices of medicine began to evolve. Most of those books were published in Prague.

Paracelsus walked the pages of nature all across Europe and as far away as Africa and Asia Minor. He gave zinc its name and popularized the improvement of the accuracy of dosage of medicine by forming it into pills. His focus on chemicals and minerals foreshadowed pharmaceutical science.

Paracelsus was influenced by Pythagoreanism, the Neoplatonists, and the *Corpus Hermeticum* or *Hermetica*. He practiced astrology not only to understand his patients better but also because he believed picking an herb on the right day at the right hour gave it more potency. He used the classic European four elements in his theories (fire, air, water, earth) but also alchemy's three elements (salt, mercury, sulfur). The elements of salt, mercury, and sulfur are symbols of qualities as well as literal substances;

in one example, the human body is salt; the soul and its projection, mind, are mercury; and sulfur is emotion. Paracelsus also invented the Alphabet of the Magi, which he used to make talismans he believed captured energies that could heal as effectively as alchemical medicines.

In a world of harmonies and signatures where every being is a symbol, the ultimate goal was the philosopher's stone. Not only could this mysterious substance turn lead into gold, but it could also heal any disease or injury, prolong life indefinitely, bring reform to society, and offer immortality to every person. This soft apocalypse of universal utopia was thought to herald the return of Christ and the commencement of the end times. While rumors of the creation of the philosopher's stone have never subsided, those suspected of solving the mystery have often disappeared, or ended badly, since others would do anything to get the secret, including stealing it and killing its possessor.

The Cosmopolitans, as the alchemists were known then, were often lonely figures on the road between castles. Many claimed to have authored popular anonymous tracts; a few actually did. In the collective imagination of Europe, these wanderers are descendants of the troubadours and cultural ancestors of the mysterious Rosicrucian initiates, said to be the secret guardians of the human experiment, whose superior powers allow them to appear and disappear, to live far longer than the average human lifespan, and to speak the languages of many places. Charlatans and adventurers masquerading as alchemists didn't last long at Rudolf's court. They received a warm welcome and then, when their ineptitude was exposed, a cold escort out of the castle and onto any road away from Bohemia.

The emperor's favorite doctor wrote the famous *A Lexicon of Alchemy*. The emperor also had what might best be described as an honorary physician, Michael Maier, a sixteenth-century Pythagorean. Several of Maier's books earned a place in the history of science as the last expressions of an era when careful observations of nature were analyzed in the light of the ideals of alchemy and astrology practiced as arts that reveal the divine perfection of creation.

Maier's authorship of the book *Themis Aurea: The Laws of the Fraternity of the Rosie Cross* has made him a popular choice as an example of that rarest of creatures, an authentic early Rosicrucian. However, at the court of Rudolf, at the time of the arrival of the Rosicrucian controversy, Maier dismissed the Rosicrucians as a scam. He changed his mind in 1616, the year that Robert Fludd published his defense of the Rosicrucians: *Apologia Compendiaria Fraternitatem de Rosea Cruce*. Two years later Maier defended Rosicrucian ideas in his book about their laws. An English translation was published in 1656, evidence of the popularity and influence of Rosicrucian ideas during the reign of Oliver Cromwell.

According to Maier, the laws of the Rosy Cross were that they must travel; cure the sick without payment; practice the customs of the countries where they live; every year on day C they are to appear at the place of the Holy Spirit or explain their absence by letter; each must choose a fitting person to be their successor when they die; the letters R.C. (Rosy Cross) will be their seal, character, and symbol; and they will remain hidden for a hundred years.

No one is certain what is meant by day C. In his essay "The Mysterious Day C of the Rosicrucians," C.R. Dunning Jr. offers fourteen plausible explanations, mostly Christian holidays including Christmas. The most popular guess for the letter *C* is that it refers to the Latin word *communio*, which refers to an intimate gathering, but also the consecration of the host and the wine. Another popular theory is that it may refer to the Catholic feast of Corpus Christi, but this seems unlikely since Luther despised that holiday, and the Rosicrucians were for the most part Lutheran.

Maier, some scholars have argued, was secretly a friend of Robert Fludd. Fludd authored encyclopedic books about the hermetic harmonics underlying music, the motions of heavenly bodies, even the functions of human organs. Fludd is another popular nomination for an actual Rosicrucian. Both he and Maier denied being Rosicrucians, but of course, that's what a Rosicrucian would do. As we shall see, Maier's relationship with Fludd was both more distant and more complicated than the legend about their secret bond.

When his twenty-year-old niece Lucy broke her arm falling off a horse, Rudolf summoned Maier, who first set her bone, and then six times, for several minutes each time, he directed healing energy into her arm. After an inexplicably fast recovery, Lucy said she felt as if a miraculous doctor had awakened her from a nightmare. Maier wrote many books, discussing them with the emperor as he composed them, but all were published after Rudolf's death.

Another popular candidate for a real Rosicrucian is the Polish alchemist Michal Sedziwój, better known as Michael Sendivogius. His book *A New Light on Alchemy* was a favorite of Isaac Newton's, whose own copy was filled with margin notes. At first, Sendivogius's time in Prague was difficult: he was imprisoned for unpaid debts. But his appeal to Rudolf was answered. Rudolf gave Sendivogius the opportunity to demonstrate his alleged knowledge of alchemy. Sendivogius claimed to have some of the real philosopher's stone given to him by his Scottish mentor, the alchemist Seton. Though he had not yet learned the secret of Seton's red powder, Sendivogius insisted he could make gold. The demonstration impressed Rudolf. He had a plaque put up on the wall for all his alchemists to see: "Let anyone else do what the Pole Sendivogius has done." Rudolf made Sendivogius a baron and gave him the right to sit with him at meals.

John Dee was Queen Elizabeth I's astrologer and alchemist, but he was so much more: a pioneering mathematician, a founding father for ceremonial magicians, an early experimenter with mediumship, and a secret agent. Dee used astrology to choose the day of Elizabeth I's coronation.

With Edward Kelley, his medium and partner in esoteric pursuits, Dee practiced natural magic to communicate with angels, who not only advised him on household affairs, but who also issued startling predictions of worldwide reform that coincided with the dramatic events Dee foresaw in the stars, astrological omens of the end of the power of the Roman Catholic Church.

Aware that the court of the Holy Roman emperor and the courts of German princes in university towns had become centers of alchemical, hermetic, and astrological experimentation, Dee may have thought that his own approach to the occult might become popular on the continent. He could gather intelligence for Queen Elizabeth I, forge alliances, and share his dream of a world led not by popes and emperors but by natural philosophers. Of course, the British would be in charge of Dee's new world order.

Past scholars, especially British ones, have romanticized Dee's trip, believing that like Orpheus he established the mysteries wherever he went in Europe, but the alchemical courts of Germany had their own rich traditions of interest in the esoteric. Dee and Kelley's earlier misadventure in Poland—when they presented the king of Poland with a prophecy from the angels, which did not come true—perhaps should have raised doubts about angelic advice. Nonetheless, when the angels ordered Dee and Kelley to visit Emperor Rudolf II in Prague, they readily complied. The travelers arrived in style with multiple carriages and a troop of guards. Rumors persisted that Dee paid for these extravagances with alchemical gold, but his lists of expenses to be reimbursed by Queen Elizabeth still exist, as does his wife's plea to the angels that they had no money for food. The angels dictated that Dee and Kelley pray seven times a day in each cardinal direction. They were to fast regularly. Even grooming had to conform to angelic standards.

Dee had dedicated his most famous book, the highly influential *The Monas Hieroglyphica*, or *The Hieroglyphic Monad*, to Rudolf's father. Rudolf was interested in the alchemical knowledge and experiences of Dee and Kelley, but Dee spent most of their meeting relaying alarming warnings from the angels, who commanded Rudolf to get his spiritual life in order, or else. If he did, they would help him unite all Europe to defeat the Turks. He would establish a new imperial order built on the truth of natural magic instead of the lies of the Catholic Church and the Holy Roman Empire. If he didn't, divine retribution would be swift and terrible.

Dee later claimed that Rudolf understood the courage and tenderness, the true loyalty and even love it required for Dee to repeat such dire messages. Perhaps Rudolf was only humoring him. How was he to get his spiritual life in order anyway? By listening to Edward Kelley's angels? Rudolf ordered a noble he trusted to investigate by attending Dee's angelic chatroom. The report must have been lukewarm since Dee was not appointed Rudolf's spiritual adviser. Instead, he was given an honorary degree from the local university. The angels wanted Dee to tell the emperor that he had the secret to the philosopher's stone. Since Dee wasn't making gold, what did the angels mean? Then the pope's delegate presented formal evidence to Rudolf that Dee was practicing necromancy and other forbidden arts. Dee was given twenty-four hours to leave Bohemia. Dee and Kelley packed up and left, as many alchemists and their families had before them.

Rudolf chose not to prevent Dee and Kelley from returning to Bohemia, where they took up residence for several years with William of Rosenberg (in Czech, Vilém z Rozmberka), the wealthiest and most powerful noble in Bohemia, second only to Rudolf. Rosenberg had been invited to sit on the throne of Poland, but the political maneuvers of his Polish rivals had prevented him.

When Rudolf was crowned in Prague in 1575, his crown was carried by Rosenberg. Rosenberg was Catholic, but when an agent of the pope complained about the shrinking numbers of Catholics in Bohemia, Rosenberg said Catholics had only themselves to blame. Their own venal behavior had alienated the people, he declared, sounding like a Protestant. While he supported alchemists and astrologers, he also did whatever he could for the Jesuits.

Rosenberg's doctor was Heinrich Khunrath, author of many books, including *Amphitheatrum sapientiae aeternae* (Amphitheater of eternal wisdom), which contains an engraving of the *Tabula Smaragdina* (Emerald Tablet), an inspiration to generations of alchemists, mystics, and Rosicrucians and even Aldous Huxley, who considered it an example of what he called the "Perennial Philosophy."

Around 1605, Khunrath would publish *De Igne Magorum Philosophorumque Secreto Externo et Visibili (On the Fire of the Mages and Philosophers Secret External and Visible)* in which he argued that the sun is the fiery presence of God. His example of how someone can be illuminated by a ray of this divine power was Orpheus. Khunrath was a Paracelsian physician and hermetic philosopher who studied the Kabbalah. He was a well-known alchemist of his time. He's been suggested as an initiatory link between John Dee and the Rosicrucians, but the proof, if it exists, is yet to be found. There is no doubt, however, that Khunrath was influenced by Dee's writing, and the influence of Khunrath's books on Rosicrucian beliefs is clear. He may have arranged for John Dee's visit to Prague. Rudolf thought enough of Khunrath to grant him something like an imperial copyright, comprehensive protection from plagiarism, for his books on medicine, alchemy, and Kabbalah.

Rosenberg had his sixth alchemical lab built just for John Dee and Edward Kelley. As 1586 came to a close, Kelley quickly produced a small amount of what appeared to be gold. He claimed the process was still unstable and unpredictable, but the bits of gold he produced kept his patrons enthralled. Historians speculate that Kelley learned metallurgical tricks for changing the color of metals.

Rosenberg also encouraged the angelic conversations, wanting advice about which woman to wed so he could father an heir and asking how to regain the emperor's favor for Dee. He was happy to receive reassurance from the angels that he would have an heir to inherit his throne for he would certainly become king of Poland. Neither prediction came true.

Kelley wore a black cap that covered his ears, which, rumor had it, had been cut off as a punishment for forgery. The tug of war over Kelley's credibility and motivations continues in academia. Some see him as a criminal who manipulated Dee, ruined his marriage, wealth and reputation, and used Dee's standing to advance his own. Others point out that Dee drove Kelley so relentlessly that by 1587 Kelley wanted their experiment in angelic communication to stop. That year Kelley claimed to have received an angelic message that he and Dee should share their wives. Could this notorious wife swap have been Kelley's strategy to dissuade Dee from continuing? When Dee resisted the swap but kept going with the experiment, the angels, through Kelley, repeatedly urged the swap. Kelley may have been surprised when Dee agreed.

We don't know much about Kelley's wife, a young widow named Jane but called Joanna. We know that Jane Dee pitied and befriended her. Jane Dee married John Dee when he was fifty-one and she was twenty-three. She had been a lady-in-waiting to a countess at Queen Elizabeth I's court. In his diaries John recorded household particulars, including their arguments (which exasperated his anxious disposition), her menstrual cycles, and their sexual encounters. Despite her distrust of him, Jane asked Kelley to help her talk with the angels. Dee recorded her plea for help: Without money for meat and drink, how could they and their children survive?

Jane not only participated in his experiments, she also managed the household at Mortlake, protected her husband's privacy, and even promoted his work, using her connections at court to help him in his never-ending quest for backers. Requiring special instruments and rare materials, alchemy was an expensive pursuit.

When Dee broke the news about the wife swap and communal ownership, Jane wept and shook for fifteen minutes. She refused to be involved. Dee patiently explained that by sharing everything, including their wives, Dee and Kelley could achieve a God-ordained purity of purpose and detachment from worldly matters. Some have theorized that Kelley and Dee viewed this as something akin to a tantric initiation. Despite his wife's protests, Dee insisted that nothing could be more important than establishing communication with the angels.

Dee signed half his possessions over to Kelley, and the gloomy wife swap went forward with unfortunate results. The wives became more depressed than they had already been. Dee and Kelley continued to argue. Some historians have speculated that one of Jane Dee's children was fathered by Kelley. While it may have gone much further than Kelley anticipated, the wife swap had the desired effect: the long sessions of experimentation with angelic presence and language stopped.

Kelley then showed off what appeared to be another advance in the process, only to disappoint everyone with more unstable and unpredictable results. In 1588 when Dee received word that the Spanish Armada threatened England, he engaged in some form of magical activity that took him to different parts of Prague. Angelic magic was said to control the weather. Did Dee involve his friends in Bohemia in a great ritual to thwart the king of Spain? If so he must have been elated when news arrived that the armada had been battered by severe weather. Dee understood that Spain's power had been broken. The wealth squandered on the war against England was supposed to have been paid for by the English conquest. Now began the slow decline of the Spanish Empire.

Dee worried that while he labored at gold making his plan for universal reform would be forgotten. Kelley showed Dee a letter in which Rosenberg wondered about how to get Dee to leave. Providentially, Queen Elizabeth I sent an urgent summons for Dee to return to England. Dee signed over to Kelley his remaining books and alchemical powder to free himself from any further debts. When he returned to England, he found his beloved house and library had been pillaged and partially burned by a mob of locals who believed he practiced black magic. The queen welcomed him home with genuine affection and a gift of two hundred gold coins called angels. She made him chancellor of St. Paul's Cathedral and warden of Manchester College to provide him support and shelter. Not long before she died, she heard he was selling silver dishes, so she sent him forty more golden angels. But then Good Queen Bess died in 1603. Two years later Dee's tolerant wife Jane and two of their children died of plague.

John Dee didn't interest the newly crowned King James. The old wizard found himself a forgotten relic of another era that seemed quaint to the new generation. Dee, the inspiration to mathematicians, natural philosophers, and reformers political and religious, had always been a pious Christian in his own Pythagorean hermetic way, but now he was merely a symbol of superstition. His last few years were spent selling off what he had left to support himself and his daughter, who devoted her life to caring for him.

About twenty years after Dee's death, John Winthrop the Younger followed his father, the first governor of Massachusetts Bay Colony, to America. He brought alchemical paraphernalia and esoteric books, including some that had belonged to Dee. Winthrop marked the barrels containing them with Dee's occult symbol, the Hieroglyphic Monad.

As for Kelley, as soon as Dee left Prague, Rudolf sent for him. The emperor seemed to believe that providence had provided Kelley just in time to solve a problem in the great work of alchemy. Kelley became Rudolf's personal alchemist with a generous salary. Rudolf gave him a patent of nobility, naming him a Golden Knight of Bohemia.

Kelley showed off just enough success making gold that he became a celebrity. Nobles from all over Europe visited to glimpse his alchemical process. Kelley sent Queen Elizabeth I the cheeky gift of a silver bedpan half transformed into gold. Rosenberg gave Kelley a town of his own, nine villages, and estates. Kelley bought a brewery, a mill, two luxurious mansions in Prague, and a dozen houses to rent out. His stepdaughter became a famous poetess in Prague whose pen name was Westonia, perhaps in honor of Elizabeth Jane Weston. Westonia described Kelley as a kind and caring stepfather.

But Kelley's good fortune ended when he broke the strict rule against duels, killing an imperial officer. Kelley tried to escape, but Rudolf had him imprisoned. Rudolf's questions, to be put to Kelley, survive in a letter from his secretary. For example, "What is the significance of the secret characters in Kelley's notebook?" and "How is the potable gold made that Kelley gave the Emperor to taste?" Kelley tried to escape but fell and broke his leg. Most of the information after that is sketchy at best. He may have returned to work for Rudolf only to be imprisoned again for treason. Dee reported that he had heard Kelley died in 1595, but some historians believe Kelley may have survived until 1600. In Rosenberg's castle to this day they say Kelley died taking poison in front of his wife and daughter because he couldn't bear to suffer imprisonment again.

THREE

The Stars in Rudolf's Court

According to a 2014 poll, one out of four Americans believe the sun orbits Earth. Rudolf knew that the Earth orbits the sun. But that belief was considered a sin by the Roman Catholic Church. Rudolf doubted that observable mathematical truth could be heresy.

As we have seen, Tycho Brahe became imperial astronomer, followed by that other legend of early astronomy, Johannes Kepler, who spent the most productive decade of his life in Prague under the emperor's wing. Tycho and Kepler made possible Galileo's contribution to what would become the science of astronomy, but they were both creatures of Rudolf's court, students of astral influences, cosmic harmony, and the omens of comets and planets. Kepler's metaphysical properties of light have more in common with Neoplatonism than the science of astronomy. Pythagoras inspired Kepler's vision of the harmony of the planets as revealed by geometry, itself a sacred art for understanding divine creation. Kepler's first book was about Pythagorean harmony. Many lesser-known astrologers and astronomers contributed, including Rudolf, who shared his own ideas.

Tycho meticulously recorded the movements of the planets in astronomical tables. Kepler devoted himself to continuing Tycho's work. Rudolf was getting firsthand accounts of the movements of the planets as seen through the earliest telescopes. He saw the planets through the telescopes of Tycho and Kepler.

Kepler was also experimenting with optics and light. He was in touch by letter with Thomas Harriot, an English astronomer and mathematician, about optics and Harriot's theory of the close packing of spheres. Harriot traveled to America with Sir Walter Raleigh in 1585 on Raleigh's second expedition to Roanoke Island, North Carolina. Harriot served as a scientific observer and adviser. Also accompanying Raleigh was the metallurgist Joachim Gans of Prague, who came from a family of kabbalists, alchemists, and astronomers; Gans was the first Jewish man to set foot in America. Back in England, Harriot was accused of being an atheist and also a Pythagorean, a grave offense and symptom of devilry, according to British authorities.

No one aroused the ire of the Vatican more than Giordano Bruno. The great philosopher was invited to debate the wisest professors of Oxford University, about whom Bruno wrote: "The leader of the academy on that somber occasion stopped fifteen times over fifteen logical propositions, like a chicken in stubble" (Boulting 1914, 87).

Bruno got into trouble with Rome when he insisted that the Earth travels around the sun, not the other way around, and that stars are not fixed lights in the sky but suns like our own. Bruno's popular lectures all over Europe gained him secret clubs of followers who shared his aims and practiced his techniques for sharpening memory. He argued that the written word had blunted the human imagination. When we think our way through complexity we find connection to the divine.

For example, he asked us to imagine a wheel, then place ideas on sections of the wheel, not unlike the American game show *Wheel of Fortune*. Now do the same thing for a second wheel. Next imagine each section of the first wheel meeting every section of the second wheel. Once you've got six of those wheels superimposed, you've completed the exercise. Less than a hundred years later, this technique inspired the philosopher Leibniz to invent one of the first calculators, an ancestor of computers.

In Prague in 1588, to get Rudolf's attention, Bruno published a book dedicated to the Holy Roman emperor he hoped would rise up, like a second Hermes Trismegistus, to restore the true hermetic religion and inaugurate a golden age. *One Hundred and Sixty Articles against Mathematicians and Philosophers* was a response to some points made by Rudolf's mathematician and astronomer Fabrizio or, as Bruno called him, that "triumphant idiot." Rudolf sent Bruno a little money to thank him but never met him. Some of the lovely geometric illustrations in this book—symbols of the intellectual principle and the principle of love, for example—look remarkably like Hindu representations of chakras.

Bruno was an enthusiastic supporter of science at its earliest stages, but that's not what got him burned at the stake. Bruno believed he understood ancient Egyptian religion, which he considered the mother of all wisdom. Moses must have learned the Kabbalah in Egypt, Bruno argued. After all, Pythagoras and Plato traveled to Egypt. To Bruno, Egyptian religion was rooted in the belief of one in all. All life blazes with the consciousness, the form, the beauty of the divine creativity at the heart of every part of creation. In Bruno's world the living planet Earth spun around the living sun, just one among an infinite number of living stars, in just one of an infinite number of dimensions of being.

While teaching in Venice, Bruno was denounced by a student. The Inquisition rightly accused him of believing in reincarnation, but wrongly of practicing black magic and spell craft. Years of imprisonment, torture, and refusal to confess earned him a dirty rag stuffed in his mouth to muffle his screams while he burned to death, in 1600, a very clear message from the pope about what free thinkers could expect from Mother Church in the new century.

Though Rudolf's grandfather had given in to peer pressure by joining his Spanish relatives in the expulsion of the Jews, Rudolf's father was a blessing to the Jews of Prague, restoring their ancestral rights and even strolling with the empress through the Jewish quarter as the residents cheered. Jews were the core of imperial finance. The richest man in Prague was Jewish and no stranger to Rudolf. Meanwhile, among the astrologers and alchemists, even among the nobles of Europe, the Kabbalah became a source of fascination.

But Christians weren't the only ones enamored of the Kabbalah. Kabbalah experienced a revival among the Jews themselves as Isaac Luria and Moses Cordovero sparked a popular movement, emphasizing expectations of imminent world reform and the belief that prayer is a creative power.

The supreme chief rabbi of Prague, Judah Loew, was a scholar respected by all the educated of Europe. He wrote books praising the irrational and the supernatural in the Torah. He used the kabbalistic masterpiece the *Zohar* to argue that neither science nor insight could be a better source of wisdom than Holy Scripture, wherein the true divine pattern of creation is revealed. But he also warned kabbalists that their study of the *sephiroth* meant that they were clinging to categories reflecting not divine reality but the limits of human perception. Loew was a friend of Michael Maier, and it's surprising how little has been made of this friendship between the alleged Rosicrucian and a confirmed master kabbalist.

Rudolf had heard of Loew for some time. He probably knew the legend that Loew had created a living being from sculpted river mud by placing in it a parchment with the word *life* written on it in the true language of the angels. The Golem haunted the dark alleys of Prague, both a distant echo of the ancient Egyptian practice of infusing statues with the living presence of deities and also the prototype for zombies and for Frankenstein's monster in movies. Loew's first invitation to the castle came after Rudolf heard him give an eloquent lecture on the need for all religions to work together for peace. No one knows what they spent so many hours discussing, but Rudolf must have asked Loew about aspects of the Kabbalah he had not yet understood. Perhaps the rabbi was surprised to find the emperor so well read on the subject.

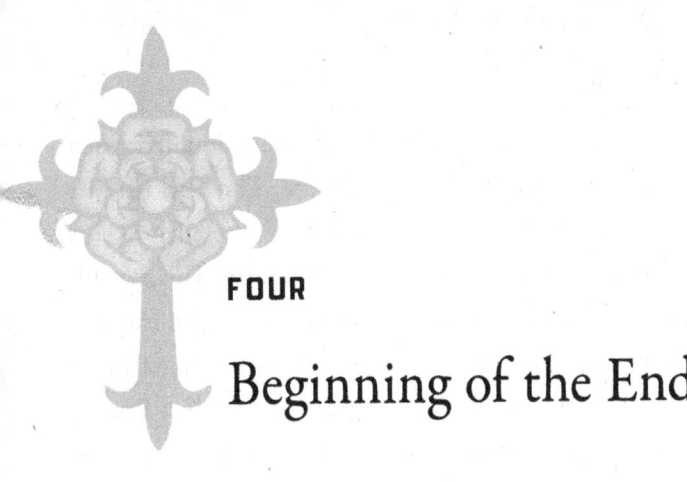

FOUR

Beginning of the End

W as the introduction of the Gregorian calendar in 1582 a bad omen? Rudolf thought so. That year Bohemia feared that the Catholics were about to attack. But Rome had chosen a more subtle approach. By 1584 Catholic power had quickly increased in Bohemia. New seminaries were built, missionaries and teachers were imported, festivals and ceremonies were encouraged, converts multiplied, enough that a representative of the pope submitted a plan to Rudolf to wipe out all heresy in Bohemia. Rudolf, of course, had no interest in pursuing such a vigorous and intolerant mission.

Plans for Rudolf's marriage to Isabella went all the way back to 1568 when she was only two years old. By 1582 King Philip became suspicious of his nephew's delays. But Rudolf managed to drag the proceedings out for another fifteen years until 1597, when Philip married the heartbroken thirty-one-year-old princess to Rudolf's younger brother Albrecht, who became known as a great peacemaker in north-western Europe, where he helped end three wars.

Rudolf reacted badly to this inevitable result, devastated even though for decades he had avoided making Isabella empress. A year later Philip violated imperial borders, giving his Spanish troops winter quarters in disputed territory.

In 1591 a Flemish priest was found hiding with a crossbow in Rudolf's bedroom. It's probable Rudolf never felt safe again. That same year the Turkish Empire demanded that their tribute be doubled, then they beheaded the diplomats Rudolf sent to negotiate. The Turkish war to conquer Europe began along the border of Hungary, where fifty years of peace ended and fifteen years of war began. In 1593, the Turks' well-prepared invasion quickly captured two of the key fortresses on the way to the old imperial capital of Vienna. Rudolf pulled himself together to raise the money from his vassals and allies to pay for war, but Prague was paralyzed as Protestants and Catholics argued about every detail of the proceedings. As he and his subjects nervously watched the successes of the Turkish army, Rudolph finally showed his strength by uniting the factions.

In 1598 Philip died, only adding to Rudolf's depression and sense of foreboding. Philip the Pious, the new king of Spain, proved to be much less zealous than his father. He's remembered as an ineffective monarch without vices but also without ambition, a man not much suited for his job.

All Europe fretted over the emperor's apparent inaction. But Kepler saw it differently, writing that Rudolf in his personal motions and his political actions moved with the elegant precision of an equation by Archimedes, applying only just enough force to stalemate the war, tiring out the Turkish army with deliberate restraint. Rudolf soon found that the monarchs of Christian Europe would not rally to him and that the war was bleeding the imperial treasury dry. And still the war dragged on.

By the late 1590s, the Catholics of Prague, led by the pope's local delegate, presented exciting new plans for Rudolf they thought would help him counter the ever-more-demanding Protestant powers of Bohemia. Locals called the agents of this attack on Protestant culture and legal rights the Spanish Party. The Spanish Party's true goal was to establish a Catholic autocracy, a spiritual dictatorship. In the 1620s, they would realize their dream. But Rudolf withdrew his support when he saw the results of the power he gave them.

Had it not been for Rudolf's apprehension that his brother Matthias was building alliances with powerful Protestants in surrounding states, he probably would have never communicated with the pope or any of his representatives. He never attended a Catholic ritual after the Spanish Party fell from power, nor did he ever take confession again. He maintained only the most minimal contact with the Vatican. Imperial bureaucrats and civil servants ruled the day. More than once the pope and his cardinals discussed excommunicating the Holy Roman emperor.

The atmosphere must have indeed been apocalyptic as the war continued, and the pope schemed while Rudolf watched one grand old Czech noble family die out after another, as if Bohemia had been cursed to produce no legitimate male heirs.

Enter, in October 1600, Sir Anthony Sherley. Sherley and his brothers traveled the world as adventurers. Sherley had explored Africa's western coast. He had visited Central America, survived a mutiny, and dined with the shah of Persia. He brought Rudolf the exciting news that as Holy Roman emperor he should unite the armies of Europe, and then Persia would attack the Turkish army, opening multiple fronts in a war the Turks could not win. Sherley had plans to bring Moscow into the war, and Rudolf was heartened to hear the distant czar considered himself loyal to the Holy Roman emperor he had never met.

Was there really such a plan from Persia? Sherley certainly profited from his adventures, gaining titles and royal audiences, for himself and his brothers Sir Thomas and Sir Robert. But the great war against the Turks never happened—perhaps only because the leaders of Europe still refused to rally behind Rudolf, who understood that he was now merely a symbol without the power that his rank had been created to wield.

The year 1600 was a bad one for Rudolf. He was convinced he would die before he turned fifty, like his father. Now time seemed to be running out. Tycho stopped calculating Rudolf's astrological transits; the emperor was nervous enough. Tycho had already warned him that his chart indicated a monk might try to kill him, or Rudolf's own family could turn against him, if he wasn't constantly vigilant. But Rudolf still found the mystical more fascinating than the practical. A note from 1600 proves Rudolf was trying to locate and purchase a copy of the kabbalistic classic *Sefer Yetzirah*.

In September 1600, the enraged Rudolf banished two of the most powerful men at his court, so powerful that one of them had been chamberlain and then high steward and president of the Privy Council. No one knows what happened, but the suspicion that they had actually been working for the Spanish, not Rudolf, was popular then and now. Rudolf became more depressed than he had ever been in his life. He berated his ministers publicly. He could not hide his revulsion toward his own court, filled with courtiers he could never trust.

Rudolf ordered the words about apostolic authority to be left out of the absolution his personal priest still gave him, and he avoided attending any public church ritual, though they were becoming quite splendid, supported by the creativity and treasury of Rome in a bid to increase papal influence peacefully. But by then Rudolf didn't have much love for Protestants either. He had grown weary of their ever-dividing sects and their hostility toward one another. It's easy to imagine that scene from Monty Python's *Life of Brian* when the People's Front of Judea scoff at the Judean People's Front.

Rudolf even lost interest in his artists and alchemists, no longer making his daily rounds. Had he given up his quest for the philosopher's stone? Rumors spread among the Catholics of his court that Rudolf was possessed by the devil. Gossips whispered that he would turn pale and tremble when passing near a cross. His chief of finance in a poignant note reports that Rudolf felt he could trust no one, that he was being bullied, and that he feared he would die any day of poison.

In his deep melancholy Rudolf was given to uttering bleak pronouncements to startled guests. "I know I am dead and damned; I am a man possessed by the devil," he is reported to have said to Philip Lang. Lang held such control over which petitioners got to see Rudolf, some historians have speculated that he and Rudolf may have been lovers. Rudolf was said to have had affairs with his chamberlain and with his valets. Other historians believe rumors of Rudolf's homosexuality were part of a whisper campaign against him to weaken his position before his removal.

The triumphant golden crown Rudolf commissioned in 1602 must have seemed ironic in its splendor, a wish fulfillment in its depiction of him on horseback leading the way to victory over his fleeing enemies. In reality, he was more fearful than ever. He obsessed on the dangers surrounding him, real and imaginary. For example, late one night, suffering his usual insomnia, he panicked and then became enraged at the idea that his dependable longtime chamberlain was actually an agent working for Matthias and the pope. Rudolf confronted the poor old man, lunging at him with a knife. Melodramatic lightning and thunder caused Rudolf to hesitate long enough for his chamberlain to escape. Rudolf reconsidered his suspicion, but this was only more proof of his dangerous instability.

Another episode occurred when Tycho Brahe complained that the bells rung by the Dominican monks at all hours were disturbing his concentration. Protestants complained that the monks were bullying the locals, forcing conversions; they were obviously sent by the Vatican to begin the purification of Prague. With the pope pressuring him to be more supportive of Catholic goals and warning him that rumors of his necromancy had spread across the empire, Rudolf decided his troubles might be due to the negative spiritual influence of the Dominican monks. He knew all too well the old prophecy that he would die at the hands of a monk. He banished them from Prague.

But these monks were shrewd. They commissioned a Venetian master to paint a masterpiece as a gift for Rudolf. Rudolf canceled the banishment. More Catholic gifts of art followed, calming the emperor's wrath. The new pope sent a new confessor, a cultured man, author of a book on the Kabbalah, a priest who also practiced medicine. He reported that Rudolf was not possessed, but he did fight melancholy, though it had never taken root in him. He even convinced Rudolf to attend communion and confession during the Holy Week of 1601, but rumors of the emperor's madness or possession persisted.

In 1604, a nova, a new star in the sky, raised expectations that the world would end, Jesus would return to rule for a thousand years, or the philosopher king would defeat the pope. But it only added to Rudolf's apprehension.

In October 1605 the long siege of the Turkish army at an important imperial stronghold succeeded. The imperial soldiers even sold their military gear to the Turks. Back home the leadership of the imperial army split between Germans and Italians. Rudolf had a war hero beheaded for killing a rival commander in a duel just after he had banned dueling. The military failure, and the execution of a popular hero, especially as the rumor spread that Rudolf had waited too long to take action, further undermined his position.

Rudolf no longer visited his animals or his gardens where he once loved to listen to music played among the trees. He didn't look at his collection of wonders from around the world anymore. The beautiful nude paintings and sculptures surrounding him may have seemed to mock this solitary sickly man in his somber palace. Rumors spread everywhere that he was already dead; only his ghost could be seen walking the castle halls.

In 1605, Rudolf gave his eldest, but illegitimate, son Don Giulio the Rosenberg estate where John Dee and Edward Kelley had talked to the angels, including the castle Český Krumlov. Don Giulio was Rudolf's favorite child. He provided Don Giulio with a good education and looked for a place for him at the royal courts of Europe.

In the fall of 1606, Rudolf's brother Matthias secretly convened his fellow archdukes declaring that Rudolf's reign must come to an end. Could a madman obsessed by alchemy and occult superstitions be allowed to lead the war against the Turks? With the blessing of the pope, Matthias was elected head of the Habsburg family, a first step toward becoming the next Holy Roman emperor.

Rudolf felt devastated by this insult and betrayal. Less money found its way to Rudolf's court and more power was exerted daily by Matthias. The following spring Rudolf pointed at three flies on his table and commented: "Ah, it's the Pope, the King of Spain, and Archduke Matthias."

Matthias negotiated an expensive peace with the Turks, giving up most of Hungary and a rich tribute. Rudolf refused to sign the treaty. He thought the terms disgraceful. Matthias arrived at the border of Bohemia with twenty thousand troops.

The leaders of Prague were as shocked to see the pale, gray old man as they were to hear his feeble voice when he finally addressed them publicly after a long absence. Rudolf's Protestants professed their loyalty, but he could only raise four thousand men to defend his throne. Peter Rosenberg, having taken over his family's great wealth after the death of his brother William, joined the Protestants opposed to Matthias, but Rudolf surrendered. He gave the crowns of Hungary and Austria to his younger brother. Matthias had himself crowned king of Hungary just outside his brother's castle wall. Rudolf remained emperor, in name only.

Rudolf was about to suffer another family betrayal. In 1607 Don Giulio asked a local barber to let his daughter Markéta move into the castle with him. The barber approved. But as time passed Don Giulio grew irritated at his commoner playmate. He beat her. Then he mutilated her and threw her out a window. The poor girl landed in a trash heap. Though parts of her were missing, she regained her health, hiding with her parents.

But Don Giulio demanded that she return to his castle. When Markéta's father refused, Don Giulio imprisoned him. After five weeks of death threats, Markéta's mother brought her daughter to the castle on a wintry Sunday in February 1608. The next day in a fit of rage Don Giulio killed the girl. He cut off her head and other parts of her body. She went into her coffin in pieces. The nobles of Europe were scandalized, and Rudolf could make no excuses. He imprisoned his favorite son for life, as Uncle Philip had imprisoned cousin Carlos.

After committing the murder, Don Giulio refused to shave, wash, or change his clothes. When food and fresh clothes were brought to him, he threw them out the window. He hurled at his servants whatever was in reach. He never left his castle, though he was allowed to take a walk or ride. By 1609 he was living in his own filth and trash and had developed an ulcer. His rooms reeked, but no one dared enter for fear of his violence. He slept on carpets and used his old, torn clothes as blankets. That summer his ulcer ruptured and suffocated him.

Rudolf wanted his favorite son buried in a manner befitting the eldest son of an emperor, but he died before he could see it done. Locals say Don Giulio is buried in a wall of the castle, which is said to be haunted by more than one ghost. Don Giulio's brother, another of Rudolf's illegitimate sons, would die young, too, in a fight with a friend over a prostitute.

In 1609, pressured by the Protestant leaders who had stayed loyal, Rudolf used what power he had left to ban all religious persecution in Bohemia. The year before, Henry IV, king of France, had granted the Edict of Nantes, guaranteeing the rights of French Protestants. Rudolf both bowed to the pressure and rose to the occasion. As if by some great alchemical transmutation, freedom of religion became legally guaranteed in the capital of the Holy Roman Empire under Rudolf's Letter of Majesty. That year a Tuscan ambassador complained that Rudolf had all but turned the imperial throne into a workbench. The emperor liked building clocks. He wasn't only visiting his alchemical workshops again, he was also back to participating in the experiments.

In 1610, Henry IV of France was assassinated by a monk, the very fate Rudolf feared, especially after he had granted the right to freedom of religion in Bohemia. To protect himself from enemies, Rudolf was known to take up his unicorn horn and his Holy Grail, both symbols of purity, and with a Spanish sword draw a ceremonial circle around himself. He also drank water from the Holy Grail, claiming it healed him body and soul.

Rudolf explored the dark arts in self-defense. His human-shaped mandrake roots and his spirit-summoning bell inscribed with magic sigils survive. At his command, a magician tried to defend Rudolf using the grimoire known as *Picatrix*. This manual preferred by aspiring sorcerers is a translation of an Arabic work on astrology, alchemy, and the *Hermetica*, including the magic of talismans. Rudolf hoped to have supernatural forces intervene on his behalf. If he could not be King Solomon commanding demons to do his bidding, he could at least receive protection as Holy Roman emperor.

When Matthias left Vienna with another army, intending to make himself Holy Roman emperor, Rudolf blundered, siding with a charming but inept nephew, whose only motivation was deluded self-interest. On his nephew's advice Rudolf hired ten thousand mercenaries his government couldn't afford to pay, who became the scourge of Prague. The Jewish ghetto suffered rape and pillage. Protestant hotheads burned down Catholic churches. Most of the citizens, Catholic and Protestant, had seen enough. The ambassador of Spain withdrew along with the pope's delegate, both reassigned to serve Matthias. In March 1611, to save Prague, Peter Rosenberg paid off the emperor's debt to the mercenaries, though it cost him his family fortune.

Trying to find a way to stop Matthias from becoming the next Holy Roman emperor, Rudolf reached out to the Protestant alliances of Europe and to powerful Protestant widows. But it was too late. By November 1611, Rudolf was forced to attend a conference about the succession. The organizers demanded he formally choose his successor, but Rudolf only thanked them and assured them he would make a decision soon. He considered this conference his death sentence.

As Matthias approached Prague to claim his throne, Rudolf stayed up all night drinking heavily, running through the darkened hallways crying out incoherently. Then Matthias marched into Prague accompanied by Hungarian and Bohemian nobles, while Rudolf cowered in his castle, unwilling to attend the coronation of his nemesis brother. Three weeks later the Protestant powers of Prague upheld the new emperor's authority, but only if he respected the agreement Rudolf had made regarding freedom of religion.

Rudolf was shocked that the people he had protected throughout his reign so readily abandoned him, and he cursed Prague, looking out over the rooftops, proclaiming: "Ungrateful Prague, I made you famous now you drive me out! Let there be revenge! Damn you, and all the

Czechs!" A curse sorrowful citizens would recall after the destruction of Bohemia a decade later.

Rudolf did not attend the wedding when Matthias married Anna of Tyrol, one of Rudolf's favorite potential empresses. Rudolf was allowed to retain the title of emperor and to live in his castle on a small allowance.

Matthias banned the court musicians, maestros collected from all over Europe, replacing them with military bands. Rifle salutes fired whenever Matthias arrived or departed tormented Rudolf. Matthias reported to Rome the rumors he heard about Rudolf using black magic against him. A dog had been baptized, given the name Matthias, and then slaughtered. His clothes had been cursed. Rudolf watched ritual sex on an altar in a circle of magical protection to counteract alleged baleful influences from Matthias. Who knows if Rudolf agreed to any of these desperate measures, or if they ever occurred?

Rudolf wanted to leave the castle but didn't because Kepler needed to stay there to complete his astronomical calculations. On infrequent visits from old ambassadors and other guests, if his brother was mentioned Rudolf would groan: "He stole my crowns, one after the other."

Jan Amos Komenski, better known as Comenius, a father of modern education, wrote after Rudolf's death that the emperor had tried to create a Society of Peace. Two ambassadors were secretly sent to forty princes, Protestant and Catholic. Rudolf urged them to end all wars by guaranteeing freedom of religion. He hoped even the Turks might be inspired to join. This peaceful compromise failed because no other prince would support him. Rudolf wished that the Society of Peace would continue and someday achieve its goal of inspiring and protecting freedom of worship, but the dream would die with Rudolf.

Comenius was a believer in dreams and visions and a follower of the great German mystic Böhme, but he was also a practical man. He outlined the system of schools we're still familiar with today: elementary, middle, high. His influence on America becomes obvious when Cotton Mather reports Comenius turned down the job of being one of the first presidents of Harvard College. Comenius took an approach to education that differed greatly from the strict Christian schooling of the time. At the beginning of his book *The Great Didactic* Comenius stated his intent to provide a method: "by which schools may be the scene of less noise, aversion, and useless labour, but of more leisure, enjoyment, and solid progress" (Keatinge 1910).

Near the end of his life when he was a recluse living in a few rooms, Rudolf had his favorite horses paraded by his window so he could sit up in bed and watch them pass. Trapped in the claustrophobic remains of his power, his only companion was the lion. But then when the old lion died, Rudolf knew his own time had come. He developed bronchitis and then swelling in his legs. He ignored his doctors and forced his shoes on every morning so he could visit his collection of wonders, his only pleasure. In pain, he kept his shoes on for two days and developed gangrene in his feet. He refused medicines, instead relying on an alchemical potion.

On his deathbed Rudolf recalled the feeling of elation that had kept him up all night when his father had recalled him to Austria from Spain. How much more excited should he be now, he wondered, when he was about to return to his true home?

Rudolf, following his father's example, refused last rites, but this time, people weren't as surprised and scandalized to learn that the mad emperor of Prague had refused the blessings of a Catholic priest. He was said to have quipped to one of his two remaining servants that he would only accept last rites from a priest of their own kind, a comment much prized by Protestants, who assumed he meant them, but probably referring to followers of the hermetic tradition. According to rumors, after his death several million gold coins, an inheritance from his father, were found in his private rooms.

Matthias kicked out the remaining astrologers and alchemists. He had Rudolf's favorite painter do his portrait as the new emperor. Rudolf's collections were lost after he died. Much of it was taken away to storage in Vienna by Matthias and those who came after him; the rest was pillaged or destroyed during the Thirty Years' War.

Matthias sired no heirs and neither did his brothers. Instead, the next emperor would be one raised by the Jesuits, a Catholic avenger who defended the faith with a vengeance: Holy Roman Emperor Ferdinand II, who drained the wealth of the Holy Roman Empire by fighting the Thirty Years' War. With his own hands he destroyed Rudolf's letter guaranteeing freedom of worship.

Thus the stage was set for the sacred marriage, for the sacrificial alchemical couple who would preside over the debacle of the Rosicrucian revolution. They would walk the halls of Rudolf's memories, strangers in his castle, the Winter King and Queen whose reign lasted one winter. Theirs was a tragic love story.

From the flaming nest of European metaphysical religion would rise the phoenix of American metaphysical religion. The freedom of religion of Rudolf's Prague was reborn two hundred years after his reign, in the colonies, where Cotton Mather read the *Hermetica*, presidents of Harvard College were alchemists, and freedom of religion would be guaranteed in the not-too-distant future.

FIVE

Queen of Hearts

A tragic romance, a lost kingdom, an audacious hoax, the history of Elizabeth Stuart, the Bohemian Revolt, and the Rosicrucian enlightenment—these events may sound like scenes from a fairy tale but they set forces in motion that still shape our world today.

In November 1572, in the constellation Cassiopeia, a supernova glowed for sixteen months. Like his friend John Dee, and most of the esoteric masters of that era, Tycho Brahe had studied Arabic predictive astrology. He knew that the great conjunction of 1603 foretold the end of an era, but he thought the new star an even more momentous omen of the imminence of divine providence.

Five years later, the Great Comet was visible throughout Europe, and astrologers speculated that it foretold the end of the world or the beginning of a new era. In 1596 a less spectacular comet crossed the night sky. In 1600 a nova appeared in the constellation Cygnus. Two years later, another small comet. Then in 1603 the great conjunction of Jupiter and Saturn was exact in Sagittarius near what astrologers call the galactic center, followed in 1604 by a supernova in the constellation Serpentario, which added to the excitement of star watchers, especially when Mars joined the great conjunction. The year 1606 brought a double comet. Inspired by these celestial events, Protestant prophets and astrologers predicted the downfall of the pope, while their Catholic cousins promised the end of the Protestant faith.

While Jesuits schemed to regain control of Germany, the Netherlands, and the United Kingdom, dreams of a world without a pope preoccupied Protestant visionaries. As the hell on Earth of the Thirty Years' War unfolded, Protestants and Catholics throughout Europe would come to know the legend of Elizabeth Stuart, wife of the Elector of the Palatinate, nicknamed the Queen of Hearts and the Winter Queen, the last queen of Bohemia.

Elizabeth was born during an unseasonably severe storm in late summer 1596. Her vivacious mother Anne, born in Denmark, had become the Catholic queen of Scotland and England, two Protestant strongholds. Anne loved theater and occasionally caused scandals; for example, when she played Athena costumed in a tunic that showed too much leg, or her stage performance while sporting a pregnant belly, or the time she painted her face and body black for her role in a masque. But Anne also commissioned artists, and art collectors, enriching the royal collection.

Among those Anne supported were the inspired lutenist and composer John Dowland, playwright Ben Jonson, and numerous inventors and musicians. Some historians have dismissed her as so frivolous and extravagant she helped create the cultural conditions that caused the English Civil War. She navigated her husband's infidelities by becoming notorious for her own. A loyal Catholic, she longed to align her children with the pope and the king of Spain. She considered her bloodline superior to her husband's. She hoped to see her daughter married to a Holy Roman emperor. When the suitor with that potential appeared, he found a chilly reception from his soon-to-be mother-in-law because he was Protestant.

King James last saw either of his parents at thirteen months of age. His father, according to rumor, had been murdered with the help of his mother, Mary, Queen of Scots, who carried a sterling silver skull watch inscribed with a saying of the Roman poet Horace: "Pale death visits with impartial foot the cottages of the poor and castles of the rich." James was silent when Queen Elizabeth I ordered his mother's execution.

As king of Scotland, James encouraged witch trials, which inspired similar terrors in England, Europe, and America. Ironically, his daughter would eventually be accused of witchcraft by her enemies.

At age sixty-one Queen Elizabeth I agreed to become godmother of the firstborn son of James. To make it easier for her, James had named the boy Henry after her father, Henry VIII. The daughter that followed eighteen months later was named Elizabeth in honor of her godmother. The queen was irked by these gestures toward the succession, but her advisers convinced her there had to be an heir to the throne in place or there would be chaos when she died. Elizabeth sent her ambassador to represent her at the christening on a cold November day, but she sent no gift. Her subjects were mortified when, at the opening of Parliament the following year, the queen staggered under the weight of her royal robes and had to be helped to her throne.

The Elizabethan age ended in 1603 with the death of the queen, who had reigned for almost forty-five years. At first, James didn't believe the news, and then the messenger gave him Elizabeth's blue sapphire ring. The throne he inherited had little wealth. James would do his best to ignore that. He would find ways to raise money, or at least credit, to support the lavish lifestyle befitting an English monarch. Mere months after he became king, he sponsored Shakespeare's company, who became known as the King's Men. The translation of the Bible he would commission still bears his name. He would publish a book attacking tobacco smoking when it first became a fad. He kept up on the latest sciences from alchemy to astronomy. He consulted astrologers and religious leaders but never blindly followed any. He took for his motto *Pacifica Rex*, the king of peacemaking. He would commit himself in domestic and foreign policy to avoiding war.

Anne, the new queen of England, and nine-year-old Princess Elizabeth traveled together from Scotland to London, touring a society in several ways comparable to our own. Very wealthy nobles bent laws in their favor to further enrich themselves. Villagers kept a careful eye on one another. A woman who had cuckolded her husband or a man who had beat his wife could wake up one morning to find his or her fellows making "rough music" outside their front door, often pantomiming the transgression and otherwise ridiculing the transgressor. On social media we still see this behavior of ganging up to ridicule and shame. But in the villages if ridicule failed, the church court was the next resort, where spying on adulterers was not only admissible but mandatory. The village culture resembled a tribal community, while in London one could disappear into the anonymity of crowds.

Never comfortable around his subjects, James put them off with his dry wit and jokes more suited to a jester than the king of England. Onlookers were shocked when the new queen refused to partake of the Episcopalian sacrament during the coronation ceremony, and the new king clowned around throughout the payment of homage.

The Haringtons, a family charged with raising Elizabeth, received a monthly stipend from the court that didn't begin to pay their expenses. They hoped to be recompensed in the future, not only in cash but with favor and influence. The princess would spend most of her childhood in their converted Catholic monastery complete with cloisters, but the inside was as modern and luxurious as any Jacobean English castle.

That same year, 1603, three conspiracies threatened the lives of the princess, her brother, and her parents. The most famous is the Gunpowder Plot. In an odd twist of fate, Guy Fawkes was made a hero by the movie *V for Vendetta* and the Anonymous movement, but his revolution intended to make Great Britain submit to the pope. Fawkes had high hopes when King James and Queen Anne took the throne of England. Anne was a practicing Catholic, while James was known to have sympathy for Catholicism. Elizabeth I never forgot the armada that the king of Spain and the Vatican had sent against her, but now many Catholics hoped they would find favor again. James did favor Catholic nobles, but he also realized that the pope would settle for nothing less than England under the watchful eye of the Vatican. When reports about Catholic power grabs reached his ears, the monarch clamped down on his Catholic subjects, more than Queen Elizabeth I had. Fawkes and his fellow conspirators decided to take matters into their own hands.

The infamous plot to blow up King James, Prince Henry, and all of Parliament is often told without an important detail. Fawkes and the conspirators planned to kidnap Princess Elizabeth. She would be raised Catholic by a Catholic regent. Lord Harington, upon hearing the first news and rumors of treason, though he received no warning of any imminent threat to the princess, decided to take her somewhere less conspicuous while awaiting instructions. Her kidnappers arrived two hours after she had been rushed away to safety. Harington recorded her precocious comment: "What a Queen should I have been by this means! I had rather have been with my Royal Father in the Parliament House, then wear his Crown on such condition." Visitors reported the depressed expressions and long silences of everyone around her months later. The princess was afraid, sleepless, and melancholy.

Elizabeth received a letter from a nine-year-old boy who would grow up to become her husband. Frederick V's letter to Elizabeth, after he heard about the failed conspiracy she narrowly avoided, illustrates the fanatic religious climate of Protestant Germany. Frederick was convinced that the antichrist himself was behind the plot, by which he meant the pope.

Having survived the tender mercies of both Mary, Queen of Scots, and Elizabeth Regina, the new king was rumored not to be keen on continuing Henry VIII's tradition of an excellent education for his daughters. "To make women learned and foxes tame had the same effect," he allegedly said, "to make them more cunning." But the source is doubtful. So much of what we know about James and his family is colored by propaganda both Catholic and Protestant.

James provided his daughter with a Scottish nurse, a personal physician, a French maid, two liveried footmen, a laundress, a seamstress, three women of the bedchamber, grooms of the chamber and stable, a dog, pet monkeys, several colorful parrots, and twenty horses for her favorite activities, riding and hunting. Her musical tutor was Dr. John Bull, said to be the composer of the British national anthem. She had a talent for playing harpsichord, or rather a virginal, as the early form of the instrument was known.

Fluent in French and skilled at Italian, the princess wrote lonely letters to her brother Henry, tying them in strands of floss silk colored gold, rose, royal blue, amethyst, lemon, and grass green, brightened by twisted tinsel threads. Although only eighteen months older than her, Henry reminded Elizabeth that he had responsibilities as the eldest son that he could not ignore, though he looked forward to their time together as much as she did. Lord Harington's son wrote a friend about the quaint way Elizabeth sent letters to the king and received his responses. A trusted dog delivered the mail between princess and monarch, running from one castle to the other.

Comparisons between Elizabeth and her famous namesake began early. The *History of Coventry* includes in its registers an account of her impressive first visit (Benger 1825, 76). Her skilled horsemanship reminded people of the late queen. The gilt silver cup they presented her was so heavy, Lord Harington had to help her hold it up. It's no wonder that Elizabeth reminded so many of that still beloved queen. She had studied with Elizabeth I's music master, with a writing master the queen had favored, and the son of the queen's dancing master taught the princess how to dance. Her hairline was plucked so that her high forehead and coif resembled her namesake. Portraits were painted in imitation of her, and as a girl she had practiced until she made her signature a replica of the Virgin Queen's regal scrawl.

As she approached adolescence, among Elizabeth's visitors were ambassadors and agents of the royal families of Europe, making first inspections of a princess who would soon become the most eligible female royal in the world. Savvy insiders felt certain she would grow up to marry Louis XIII and so become the queen of France. Her brother Henry would most likely wed a Spanish princess. In this way, James would keep a balance between Protestants and Catholics, preserving peace and postponing the inevitable war.

Visits to the court where her father doted on her cheered up Elizabeth. He surprised her with lavish gifts of jewelry, dresses, and dazzling toys. Elizabeth and Henry were known for their good sense and gracious ways. At age thirteen she was invited to watch her brother joust and then to attend his banquet. Before the guests arrived, she and Henry previewed the feast, walking twice around the 120-foot table of sweetmeats arranged to resemble windmills and flower gardens, creatures crafted from food, rosewater fountains, and pastries patterned in imitation of the constellations.

Ben Jonson wrote speeches for the event, which included generic prophetic lines delivered by a Merlin to Henry, Elizabeth, and their little brother, Charles. Merlin missed completely on his prediction for Henry. He was right about Charles when he said he would "shake a sword and lance against the foes," but he did not mention that the enemy would be English and that Charles would lose his head. As we shall see, Merlin's prophecy for Elizabeth came true: "That most princely maid, whose form might call the world to war, she shall be mother of nations."

The charismatic crown prince Henry jousted with such skill that day that the court buzzed with comparisons to the young Henry VIII. James had given his son a set of golf clubs and tennis rackets, which he began using when only six years old, so he excelled at both sports, the one beloved by the Scots and the other by the English. At age fourteen, Henry kept a charity jar to which any of his servants who used vulgar language contributed. As he grew older, but still a teen, Henry commissioned a garden to showcase the wonders of ancient engineering recovered by the French Huguenot engineer Salomon de Caus, one of Princess Elizabeth's tutors.

Imprisoned in the Tower of London for treason, Sir Walter Raleigh, who had been a great hero of the Elizabethan Age, was suicidal at first but he soon made the best possible use of his predicament by writing books and turning his cell into a center for intellectual discourse and alchemical experimentation.

Prince Henry encouraged Raleigh to write his audacious classic *The History of the World* (1628). Raleigh dedicated the book to Henry, who had defied the king to show him favor. Henry's comment about James condemning Raleigh—"only my father would keep such a bird in a cage"—became well known. Henry sponsored the exploration of the fabled Northwest Passage, a way from the Atlantic to the Pacific through the Arctic Sea. He had libraries built, and a gallery for his collection of paintings by Hilliard and Holbein.

As for Raleigh, he and John Dee were friends who shared a deep interest in esotericism. In *The History of the World* Raleigh wrote: "Magus is a Persian word primitively, whereby is expressed such a one as is altogether conversant in things divine." Raleigh tells us that according to Plato, magic is worship of God. Raleigh quotes from a letter of Apollonius that tells us *magus* has two meanings. The lower meaning designates men who are like gods. The higher is the title of those who are deeply devoted to serving God. Raleigh then refers to Matthew 2:1, the story of the Magi at the birth of Jesus. Raleigh continues: "These Wisemen the Greeks call Philosophers: the Indians, Brahmans . . . among the Egyptians they were termed Priests; with the Hebrews they were called Cabalists, Prophets, Scribes, and Pharisees: amongst the Babylonians they were differenced by the name of Chaldeans: and among the Persians, Magicians." Filled with unsubtle jabs at King James, the *History* was banned by royal decree but was too popular to disappear.

Young Henry and his friends studied Neoplatonism, kabbalism, and hermeticism, inspired by the Elizabethans and by Italian philosophers Ficino and Pico della Mirandola and also influenced by prominent writers on esoteric subjects, such as Agrippa and Michael Maier, who visited England. Although James wrote *Daemonologie* (1597), a book warning his subjects about the dangers of witchcraft and black magic, he, like most of the Englishmen of his time, found no contradiction in condemning witches while praising alchemists and astrologers, though he feared that an astrologer might predict his death and somehow therefore seal his fate. Neoplatonism influenced the art of the great poets of the time, including Shakespeare, and the theories of pioneer scientists, including Isaac Newton.

As Princess Elizabeth matured, delegations arrived representing European nobility: the Prince of Hesse, the future king of Sweden, and even the newly widowed king of Spain. The delegation on behalf of the crown prince of Savoy presented James with the gift of a rare snow leopard. However, the gift backfired when the big cat ate one of the king's favorite pets, a white deer.

In 1611, when Elizabeth was fourteen, James received a document from the influential Duke of Bouillon, the ruler of a small semi-sovereign state located between Luxembourg and Champagne. Bouillon sang the praises of his nephew Frederick V. Born three days before Princess Elizabeth, Frederick was dark haired with large dark eyes. Surprisingly athletic despite appearing younger than his years, Frederick was an excellent horseman. He was not the son of a king, but he would inherit his father's role as the most powerful of the seven electors who elected the Holy Roman emperor. As palsgrave, Count Palatine of the Rhine, Duke of Bavaria, imperial knight, high elector, and ruler of the Palatinate—a constituent state of the Holy Roman Empire—only he had the power to veto decisions made by the emperor. Should the emperor be accused of violating the constitution of the Holy Roman Empire, the Elector Palatine would judge him. And, along with the Elector of Saxony, the Elector Palatine would serve as interim co-emperor between reigns.

Rumors from Bohemia suggested Frederick might be chosen king. As king of Bohemia and Elector Palatine, Frederick might be elected Holy Roman emperor. Though it seemed unlikely that a German Protestant prince could ever sit on the ultimate secular Catholic throne, Frederick's bloodline was among the oldest and most royal in Europe. His family had ruled Bavaria since Charlemagne. Palatine was derived from the Latin word *palatinus*, for "imperial" or "of the palace." Palatine Hill was the hill at the center of ancient Rome. Empress Elizabeth? King James must have thought that a delightful if improbable possibility when, as he claimed, a plan for electing Frederick emperor was first proposed to him in October 1610—but he never said by whom.

Rumors reported by Sir Walter Scott, in his gossipy *Secret History of the Court of James the First*, suggest that Prince Henry had strongly encouraged Frederick as the right choice for his sister. If Henry then married a German princess, he would have a German army. He could begin his war against the Vatican without having to wait for his ascension to his father's throne. Scott portrays Henry's cruel side, as the crown prince teases his little brother Charles, telling him he should join the priesthood to hide his crooked skinny legs under a robe, making the boy cry. But Scott confirms Henry's devotion to his sister.

By the time she turned fifteen, the ambassadors from the royal courts of Europe were describing Elizabeth as beautiful, intelligent, dignified, and gracious. The princess began exchanging letters with Frederick. They wrote in French, the only language they both knew. Other suitors exchanged letters with Elizabeth, but the possibility of marriage was mentioned only when writing to Frederick.

Elizabeth had her own barge as all of London took to the river Thames to celebrate Henry's status as the new Prince of Wales. Two mechanical wonders delighted everyone: a whale and a dolphin, both bearing on their broad backs actors costumed as deities of classical antiquity. Many barges were decorated with flags, banners, and streamers. Musicians on board filled the air with music.

A month later Elizabeth was invited to participate in one of her mother's masques, a story about Tethys, queen of the ocean, the wife of Neptune. Elizabeth would play the Nymph of the Stately Thames. She wore a sky-blue taffeta bodice decorated with symbols of the sea. Charles, a frail child who most expected would not survive long, had grown into a fine ten-year-old boy. He played Zephyrus, god of the west wind, in a short green satin robe embroidered with golden flowers. Silver wings and a multicolored flower garland in his hair completed the costume.

Phineas Pett was a shipbuilder who took to heart a friend's advice that he should build Prince Henry a pleasure yacht. Henry was pleased, even more so by the plans for another ship Pett presented. Pett found himself chatting over his plans with the king of England. The royal shipbuilders, alarmed by the sudden rise of this newcomer, schemed against him, accusing him of using bad lumber and otherwise endangering his own projects because of his ignorance. A grueling examination followed, during which only Henry offered moral support and only in the most subtle ways. James decided the accusations were false.

By way of consolation, Henry and his sister visited Pett at his home. Elizabeth's kindness impressed Mrs. Pett. Elizabeth and Charles journeyed with their mother and father to watch Prince Henry christen Pett's warship, which would be the pride of the English fleet. But the dock gates had been badly built, and the ship got stuck between them, so the royal family had to go home. Prince Henry returned later that night at high tide. He personally supervised the launch and christened the ship, giving it the name *The Prince Royal*. On that ship Elizabeth would leave England to begin her ill-fated life in Europe.

While the English were not especially fond of their new king and queen, they adored the royal children, especially Henry. He made no secret of his intent to someday unite England, Germany, and France in a war against the Vatican and the Holy Roman Empire. But then a Catholic with a knife murdered the king of France in the streets of Paris. He had been a champion of the Protestant cause and was to set off to war that day as an ally of the Protestants of Germany. Henry IV's wife, Marie de' Medici, whose coronation took place the day before, would arrange marriages for their children with Catholic royals only.

James was not willing to send Elizabeth to a Catholic court, and there weren't many good prospects among eligible Protestant princes and kings. So James nominated Frederick of the Palatine against Queen Anne's protests. Anne allegedly asked her daughter how she would like the title "Goodwife Palsgrave." But Elizabeth defended her father's choice. When her mother insisted she marry for a king's crown, Elizabeth said she would "rather be the Palsgrave's Wife, than the greatest Papist Queen of Christendom."

Frederick's father, Frederick IV, had been the first director and a founding member of the Protestant Union, a defensive pact between nine princes and seventeen imperial cities. Christian of Anhalt, his prime minister and general of the war council of the Protestant Union, was now Frederick's mentor and prime minister. Frederick IV had been a skilled negotiator, often able to create agreements where none had been thought possible. His personal charm and common sense helped prevent wars. He also helped make Heidelberg University one of Europe's centers of learning, but he enjoyed the wonderful wines of the Rhine produced by his nation of vineyards so much he drank himself to death at age thirty-six. Frederick V was only fourteen years old when his father died.

In May 1612 the Duke de Bouillon represented Frederick V as documents were drawn up in London promising him marriage with Elizabeth. When the Spanish ambassador wondered if Frederick was, after all, an inferior match for such a fine princess, King James was indiscreet enough to bring up the possibility that his soon-to-be son-in-law might be elected king of Bohemia. Yet by the time the predicted election occurred, James did not want Frederick to accept, and when he did anyway, refused to formally recognize him as king. Meanwhile, Queen Anne continued to insist that the king of Spain had been the only reasonable choice for Elizabeth.

After a difficult voyage through stormy October seas, Frederick's first attempt to reach England with a small fleet failed. So the English sent three ships to fetch him. That journey went smoothly and Frederick arrived in the United Kingdom with a retinue of 420, including 12 royals and 30 nobles. Crowds cheered as they watched 150 boats and barges float up the Thames to the tune of trumpets and drums, a two-hundred-gun salute from the Tower of London, and cannon volleys fired by nearby ships.

Frederick met his future brother-in-law Henry at Whitehall Stairs. They walked together past the pillars under the lofty ceiling of the Banqueting House built by the brilliant engineer and architect Inigo Jones. There before the gathered nobles in their best finery and jewels, with guards in gold and velvet, Frederick met his future wife and in-laws. First, he bowed deeply to James, who embraced him. The queen refused to look at him as he bowed so low he missed her subtle invitation to kiss her hand. Prince Henry and Frederick exchanged smiles and greetings. Prince Henry looked pale and ill, but he was in good spirits. When he came to Elizabeth, Frederick stooped to kiss the hem of her gown, but Elizabeth curtsied so low she was able to reach out and stop him. He kissed her hand. She blushed.

Frederick refused invitations to play tennis or ride with Prince Henry. He avoided the activities his entourage enjoyed. He wanted only to be in the presence of Elizabeth, to talk with her and to take their meals together. Then commenced a series of interviews, ceremonies, and celebrations. Even the queen had to admit, while a bit homely and certainly not dashing, neither heroic nor exceptional, Frederick was intelligent and charming. His large dark eyes were sensitive and expressive. Sir Walter Raleigh in the Tower wrote that Frederick was the only choice. Henry and Frederick agreed on so many matters they became friends. Henry enthusiastically endorsed Frederick. He told Elizabeth he would travel with her to pick out a German princess to be his bride.

Though he became a favorite of the king, the British nobles mistook Frederick's dignity for arrogance, and his retinue, instead of impressing the court, caused derision because of their foreign ways, which were considered prudish and uncultured. But in Europe, especially Germany, the match became a symbol in the imaginations of reformers, prophets, radicals, and poets of a sacred marriage dedicated to reforming the world.

Then tragedy struck. Even before Frederick had arrived, Prince Henry had suffered two bouts with fever, and then dysentery. The eighteen-year-old prince probably had typhoid fever, caught when he went swimming in the sewage-polluted Thames, where he was busy with his latest project, building the first bridge to cross the river at Westminster. It was not the first time he had caught fever after overindulging in food, and then diving into the unsanitary river.

Henry refused to ruin the festive atmosphere of his beloved sister's nuptials, so he forced himself out of bed to play cards the next two days. The doctors bled him. On November 1 he seemed to be improving and was well enough to get a visit from Elizabeth, Charles, Anne, and James but in his accustomed place now walked Frederick.

On November 3, the heir to the throne of England faced the cold weather in a shirt to play a game of tennis. But at a sermon the next day he appeared thin and pale. The court worried about the prince's dull, hollow eyes. Henry and Frederick were to attend a feast organized by the City of London on November 8, but only Frederick attended. Soon Henry was bedridden with a severe fever. Rumors that agents of the pope had poisoned him spread as fast as the news that he was sick. Even James would be accused by the conspiracy theorists of the day of having poisoned his own son. More bloodletting was prescribed.

James, Anne, and Elizabeth visited Henry daily. His health seemed to be improving. November 11 was the last day of optimism. James looked into arranging an immediate marriage so that even a brief recovery might produce another heir to the throne, in case his own youngest son Charles should become sick again.

So desperate was the search for a cure for Henry that of all the alchemical and cunning remedies sent to save his firstborn son, King James allowed Sir Walter Raleigh's elixir to be administered. Raleigh, with perhaps more shrewdness than sincerity, confidently announced that his concoction would restore Henry's health, unless the prince had been poisoned. The elixir caused Henry to break into a sweat that was at first considered a good sign, but the fever raged on. As he worsened, the doctors bled him again and gave him enemas and laxatives.

Becoming delirious, Henry cried out for his sword, declaring he must be gone. More drastic methods of healing were applied. The doctors shaved off his dark blond hair. Cupping glasses reddened his skin. The halves of a rooster cut down the back were lashed to the soles of his feet. The Archbishop of Canterbury prayed for him.

Elizabeth was no longer allowed to see her brother, in case he might be contagious. She disguised herself, twice attempting to sneak into his room. She wanted to comfort him as he died. Mortified, James retreated from the court to his sanctuary in the country. The day before the eighteen-year-old's death, the rumor of it had already spread across the countryside. In towns people mourned and cried out in the streets.

Phineas Pett, the shipbuilder Henry had championed, found at St. James "a house turned to the very map of true sorrow, every man with the character of grief written in his dejected countenance, all places flowing with tears and bitter lamentations." Twelve-year-old Prince Charles gave his older brother a poignant last gift: a small bronze toy of the equestrian statue of Cosimo de' Medici. Cosimo was not only a great ruler, but also a renowned patron of the arts and of philosophy. Cosimo commissioned Ficino's translations of Plato and the *Hermetica* that helped inspire the Renaissance. Crown Prince Henry Frederick died on November 16, 1612. The last thing he said was: "Where is my dear sister?"

No matter how terrible the grief, no one as yet understood how grave the loss of Henry would be for his sister and for the Protestants of Europe. The ambassador from Venice reflected on the measure of what promised to have been a great king when he wrote of Henry: "His authority was great. . . . His designs were vast; his temper was grave, severe, reserved, brief in speech. All the hopes of these kingdoms were built on his high qualities." Thousands mourned in the streets of London, "weeping, crying, howling and wringing their hands" (MacLeod 2012). The great writers and composers of the day eulogized and lamented. Heartbroken, Elizabeth wept for two days, refusing to eat. Charles fell ill. At Henry's funeral procession, led by his brother Charles, the crowd responded most to the bereaved sister and her husband-to-be. James and Anne were too grief-stricken to attend. Months later, in a meeting with diplomats, James would break down and weep, crying: "Henry is dead, Henry is dead."

After Henry's death, Frederick was so genuine James was moved to announce that his future son-in-law was a gift from God to console him for the loss of his son. The love of Frederick for Elizabeth, obvious in his tenderness, became an important emotional support for her as grief bonded them. With her help, Frederick hurried to learn enough English so that he could speak his lines for their wedding ceremony. He and Elizabeth played two of her favorite games: billiards and gambling with cards.

On December 18, Frederick became a Knight of the Order of the Garter, though the king, suffering gout, performed the ceremony from his bed. The ribbon and diamond star awarded to him had belonged to Prince Henry.

At their betrothal ceremony on December 27, the teenagers giggled slightly at the atrocious French of the presiding official. After a boring sermon James attended the dinner, which was not a celebration since the court was in mourning, yet James told jokes. After the ceremony Frederick's name was added when prayers for the royal family were said.

On New Year's Day an old tradition was revived, and gifts were exchanged. Frederick gave James diamond-encrusted swords and an agate bowl. Elizabeth received her engagement ring. As the pageantry of masques and dances presented by the court, the mayors of cities, and the students of Gray's Inn occupied her attention, the queen warmed up to Frederick enough to promise she would help plan the wedding ceremony. Some at court were surprised that the parents of Prince Henry were occupied in frivolous entertainments so soon after his death. But James and Anne sought solace not only in habit but also in their duty to support the marriage of their daughter, and the alliance with the Protestant Union.

The betrothed royal teenagers rode horses, hunted, and took boat trips. Painters attempted to commit their charm to canvas in officially commissioned portraits. The King's Men were paid for "presenting before the Princess Highness the Lady Elizabeth and the Prince Palatine Elector fourteen several plays," which included *Much Ado about Nothing, The Winter's Tale, Julius Caesar, Othello, The Merry Wives of Windsor,* and *The Tempest.* Some scholars believe Shakespeare rewrote the masque scene in *The Tempest* in honor of Frederick and Elizabeth, others that he was inspired to author or coauthor *Henry VIII,* the play that was performed on their wedding night. The play's climax, the birth of Queen Elizabeth I, is celebrated by a beautiful prophecy:

In her days every man shall eat in safety
Under his own vine what he plants, and sing
The merry songs of peace to all his neighbors.
God shall be truly known . . .

This is not only a eulogy for the Elizabethan age, but also a hopeful prayer for Princess Elizabeth. The prophecy of the rebirth of the phoenix is addressed to James. Perhaps Shakespeare believed, as did many others, that by marrying his only daughter to the head of the Protestant Union, the king of England was committing to the independent policies of Henry VIII and Elizabeth I.

At 10 a.m. on January 6, a Sunday, Frederick and Elizabeth were married privately at Banqueting House. A tapestry of the English victory against the Spanish Armada decorated the room. At dawn her retainers had begun the work of preparing Elizabeth. They wrapped her in a diamond-studded black satin gown embroidered with silver lace. They carefully detangled her waist-length amber hair letting it flow free. Gold spangles, rubies, emeralds, pearls, and diamonds woven into her hair sparkled. Thirteen young ladies with their hair flowing free, all in white, carried her long train. A golden crown decorated with pearls and diamonds and a plume of white feathers completed her wedding apparel.

Frederick wore purple velvet decorated with gold lace, his cloak lined with "cloth of gold." He also wore the glittering diamond insignia of St. George that had belonged to Henry. James wore a black Spanish suit and cape, with long stockings, and a single big diamond in his hat. Queen Anne did not attend. She blamed her absence on a case of gout.

On February 11 a grand exhibition of fireworks lit up Whitehall. The narrative they told was inspired by Spenser's Elizabethan tribute to Elizabeth I, *The Faerie Queen*. Evil Mango the necromancer fought Red-Crosse Saint George and the Lady Lucida. To the thunder of nearby cannons, St. George and the dragon battled. Emblazoned in fireworks, a pack of hounds chased a hare darting across the waters. Fireworks took the forms of birds, fish, men, and women. Finally, a fleet of ships rigged with flags and streamers sailed into view for a naval battle under the stars. Firefighters stood on the banks of the river.

On February 13 the entertainment was a pretend naval battle between a Venetian man-of-war and seventeen smaller Turkish boats. It told a tale of a damsel in distress. The late Prince Henry had helped design it. It turned out to be a more dangerous event than the great fireworks show. One man was blinded, and another lost his hands. A sailor commented that the entertainment had been more dangerous than an actual battle. But after the fireworks, the show was a letdown and the king looked bored.

The late prince figured more prominently in the *Masque of Truth*, written by a member of Frederick's entourage, with costumes, sets, and special effects by Inigo Jones. A sketch survives of the costume to be worn by Elizabeth and her ladies. Breasts almost bare behind transparent cloth, meant to symbolize innocence, undoubtedly would have scandalized Frederick's entourage. Henry was not only to have played a prominent role, he contributed many ideas to the masque and so did Elizabeth. A metaphorical prophecy about the alliance between the Palatine and the United Kingdom, it predicted that Protestantism would eventually win over all Catholics. Elizabeth rehearsed for two months but the masque was canceled. Nadine Akkerman describes the theatrical marvels of these masques: "Accounts talk of machines that enabled almost magical scenery changes, with architecturally fantastic buildings vanishing only to be replaced by others within seconds, to the delight and amazement of their audiences" (2021, 78).

Five full days of celebration included a ballet attended by over three hundred noble women wearing dresses embroidered in gold and silver lace. The ambassadors of almost every nation in the world were astonished by the splendor.

The solemnization, the wedding for the public, was to take place February 14 at Westminster Abbey, but it was moved to the Royal Chapel so the bride would not have to marry in the place where her brother had recently been entombed. The morning of St. Valentine's Day, bells rang in the church towers. Cannons and muskets fired. Frederick wore a white satin suit decorated with gold and pearls. The bride in one account wears the only white dress at the event. White was the color of mourning for women of the royal family. Another says her gown of silver thread and pearls was spangled with jewels, her very long train carried by ladies in white and silver gowns. Between the plaits of her hair, diamonds, gold, and precious stones once again gleamed and glittered. Her crown alone was valued at one million pounds.

Frederick handled his English lines awkwardly but sincerely. Nobles from across Europe filled the hall, but none from Spain. Even the Spanish ambassador refused to attend, excusing himself with a polite lie about his health. A boring sermon followed a tedious service, but the ceremony was short, notable only for the choice Frederick and Elizabeth made to leave out obedience in the list of marital pledges, vowing to love, cherish, and honor but not to obey. Elizabeth's face was said to have been glowing with sparkling lights of joy that the common folk considered a bad omen.

After the ceremony Elizabeth changed out of her weighty gown into a more comfortable and becoming dress of gold threads. Trumpets summoned the guests to dinner. Fifty-two sat at the table for a three-hour feast. In the evening a three-hour ballet on the theme of Orpheus received the damning royal criticism that it was "several hours too long."

Leading lights of the time celebrated at the after-party. The great poet John Donne wrote a poem about the wedding night that ends:

Oh let not this day but this night bee thine
Thy day was but the Eve to this O Valentine.

The next morning James embarrassed Frederick with his questions about the wedding night. Any doubts anyone may have had about the consummation of the marriage would be dismissed when Elizabeth became pregnant before leaving England in April.

On February 15, *The Memorable Masque of the Middle Temple and Lincoln's Inn*, written by George Chapman, once again with costumes, sets, and stage effects by Inigo Jones, was performed. Inspired by the bold inventions of the masters of Italian theatrical stage effects, Jones innovated breakthroughs in the optics and mechanics of live theater that helped open the door to the modern era of spectacular special effects.

Chapman, a follower of the late Prince Henry, and therefore an enthusiastic supporter of the Virginia Colony project, based his masque on the theme of Native American sun worshippers arriving in London to honor the newlyweds by converting to Christianity. The festivities commenced with a torchlit parade down Chancery Lane: fifty gentlemen on horseback, followed by boys dressed as baboons in Neapolitan suits with exaggerated ruffs, and then musicians and masquers in chariots.

Jones's stage set featured a golden mountain with a silver octagonal and domed temple on one side and a hollow tree on the other. The mountain moved toward the spectators, then split open to release the baboons. The mountaintop opened revealing fire dancers whose torches were lit at both ends. The elite of the court played highly stylized native chiefs. In the dedication when Chapman refers to "thrice gracious Princess Elizabeth," it's an obvious pun on "thrice greatest Hermes."

More masques followed, including *Marriage of Thames and Rhine*, organized by Sir Francis Bacon, and productions of theatrical masterpieces, including Beaumont and Fletcher's *Philaster or Love Lies A-Bleeding*, a tragicomedy about love, lies, and revenge, complete with a Spanish villain and a rebellion by good citizens to save their princess and her true love.

As one exhausting entertainment followed another, the king began to droop and yawn openly, and the queen began spitefully referring to the bride as Goodwife Palsgrave. Two days after Bacon's masque, James left the court, retreating to his country house. He now considered it urgent that he marry his younger son Charles to a Catholic princess. Thereafter, knowing that the Spanish despised him, James nevertheless did whatever he could to appease them, including ordering the beheading of Sir Walter Raleigh.

England resounded with prophecies of the glories to be born from this marriage of the Thames and Rhine. How hollow these prognostications of happiness and dominion would seem in a few short years. Poets composed solemn declarations. Neoplatonic and alchemical themes of the union of opposites appeared in art, writing, and theater as the blonde princess and dark-haired prince were recast as the hermetic marriage. About Elizabeth, John Donne wrote, in his poem "An Epithalamion, Or Marriage Song on the Lady Elizabeth and Count Palatine Being Married on St. Valentine's Day" (1613): "Up then, fair phoenix bride, frustrate the sun." Referring to the wedding he wrote, "And by this act these two phoenixes / Nature again restorèd is" and "Here lies a she sun, and a he moon there" (Donne 1896, 83–87).

In his *Epithalamia: or Nuptiall Poems* (1612), George Wither, who would later author the obscure oracle *A Collection of Emblemes, Ancient and Moderne* (1635), wrote that Queen Elizabeth and Princess Elizabeth were two phoenixes "being both one." Oxford University published its own book of *Epithalamia* in 1613, an influential and multilingual collection of 238 poems about the royal bride and groom. Cambridge published another 146 poems. A flurry of pamphlets heralded a new era. As Akkerman writes: "Taken as a whole, the English and Neo-Latin verse and prose written on the occasion of the marriage would coalesce into a propaganda program for a unified militant Protestantism." As she summarizes it: "The Palatine wedding had turned Elizabeth Stuart into their new warrior queen, a mystical heir to both Henry and the late queen Elizabeth her godmother" (2021, 88).

By the end of March, the royal mood chilled further. James had spent the equivalent of roughly fifteen million in 2022 dollars on the wedding, an enormous fortune in those days. Now with everyone clamoring for their money, he suddenly dismissed without warning two-thirds of Frederick's retinue, to the relief of many who complained that English women were debauching their young men.

Elizabeth was mortified by her father's rude action, but the entertainments continued. A joust the next day was followed with a visit by the newlyweds to the Tower, where Elizabeth charmed onlookers by insisting on lighting the ceremonial cannon and then, instead of flinching, beamed with excitement at the powerful explosion. Comparisons between her and her namesake made the rounds again.

But James wasn't done cutting costs or mortifying his daughter. When the Haringtons asked to have their generous expenditures reimbursed, repayment for wedding preparations, and for having raised the princess, James refused them. However, he did grant Harington the right to mint brass farthings, pocket change nicknamed Haringtons.

The royal cold shoulder left Frederick complaining that his father-in-law treated him more like a page than a son. But James tended to sour whenever he ran out of money. The loving couple he had such affection for only a few weeks earlier were now a burdensome expense. The king and queen accompanied the newlyweds only partway to their port of departure. Locals flocked to see the royals. On their last night together, Anne excused herself from dinner. Gossips wondered if she was overcome with emotion at the departure of her daughter, or perhaps simply bored.

James dined with Elizabeth and Frederick. They did not know this would be the last time they'd ever see each other again. As they said good-bye, Elizabeth wept. Her new husband, a mere boy, and her younger brother Charles tried to comfort her. A sixteen-year-old girl, she had never been to the continent.

When the weather forced them to postpone their departure, the superstitious whispered that it was a bad omen. The delay spoiled a book about their eventful arrival in Heidelberg that was published, much to the embarrassment of the publisher, eight days before they set sail. The king and queen behaved as if their daughter was already at sea. Anne got back to organizing her amusements, and James returned to his favorite country house to enjoy his everyday pleasures.

Nobles and commoners alike tried to warn Elizabeth not to meet her future on her late brother's ship *The Prince Royal*. They feared his ill fate would somehow become contagious and infect her, but the vessel proudly flew Prince Henry's royal insignia. Elizabeth presumably felt comfortable on board the ship that had been championed by and named after her brother. Perhaps she thought in some way it represented his continued presence and protection.

SIX

The Eighth Wonder of the World

Seven ships sailed across the sea, commanded by the last surviving hero of the victory against the Armada; this was the Earl of Nottingham's final service as Lord Admiral. Arriving in the Netherlands, Elizabeth found that her enjoyment of military spectacle had been noticed. Trumpets and exploding ammunition of various kinds welcomed her. Elizabeth, unveiled and smiling enthusiastically, walked through the streets, ignoring all court etiquette, the very picture of the liberated young English royal.

For eighty years the Dutch, rebelling against their Habsburg rulers and the heavy taxes of the Holy Roman Empire, had fought the Spanish and had relied on help from English monarchs, especially Elizabeth's namesake. The navy, the musketeers, and the city garrison competed over which of them would honor her first. They were charmed when she requested to see the sites of the famous battles where they had defended their liberty.

In the home of Maurice of Nassau, a powerful Dutch leader, nicknamed the Brazilian for his profitable governorship of Dutch Brazil, eighty guests, including local officials and members of Frederick and Elizabeth's entourage, enjoyed a two-day feast that illustrated the excess of royal celebrations and their impact on local economies. The guests consumed 1 hare, 12 geese, 12 sparrows, 18 peacocks, 19 lambs, 24 turkeys, 48 mature rabbits, 60 chickens, 78 young rabbits, 120 capons, 122 quails, 178 chicks, 30 pounds of beef, 263 pounds of veal, and 420 pounds of sheep.

Frederick provided Elizabeth with a boat to sail up the Rhine, featuring a crowned lion on the bow. He also warned her about which towns to avoid because of plague. While he went ahead to make preparations, Elizabeth progressed slowly toward the Palatinate, from one celebration to the next. As they glided down the Rhine, people lined the banks offering their hospitality. Pantomime comedians performed in a hastily built theater on a bridge. Elizabeth enjoyed listening to stories of local mythology and the lore of battles. A local noble provided her with a picturesque picnic on an open field near a quaint village. During a hunting expedition she inspired gossip when she shot three stags herself. Triumphant arches depicted her as a Greek goddess.

Everywhere she went, Elizabeth presented gifts as a new monarch introducing herself to her people. But soon she had no more gifts to give, so she pawned some of her jewels to get the money for more, the first of many times she found herself facing that indignity. One observer, a military officer, commented approvingly of their reunion when Frederick returned to escort her to her new home. Elizabeth "threw herself into her husband's arms."

Elizabeth entered the Palatinate in a six-horse coach with a red velvet interior. Musicians played and Latin orations filled the air with rhetorical flourishes carefully prepared to honor her. The Palatinate was a cosmopolitan culture of villages surrounding twenty-six walled towns. To celebrate her arrival the locals dressed up in their traditional costumes: German, Swiss, Turkish, and Polish. Women and children tossed flowers in the street. Musketeers, dressed as Romans and as Turks, marched in opposite directions. Wearing the green uniforms of rangers, archers demonstrated their skills. The goldsmiths' guild decorated the facade of a theater and sponsored music. The decorations personified faith, constancy, fortitude, and generosity, showing Solomon and his bride, and Elizabeth herself, hair flowing free, with the star of Britain on her left and Frederick on her right.

An entourage of four thousand on thirty-four decorated barges traveled up the Rhine, reaching Heidelberg on June 7. On the way to the castle the army provided a spectacle of guns fired in the air and cannon booming in a sham fight, representing the siege of Troy with artillery. Just outside the gates of the city, boats engaged in another staged fight. The English traveling with Elizabeth marveled at the beauty of the banks of the brooks and rivers. Over the city gate hovered a sculpted angel with spread wings and the motto "God Unites." The streets were strewn with green grassy turf, and the roofs of the houses were decorated with boughs of May. Festoons of flowers hung from the walls. Inside the town they passed through another triumphal arch, but here progress halted while a ceremonial crown was accidentally dropped on and then lifted from her head. This too was considered a bad omen.

At the town hall the four colleges of the university displayed their globes, mathematical instruments, and medical grotesqueries. A boy in a long cloak offered a basket of fruit, adding in French "Behold, Madame, the tribute of the goddesses Flora and Pomona." Later, onlookers proudly noted that she ate some of the fruit in her coach. The last and most magnificent triumphal arch waited for them just outside the palace. It showed Frederick's ancient lineage, with emphasis on his ancestors who had married English princesses. As Elizabeth arrived in her new home, Frederick's mother, the dowager queen, Louise Juliana, daughter of William of Orange, met her. They embraced with tears in their eyes.

Heidelberg Castle, built of red brownstone and ornamented with many fine statues, stood on barren rock looking out over two rivers: the Nekar nearby and in the distance the winding Rhine. The most ancient part was a tower raised on a cliff in which a prophetess had lived named Jetha Behel. Though she never let them see her, people had come to her room daily asking for advice about future events and receiving oracular responses. The tower had been converted into a library that contained some of the rarest books and manuscripts in Europe, with floors of porphyry and golden pillars, cornices studded with jewels, beautiful tapestries, fresco paintings, and a silver room. The palace in the bright light of summer must have been dazzling. June was beautiful in the Palatinate. Elizabeth feasted on nectarines.

The next morning a pageant delighted Elizabeth: *Jason and the Golden Fleece*, with Frederick himself in the role of Jason. From Pallas in a chariot drawn by dragons to Orpheus riding a unicorn, the special effects dazzled. Jason and his two companions appeared in the contrivance of a slow-moving boat. Each spoke a poem praising Elizabeth. But something about the Golden Fleece itself aroused the superstitions of the onlookers who one after the other lost their smiles in a contagious melancholy. Perhaps they realized that since the emperor was a member of the Catholic Order of the Golden Fleece, the pageant presaged dangerous times just ahead. Whatever the cause, their foreboding proved accurate.

Frederick's role as Jason the Argonaut could not have made a stronger statement about his intentions: Jason stole the Golden Fleece. The Order of the Golden Fleece—a Catholic knighthood that upheld the faith and chivalric code—was the highest honor bestowed by the Spanish Habsburgs. Frederick in another pageant played Scipio, the great Roman general who defeated Hannibal and conquered Carthage. In Spain, so influenced by the north African Moors, was the city of Cartagena. So the Scipio costume may have been another veiled threat against the Habsburgs. But Frederick's boldest statement was appearing as Arminius, the liberator of Germania, who destroyed three Roman legions in 9 CE. In his choice of roles Frederick clearly cast himself as an enemy of the Holy Roman emperor.

One pageant followed another. Here is a description of one from Miss Benger's *Memoirs of Elizabeth Stuart, Queen of Bohemia* (1825, 202):

Masculine personifications of the sun and moon came upon Mount Parnassus—the representative of the sun was in gilt trappings, whilst the moon's squire was clad in a suit of grey armor: presently Mount Parnassus itself appeared in motion with living animals springing through its cliffs—the eagles, the wolf, the bear, all dwelling in concord. Apollo entered in a long white gown. The Muses in green quilted vests, played on various instruments; Pan piped; Diana hunted; the old German hero Arminus, passed over the stage.

Songs sung for Elizabeth were said to have been composed by Orpheus and Venus.

What did Elizabeth think when she heard in the midst of the continuing festivities the news that twenty-two days after she ascended the throne of the Palatinate, the Globe Theater burned down in London during a performance of *Henry VIII,* a play Shakespeare wrote for her wedding? Did anyone feel a shiver of premonition?

Despite all the entertainment, conflict beset daily life in the castle. Elizabeth and Louise Juliana fought over who should receive the honors and privileges of precedence. Elizabeth complained that Louise Juliana wanted her to adopt German manners and customs; everything had to be done the German way. Elizabeth expected to be treated with the respect due to the daughter of the king of England. They both demanded that poor Frederick do something about it. Frederick, who had been raised by his uncle in France, was not familiar with the details of his own court. Louise Juliana was accustomed to running what amounted to a complex organization of a thousand officials, courtiers, and servants. Frederick depended on her for guidance.

The English were apt to joke about what they considered a prudish and culturally deprived German court in comparison to home; Elizabeth's entourage of thirty-five men and thirteen women cast a long shadow. The Germans were offended that their traditions were challenged by foreigners of dubious morality. Not only did the English have difficulty accepting German customs and vice versa, but the Scottish, who saw Elizabeth as one of their own, represented yet another culture. They fiercely defended Elizabeth's rights, causing more conflict in the castle.

Away from the wearying politics of the court, Elizabeth enjoyed hunting. In one especially aggressive hunt, mere days after she moved into Heidelberg Castle, she used a crossbow to shoot twelve deer. A witness reported that Frederick and the other princes present were astonished when she brought down a stag with one shot from horseback while pregnant. Her people nicknamed her Diana after the ancient Roman goddess of the hunt. A Dutch poet who watched the sixteen-year-old princess hunting wrote a poem in which he compared her, as Akkerman writes, "to both an Amazonian warrior and Diana the huntress-goddess while conjuring the memory of Alexander the Great" (2021, 76).

Within the year the young royals had their first child, Frederick Henry. He looked like his father, so Elizabeth called him her "little black baby." Germany and England rejoiced, and the enthusiastic celebrations in Scotland were rumored to have inspired jealousy in James and Charles. But the conflicts at court may have alienated Frederick and Elizabeth. Their next child would be born three years later.

Not long after his eighteenth birthday, and his assumption of full power as Elector Palatine, Frederick attended a meeting of the Protestant Union. The long-expected war seemed about to break out as a Catholic German noble sided with the Austrians and Spanish against the Protestants. His first decision could have been to go to war, but Frederick suffered a malaria-like illness. Fever and chills incapacitated him.

With the memory of Henry's death by fever at the same age haunting him, Frederick became melancholy. Like his father, he gave most of his responsibilities to his chancellor, Christian of Anhalt. In 1591, Christian led a successful military expedition in support of the French king Henry IV in his war to break the power of the Vatican in France. But then, as we have seen, Henry was assassinated.

As for the Protestant Union, Calvinists cast a judgmental eye on mere Lutherans; they accused them of drinking too much and doubted the virtue of their women. Lutherans found a hint of extremism, the fanaticism of the Catholic Church itself, in the strict conformity of the Calvinists, who preached against even hunting, fishing, and hawking, especially because the Lutherans were said to prefer these activities while drunk. So severe was the religious discipline that German musicians were rare and English minstrels the main source of music in Germany. The Bible and the writing of Luther may have been known widely but no literature, classical or contemporary, made the reading list. In England, theater and romantic poetry flourished, while in the homeland of Luther such entertainments were considered vulgar.

Yet German princes could be as extravagant as their British and French cousins. Pageantry required that the lavish tables of royal feasts include artistic decorations, often edible. A splendid peacock with tail in full display made a centerpiece. At one such celebration Frederick's table featured a statue of Minerva, to represent his love of learning. Fish were gilded to make their scales glitter more richly. Nobles boasted of six-hour eating and drinking contests.

For all its luxury and its panoramic view, Heidelberg Castle was situated in stark surroundings, positioned on a rocky cliff. When Elizabeth expressed her dissatisfaction with the barren setting and then suggested building gardens, Frederick approved. She chose Salomon de Caus to help her design and build what became a legendary garden. De Caus seems to have been an art and music teacher to Prince Henry and Princess Elizabeth just before Henry's death and the wedding. He had designed their mother Queen Anne's French garden. He had also designed Prince Henry's small but astonishing English garden in which mechanical statues moved and made sounds, demonstrating the technological advancements made possible by mathematics.

That other inventive genius of the Stuart court, Inigo Jones, joined de Caus in designing elaborate settings for masques with mechanical elements for startling effects. Elizabeth had grown up participating in these theatrical events so beloved by her mother, and she intended to establish the tradition in Heidelberg. Like her late brother, she shared in the creativity of inventing them.

Elizabeth and de Caus leveled a ridge and filled chasms, converting the craggy bleak landscape into a flowering paradise. Full-grown trees were transplanted. A wonderland bordered by trees and hedges appeared so suddenly, enemies whispered it must have been done by black magic. The scent of lime trees and thirty-six orange trees filled the air. Statues, fountains, pergolas, pavilions, a maze, and a grotto provided a variety of amusements. In summer delicate exotic plants, including flowers from the recently discovered tropics, bloomed in luxuriant colors.

A replica of an English orchard gave Elizabeth the sights and scents of home. At center a magnificent fountain watered the soil. Small lawns like green velvet and manicured walkways contrasted with the rocky peaks still visible above the new tall trees, striking a picturesque contrast. An artificial waterfall added excitement and refreshing negative ions, while cleverly creating silvery ribbons of fresh water meandering through the lawns. A monkey house, mazes, a menagerie, a water organ made according to the Roman writer Vitruvius's design, clockwork-driven automata birds moving and singing like nightingales, and statues that spoke or moved added to the wonderment. Hidden musicians provided accompaniment in this prototype of an amusement park. The stones of the majestic entrance bore a Latin inscription:

FREDERICK V
TO HIS BELOVED WIFE
ELIZABETH
1615

The garden became known as the Eighth Wonder of the World, but Catholic propaganda portrayed it as a gate to hell.

Watching the tranquil river Nekar flashing light as it flowed below, Elizabeth listened to the astro-theological theories of Abraham Scultetus, Frederick's chaplain and a driving force in the project to write down the first one hundred years of the Reformation. As she listened to the mysterious oracles of Jetha Behel, she gazed at the old tower where the sybil had lived.

The gardens of de Caus have been said to contain hermetic and astrological symbols. In the twentieth century some scholars argued that de Caus was a Rosicrucian and perhaps a liaison between the secret order and the court at Heidelberg. However, in *Nature as Model: Salomon de Caus and Early Seventeenth-Century Landscape Design*, Luke Morgan, after a thorough examination of the historical records, found no evidence of such interests. De Caus appears to have been a practical Huguenot, not a brother of the Rosy Cross. Inventive explorations of mathematics and geometry inspired his designs.

The political realities underlying this earthly paradise were as ugly as the garden was beautiful. The Twelve Years' Truce would expire soon. Spain and the Netherlands were expected to resume the Eighty Years' War. A terrible power struggle brewed in Germany. German Catholics, though they had failed for a hundred years to stamp out Luther's Reformation, were ready for war, while among the Protestants a movement arose that hoped to crown a ruler of united Calvinist and Lutheran states to stand in opposition to the Holy Roman emperor. Failing that, they planned to at least tear their chunk of Europe out of the grasp of the pope once and for all.

Frederick stood to gain or lose the most. Though an inexperienced boy, he seemed the best choice, given his ancestry and alliances. With astrologers and evangelicals assuring him of God's assistance in this holy mission to stop the Counter-Reformation, Frederick must have believed it possible that he could eventually be crowned as something like the king of Germany. But he knew if the mission failed, he could lose the Palatinate and Heidelberg Castle. His lands bordered Habsburg territory, and the most powerful of all royal families perpetually schemed to take the fertile agricultural fields of the southern Palatinate and the rich mines of the north.

SEVEN

The Bohemian Problem

In London, in 1617, Pocahontas, now married and known as Lady Rebecca, a finely mannered Christian woman, attended *The Vision of Delight* masque written by Ben Jonson. In Sweden, seven women were burned at the stake for witchcraft. In Bohemia, the Austrian Archduke Ferdinand II, next in line to become Holy Roman emperor, was elected king. Rumors that the election was rigged were exacerbated by the heavy-handed Catholic agenda Ferdinand imposed.

Elizabeth's mother-in-law Louise had retired, reducing conflict in the castle, but the issue of precedence continued. Elizabeth demanded equal precedence with her husband at public events. Frederick explained to her that other German princes had married daughters of kings, including other kings of England, but the husband had always taken precedence in Germany. However, at home he granted her precedence.

Then came the comet of 1618. The French feared it meant another massacre like St. Bartholomew's Day. The Dutch believed it confirmed the impending death of a patriot. At the imperial court the comet was interpreted as the promise of the imminent defeat of the Protestant Union. But the astrologers and prophets of the Protestant Union predicted a new and reformed world order and the downfall of the last pope.

In 1618, Europe didn't appear to be on the brink of a three-decade war. The tensions between Catholics and Protestants were for the most part resolved through diplomacy, and both sides valued peace.

Meanwhile in the Palatinate, astrologers whispered into one royal ear, and evangelical Protestants into his other, that Frederick was born to accomplish extraordinary things.

In May 1618 an assembly of Protestant noblemen and supporters stormed Prague Castle and threw the two leading representatives of the Holy Roman Empire out the windows of the chancellery; they landed safely on a dunghill. The rebels claimed Ferdinand had exceeded his authority. They established a government that tolerated all classes and religions; even Catholic priests were allowed to stay. The rebel leader could have claimed the throne for himself, but he wanted to pass the scepter to Frederick.

From a young age, Frederick was viewed as the key to a potential unification of all the various and divided powers of Germany. The most radical resisters against Catholic domination believed that only by unification could the Protestant faith survive and perhaps even break the power of the Vatican. But such schemes had always failed, quickly detected and opposed by more conservative leaders who preferred fragmented power to a centralized government. The old states' rights versus the power of the federal government argument so familiar to Americans is a recurring theme throughout history and never more so than in Germany just before the Thirty Years' War.

Frederick's uncle William of Orange's military and political successes, as a David taking on the Goliath of the Holy Roman Empire, made him the sweetheart of Protestant girls' romantic daydreams. William's victories had added luster to his nephew's reputation. The cultivation of oranges in the gardens of Heidelberg had become a symbol of civilization and the blessings of freedom from Catholic oppression. The nobles of Bohemia didn't choose Frederick to be their king because he was a charismatic leader and brilliant general like his uncle. They chose him for his lineage. As a relative of British and Danish kings and of leaders of the Dutch Republic, as head of the Protestant Union, chief elector, and Count Palatine, he seemed to represent a community of powerful allies. The nobles of Bohemia saw this as their chance to push back against the power of the Austrian Habsburgs, whose incremental suppression of their guaranteed rights they struggled to stop.

Most of the Protestant powers understood and opposed the Habsburg attempt to make the elected throne of the Holy Roman emperor their own by hereditary right, but the pope would not be satisfied until a Catholic monarch ruled all Europe. In England the Protestants quoted Dante. The great poet had appealed to imperial power for relief from a corrupt church: Henry VIII's principal justification for defying the authority of the Vatican.

A third child, the first princess, was born; she was named after her mother. Elizabeth's menagerie of dogs and monkeys romped over her bed in the morning, reducing her and the children to helpless laughter. Though Frederick still suffered bouts of melancholy, visitors to their court commented on the depth of the attachment between them; one wrote that Elizabeth was "so dearly loving and beloved of the prince her husband that is a joy to all that see them." Nevertheless, news arrived at the court of James that his daughter was homesick.

Frederick visited his rival Maximilian I of Bavaria (1573–1651). He promised he would vote for Maximilian to become emperor. But the shrewd Bavarian politician declined; he would not break his oaths of loyalty to the empire and the church. Maximilian understood that if Frederick was naive enough to accept the Bohemian crown, Bavaria might be able to acquire the lands of the Palatinate and perhaps Bohemia in the war that would inevitably follow.

On the same day, March 20, 1619, two deaths occurred that had great impact on Elizabeth's life. Her mother died. Rumor had it that she had left nothing to her daughter, not a single jewel. But the fate of Europe hung in the balance as the reign of Holy Roman emperor Matthias, the brother of Rudolf II, came to an end. Frederick had now become one of two imperial vicars, essentially interim emperors.

Ferdinand II was the elected king of Bohemia, but the illegal power grab that accompanied the new emperor's election outraged the Bohemians. They banded together into a confederacy, refusing to recognize imperial authority over them. A small group of Bohemian revolutionaries cornered Ferdinand in his own bedchamber. They tried to force him to sign abdication papers on the spot by threatening to kill him, but he was saved by the arrival of a squad of imperial guards. This experience reinforced the bigotry Ferdinand had learned from his mother, which would later fuel his ruthless and successful effort to convert or expel the Protestants of Austria and Bohemia. But for the moment he left Prague for safer ground.

Frederick's duty as imperial vicar was to protect the constitution. He argued that electing Ferdinand, yet another Habsburg after so many Habsburg emperors, would seem to confirm that the throne had become a hereditary dynasty, a violation of imperial law. He offered other possible choices for emperor, excluding himself from the list. The Protestant princes disapproved of not only his flirtation with Bohemia but also his strategy as imperial vicar. Ferdinand II was elected Holy Roman emperor in August of that year and crowned in Frankfurt in September. Staging the coronation in a German city was perhaps a message from Ferdinand about the reach of his power. Frederick was the only elector who voted against him.

The idea of his daughter becoming queen of Bohemia seems to have alarmed King James. He advised Frederick to say no. But Frederick sent mercenaries to the city of Plzeň in Bohemia, defeating remaining pockets of resistance by Catholic forces there, putting the entire country under Protestant rule. Frederick was shrewd. No one but the rebels of Prague could be certain who sent the mercenaries. But was he shrewd in his choice of Ernst von Mansfeld as his general? No doubt Mansfeld was skilled, but he was also a Catholic.

Count Mansfeld was the son of a marriage between a noble and a commoner. Illegitimate because of the difference in their ranks, he had no inheritance. The late emperor had rewarded his martial prowess by declaring him a prince of the empire but without lands to go with the title. Mansfeld had to make his own way in the world. A skilled strategist and warrior, he never had a problem attracting soldiers to his banner. He had a unique code of honor. For example, he demanded that the lands and towns he passed through provide supplies for his army; he explained that while this was still unfortunate for the locals at least he could guarantee that they would not have to suffer rape and burned houses and fields. Raised Catholic, he took pay to lead the Protestant rebellion. But claimed to have no scruples about fighting for either side.

Perhaps Mansfeld was sincere. He was one of four men who wore a lock of Elizabeth's hair in an earring. The others were Frederick, Christian of Brunswick, and her maternal uncle, Charles IV, king of Denmark.

Frederick's counselors told him that the numerous Protestants of Austria were rumored to be ready to join the revolution that had already swept through Bohemia, Hungary, Moravia, and Silesia, which had sent three thousand troops to support the rebels. They would all welcome Frederick as their leader. His ally the king of Denmark would certainly join the war, and with him the princes of the Protestant Union. King James could be expected to support the fortunes of his own daughter and son-in-law. The Dutch would soon be keeping Spain busy with the resumption of the Eighty Years' War.

Even the royal court of France, currently paying lip service to the pope, could be expected to at least rejoice if not join in. Not only would all these powers be eager to participate in such a glorious cause but none of them would allow the ancient Palatinate and Bohemia to fall out of Protestant hands. The new emperor had no army with him in Austria. He would be forced to flee and to fight his way back to Italy. Who would support him? Would Spain be willing to risk all-out war against Germany, Bohemia, the Netherlands, and England?

A story is told that Louise Juliana, Frederick's mother, reminded the court that the Austrian army was still in imperial hands, Denmark too far away to help, the Protestant princes jealous and cautious, and James unwilling to threaten his truce with Spain. She insisted they shouldn't trust the loyalty of the Bohemians. She reminded them that Frederick had no real army. He would be facing professionals, and the might and wealth the Vatican would rally against the rebels. The daughter of William of Orange convinced the court that the Bohemian invitation was too dangerous. Until Elizabeth spoke.

Elizabeth allegedly declared that she considered caution cowardice; this was the time for courage. Opportunities to make history, to liberate entire countries, are rare and must be taken whatever the risk. The generals, of course, supported her, but so did Frederick's chaplain. Calvinists believed they had found in the book of Revelation a prophetic biblical reference to Frederick. The story is suspiciously melodramatic. Akkerman reports what really happened. When asked, Elizabeth would not give her opinion because it was Frederick's decision to make, an example of propaganda's distortion of history.

In October Emperor Ferdinand signed a treaty with Maximilian of Bavaria. Maximilian and his army would lead the imperial attack against Frederick. His reward would be the Palatinate, Frederick's electorship, and Bohemia. The princes of the Protestant Union promised to support Frederick. Frederick sent letters to London asking for guidance, but James didn't respond. The Archbishop of Canterbury did: he urged Frederick to take this glorious opportunity. Elizabeth sent letters, but Frederick made his decision before they were answered. In late September he accepted Bohemia's invitation to be their new king, declaring it a calling from God.

While Frederick and his generals debated their next action, Elizabeth was said to have lamented that they didn't simply strike, trusting faith and surprise. It may be true that if Frederick had quickly attacked Austria at that time, he might easily have captured Ferdinand and seized control over the eastern half of the Holy Roman Empire.

But in their letters she is melancholy despite Frederick's insistence that she have more faith in him. She mocks Emperor Ferdinand, writing that his lice-infested clothes show he doesn't have money, implying that he lacked the wealth to pay for an army. Frederick had Elizabeth's dowry and the interest it had accrued, kept in bond by the Dutch Republic. Frederick had realized James would not support him, but he still thought the Dutch and the Protestant princes of Germany would. Not only did he consider the crown of Bohemia God's will, he also understood the strategic and economic advantages of the combined resources of the Palatinate and Bohemia.

Away from Elizabeth, surrounded by an army of twelve thousand mercenaries, Frederick in the privacy of his tent wrote a letter filled with love and longing: "I am as impatient as you to have the happiness of seeing you again." He sounds lonely, not heroic. There's a sense of foreboding in his signing off "until death."

Meanwhile, in her chapel, Elizabeth listened to Chapman preach a poignant text: "Go to now, ye that say today or tomorrow we will go to such a city, and continue there a year, and buy and sell, and get gain; whereas ye know not what will be in the morrow; for what is your life? It is even but as a breath, that appeareth for a time, and then vanisheth away; for that ye ought to say, if the Lord will we shall live and do this" (James 4:13, KJV).

Frederick ceased all pleasantries to devote himself to his mission; he even gave away his pack of hounds. Elizabeth walked through her magical garden one last time. An English visitor wrote a letter describing the day before their departure, later published in *Tracts on German History* (1620): "A portentous gloom overspread the face of nature—the people wept, the clouds poured down torrents—nowhere was seen the smile of joy. A tearful Frederick pronounced a solemn valediction to the people, who, with an involuntary movement, clasping their hands in agony, implored for him and his house the divine benediction. When he passed through the church, sighs were sobbed forth, grief was audible; every eye followed his steps—."

The writer continued, comparing Elizabeth first to her namesake, and then to the fair virgin the Moors would place before their army at their deadliest battles because their soldiers would fight to the last man to protect her. He understood the terrible danger Elizabeth had put herself in for what they agreed was the noblest of causes: the Protestant Reformation. His confidence that England must follow their beloved princess into the field of battle is so impassioned it rings hollow with doubt: the writer is trying to convince the reader. Told that the king of Bohemia should be added to Frederick's titles when prayers were said for the royal family, James refused to allow it.

Despite another pregnancy Elizabeth accompanied her husband on his journey to their new kingdom. She even broke her lifelong custom of never traveling on Sundays. On the way to Bohemia a messenger arrived from the emperor to warn Frederick that he would suffer dire consequences unless he turned back, but the 152 baggage wagons continued rolling down the road to Prague. The Bohemians were happy to see this young king who had taken up their cause at great risk to himself and his family. Vast crowds greeted them.

The manifesto Frederick delivered as he entered Bohemia was a significant and early precursor to the freedom of religion enshrined in the American Constitution. Echoing the *Edict of Torda* (1568), he promised that throughout his reign he would not hinder or oppress anyone because of their religion, and he would not allow others to do so. As long as everyone lived peaceably and obeyed the laws of the kingdom they were free to worship without fear.

Calvinists, Lutherans, and even Catholics impulsively ran from their homes as the royal couple arrived at Star Park, where they first set foot in their new capital. In Prague, Obora Hvezda (Star Park), where the aforementioned Star Villa was located, was considered the most beautiful spot. Among those in the crowd was Jakob Böhme (also called Jacob Boehme), already the author of what would become deeply influential mystical books. Jews, not allowed to attend the spontaneous festival, stood off to the side quietly watching.

Elizabeth's beauty and her unpretentious grace and candor soon won the affection of the citizens. Old men gave thanks that they had lived to see the rescue of their country. Young men brandished their swords, eager for war. Girls wore flowers in their hair and spread flowers on the street wherever the royal couple went. On all public ensigns, and on the royal plates, the Austrian eagle was replaced with Frederick's lion. Talk of a German emperor and a Protestant empire to rival the Catholic empire of Spain made the rounds.

The prophecies of Paracelsus, collected from his books on divination and astrology, were published around this time as *Prognosticon Theophrasti Paracelsi*. A prophecy falsely attributed to Paracelsus circulated about a Midnight Lion or Lion of the North that would kill the papal eagle and reform the church and the world. Frederick had become the leading candidate for the Midnight Lion.

On November 4, 1619, the Bohemians crowned Frederick their king. Rumor had it that not a single person died in all of Prague that day. Three days later Elizabeth wore ermine as she was crowned queen of Bohemia. The coronations were so inclusive even Jews were invited to pay homage. Prague celebrated by night with wine drinking and dancing in the streets. For the Bohemians their rebellion was not a rebellion but the defense of their constitutional religious rights. They hoped that electing Frederick king of Bohemia would defend not only Bohemia but the empire.

Frederick was twenty-three years old. Why did he take the throne? Most Catholic historians have blamed Elizabeth, suspecting her eagerness for the title of queen as a way to prove something to her late mother, or because of her late brother's ambitions on behalf of the Protestant cause, ambitions she had shared with him and perhaps wished to further however she could. But as we have seen, she believed her husband had to decide for himself.

Frederick claimed that he made the decision because he felt this was his calling, to rise to the defense of his fellow Protestants, to protect them against the avarice of the Holy Roman Empire and the injustice of the Vatican. Christian of Anhalt, one of the most enthusiastic promoters of the Bohemian venture, also understood the economic advantage. With the north Palatinate as Germany's center for iron, combined with Bohemia's tin and glass trade, the rich could become much richer.

Like Heidelberg Castle, Prague had its own ancient tower where an oracular prophetess once lived, Lilybussa, an enchantress who became queen by choosing who should be king. But this dismal castle was haunted by the unfinished construction and what was left of the collections of Rudolf II.

Life became much lonelier for Elizabeth than it had been in London or Heidelberg. Frederick was in the field with his army. Elizabeth didn't speak Czech. The nobles of Bohemia were of a different sort. They didn't enjoy French comedy or English theater. They had no public festivals, masques, or pageants, only old-fashioned balls where the boisterous dancing bore little resemblance to the comparatively graceful etiquette of the court of James. Though Bohemia under Rudolf II had been a city of art and science, alchemists and astrologers, under years of Catholic rule the taste for esoteric knowledge and for literature in general had declined. Women held fewer rights than elsewhere in Europe. Prague had the feeling of a city lost in an earlier time. Crossing the great bridge that was the pride of Prague, Elizabeth asked to be taken the long way around so she wouldn't see the naked men and women bathing in the river. It must not have been very reassuring to the princess who had survived the Gunpowder Plot that a feud between nobles resulted in a castle being blown up just ten miles from the city.

Unfortunately, the English who came to Prague with the royal couple were not shy about showing their amusement at what they considered the corny customs of a quaint culture. For example, to honor their new queen a group of wives presented her with breads they had baked in the shapes of flowers. The ritual commemorated Queen Elizabeth of Hungary, a saint known for her charity, whose husband had tried to stop her generosity to the poor. When he caught her with her apron full of breads she had baked for the hungry, she lied and said her apron was full of flowers. He demanded to see, and to her own surprise where there had been bread there were now flowers.

Elizabeth's English retainers found humor in the humble gift of bread. One even picked up a loaf of bread and twisted it as a garland for his hat. The matrons later returned to make up for what they considered their faux pas; they provided an exquisitely carved ebony cradle inlaid with gold and jewels, just in time for Elizabeth to give birth to her most famous child, a legendary Royalist soldier of the English Civil War, who would be remembered as Prince Rupert of the Rhine. Rupert was named after an ancestor who had very nearly become emperor. The family's ambitions seemed obvious in the choice of his name.

The royal couple invited twelve local Bohemians to join the royal household as servers and helpers. On the first day these men began working in the castle one managed to jostle Elizabeth while she was drinking wine, spilling it on her dress. Another, carrying a sugar basin, was so startled when Elizabeth's pet monkey jumped on his shoulder that he lost his grip and the basin crashed to the floor, spilling sugar everywhere. A third managed to lose the contents of the plates on his tray without noticing it, so he served the queen an empty plate. The superstitious locals considered these bad omens.

At first their new queen's vivacious personality charmed her subjects, and the royal couple remained popular, but soon complaints were heard. The English ladies revealed too much cleavage. Elizabeth's love of theater scandalized the locals. She advised her ladies to wear ruffles for discretion, but she continued to dress as she pleased. As for theater, the locals would have to get used to it.

Frederick discovered that the king of Bohemia had restricted powers. The kingdom was divided between factions. The economy reflected the fractured, depressed state, depleted by the long war against the Turks and battles with the German Catholic League. Frederick was not allowed to raise taxes. He had to depend on the nobility for his funds. Meanwhile, the nobles expected gifts, the traditional gesture of a new king appreciating the loyalty of his most important subjects.

Frederick's chaplain, Scultetus, made matters worse. A strict Calvinist, he abhorred the Bohemian tolerance for sacred art and religious relics. He considered them all idols. A few days before Christmas, a famous altarpiece of the Virgin Mary by Lucas Cranach the Younger was destroyed. The precious crucifix Emperor Rudolf II had provided for the altar was removed, and the holy relics of the saints were trampled.

Frederick claimed he did not approve of this act of vandalism, but then on Christmas Day he gave a Calvinist sermon. The Bohemians were convinced their new king was planning to force Calvinism on them.

Scultetus wasn't finished alienating the Bohemians. He organized a few zealots, and one night on the great bridge that was the pride of Prague, they removed the massive cross that had stood there for hundreds of years. In the morning, confronted with the vandalized bridge, women wept hysterically and men ranted in the streets, wondering if Ferdinand could have done any worse by them than Frederick had. Elizabeth's modesty, which turned her carriage from the bridge so she wouldn't embarrass or be embarrassed by the nude bathers, was misinterpreted as an expression of shame for having ordered the cross removed. Frederick ordered the cross returned and again denied having anything to do with the vandalism.

Young Frederick Henry was sent away with an entourage so large it resembled a small army. He feasted his way from town to town, the royal heir to the throne of Bohemia on display to reassure Protestants everywhere that whatever might happen to Frederick in the war, there would be continuity.

Frederick decided to visit the adjoining provinces, taking Scultetus with him. In the towns he visited, where Calvinism had taken root among the farmers, Frederick found himself greeted by smiling subjects who showed no servility and no court etiquette, who treated him like any other man, though he inspired more curiosity than most. This trip must have been for Scultetus the highlight of his life. He had come from one of these country towns, Having grown up poor and obscure, he returned as the honored spiritual adviser of the king. Scultetus gave sermons in evangelist churches that had once been Jesuit outposts.

Two local prophets visited Frederick on his journey through the Bohemian countryside. Christopher Kotter of Silesia was famous, Christina Poniatovia, a Polish noblewoman and visionary, less so. A member of the Bohemian clergy, Kotter had been seeing visions of Frederick on the imperial throne since 1616. Scultetus eagerly approved this latest prophecy as he had the others, while Frederick remained complacent. But Kotter also warned Frederick to avoid the use of force. Kotter and Poniatovia agreed: soon the first Protestant emperor would unite the world.

A Catholic historian writing in 1821 included Kotter and Poniatovia in a list of visionaries about whom he wrote: "it is not necessary to enter into a more circumstantial detail of the history of this visionary tribe, since none of them arose to such a degree of reputation and consequence, as to occasion any considerable tumults by their predictions. It is sufficient to have observed in general, that, even in this century, there were among the Lutherans certain crazy fanatics, who, under the impulse of a disordered imagination, assumed the character and authority of prophets sent from above to enlighten the world" (Mosheim 1842, 412). But the false prophets were in good company, the great mystic Jakob Böhme's "distorted imagination" having been dismissed in the previous paragraph.

What could Frederick do? He raised taxes drastically and began drafting soldiers. The Bohemians were good fighters but not an organized army. They loved to literally leap into their saddles, often going into battle drunk. They had no interest in the disciplines Frederick tried to teach them. Frederick rallied his allies. Good news came when Transylvania and Silesia reaffirmed their loyalty to the king of Bohemia. To provide a good example and to prove his commitment, Frederick moved all the gold of the Palatinate to Prague, leaving his homeland bankrupt. He even pawned the royal jewels to pay for his army.

Elizabeth begged her friends to convince her father to help them. News arrived from England. James offered no solace to his daughter now surrounded by enemies. Though many in England wanted to fight, James was not about to start a world war. He couldn't. Only Parliament could authorize the expense of an official war. Also, James didn't dare jeopardize the negotiations for the marriage of his surviving son Charles to the daughter of the king of Spain. Nor did James care for the strategic situation of the landlocked Palatinate. His only gesture of support was his approval of a force of twenty-five hundred volunteer musketeers, led by Scottish Catholic Sir Andrew Gray, to prove his loyalty to the Stuarts, but they were underpaid and poorly equipped. Worse, James had made statements separating the Protestant cause from Frederick's predicament. The Netherlands sent only a token force, and the money they pledged was so meager as to seem insulting.

Still, the great army of the German princes of the Protestant Union had taken the field and now faced the Catholic League's smaller army under Maximilian of Bavaria. In Prague, Elizabeth and her ladies imagined how splendid the banners of the combined chivalry of Germany must have looked camped around the city of Ulm.

French diplomats held the armies apart as they argued for peace. Did the princes really want to unleash war all across Europe? Did they know that a Spanish army was marching toward the Palatinate? Why get involved in this fight between Frederick and Ferdinand? Let them fight it out for themselves. This argument had built into it some convincing legal subtleties. Bohemia was not part of the German Union. Though the princes were pledged to protect Frederick, they were not pledged to protect Bohemia. Spain, as the most powerful ally of its fellow Habsburg state Austria, was not going to war against all Germans, only the upstart in Bohemia. The Protestant Union, although they had encouraged Frederick to take the Bohemian throne and promised him their support, had no legal commitment to fight the battle about to begin. July 3, 1620, the Protestant Union signed a treaty with the Holy Roman Empire. They would stay out of the war against Frederick. The German army went home, and Maximilian began his march to Prague.

The French continued their diplomatic mission to isolate Frederick, convincing many of the Hungarian and other allied warlords that Bohemia counted on that they should avoid this war over a technical point of succession. Frederick had overstepped his boundaries and now he must suffer the consequences. Why make trouble for the emperor when the emperor has no problem with you? The French understood how the dominos would fall. They understood that by refusing to support his daughter James had given them all the proof they needed that Frederick was wrong.

Saxony invaded Silesia. This invasion not only deprived Frederick of the Silesian troops, he now had to send some of his own men to help the fight there. His only hope was James. Few believed that James would leave his only daughter to face the imperial artillery.

As we have seen, Scottish and English volunteers were already part of Frederick's army. Many of them had dedicated their lives to Elizabeth. In England his ministers were imploring James to go to Frederick's rescue. The military, Parliament, and the people supported this intervention on both patriotic and religious grounds. They wanted to help their princess, and they must stand up for their fellow Protestants. James reminded them that wars are unpredictable and costly.

In early August 1620, Austrian and Spanish troops entered Bohemia. Two weeks later the imperial forces turned their attention to the Palatinate. Two thousand English volunteers were no match for an army of twenty-five thousand professional imperial soldiers. Helpless in Prague, Frederick heard reports of the rape, burning, and pillage of his ancestral homeland. He managed to raise fifteen thousand poorly equipped and poorly fed soldiers. Having so little experience of war himself, Frederick left their command to his generals, including Mansfeld. Arrayed against him were several of the best generals in Europe.

Frederick wrote to Elizabeth that traitors and spies surrounded him. His enemies knew his every move. When he offered to meet with his enemy and kinsman Ferdinand, he was refused. Frederick asked for Elizabeth's opinion on their hopeless predicament. She was pregnant yet again, and he was worried for her and for the child, urging her to take care of herself and not to give in to despair. He begged her to leave Prague immediately. He joked about his funeral shroud and signed his letter "your devoted friend in life and death." But Elizabeth refused to abandon Prague.

Frederick then attempted a military assault of great daring. The Bohemian army would attack the army of the Catholic League in the night. In one move, Frederick could regain the upper hand. If Frederick's army defeated Maximilian, Bohemia might be saved. Planning and execution were brilliant, but Frederick was right, spies surrounded him. The enemy knew exactly when and how the attack was to take place, and so Frederick's forces suffered a bloody defeat.

In desperation Frederick turned to unexpected allies. He negotiated with the Ottoman Empire. The Turks agreed to send Frederick an army of sixty thousand cavalry to fight the Habsburgs. An army of four hundred thousand would invade Poland, which was already at war with Frederick's ally Sweden. In return, the sultan demanded only yearly tribute. Many Europeans, Protestants, and Catholics were horrified by this desperate alliance. But Frederick would suffer final defeat before his Turkish allies could cross the border.

At first spirits were high. Frederick intended to make Elizabeth laugh when he sent her an intercepted letter Maximilian of Bavaria wrote to his wife, promising the "rich spoils" of Prague. This was not indicative of Frederick's confidence in his army, since the jewels and other valuables were in the process of being packed in case of retreat. With supplies running out and money for his soldiers all but gone, Frederick avoided a mutiny only by appearing in person to rally the men.

Elizabeth had already sent away Frederick's heir, her firstborn son, Frederick Henry, and now she sent baby Rupert to live with his grandmother, Louise Juliana, who had retreated to the lands of relatives in Prussian Poland. As a hot-tempered child, he would earn the nickname Rupert the Devil. As we shall see, he grew up to become a war hero to Royalists, an evil wizard to Catholics, a pirate, a fine artist, an inventor, a colonial governor in Canada, an architect of the slave trade, and an alchemist.

As the war spread, foreshadowing the Thirty Years' War, atrocities were committed by both sides. In the aftermath of defeat soldiers and refugees froze to death. Disease and starvation killed thousands. In the decades that followed, they would kill 20 percent of the population of Europe. The only good news was that the enemy was in the same predicament regarding scarce supplies and cold. The sizes of the forces were roughly equal, though the imperial army had two thousand more men and two more cannon. A significant portion of Frederick's cannon were still in Pilsen with the British volunteers. Mansfeld either did not anticipate the speed of the imperial army's arrival near Prague, or he deliberately held them back, as he was negotiating his defection, but too late.

White Mountain was not the towering snowcapped monument the name implies. It was more like a plateau. Frederick's army took up position on a ridge, but instead of digging in as ordered, the exhausted soldiers complained that they were too tired to do work that should be performed by serfs and peasants.

With an army of nearly thirty thousand between Prague and the enemy, on the eve of the decisive battle, Frederick met with the ambassadors of King James. They agreed it seemed likely that because of the lack of supplies on both sides and the arrival of winter, the armies would not fight. The war would resume in spring. The leaders of the imperial army were about to arrive at the same decision, when a priest burst into the meeting. He had recently found an icon of Mother Mary. A Calvinist had gouged out the Madonna's eyes. The morale of the imperial army had already been higher than Frederick's crew of mercenaries and unprofessional volunteers. As outrage over the act of sacrilege spread, the imperial army's morale rose even higher, and the attack was ordered.

Just after noon on November 8, 1620, the battle began. Frederick was taking lunch with Elizabeth in Prague. Frederick's mood was described as "gleeful," but it only took an hour for Frederick's army to melt away. The cavalry disengaged the enemy flank, causing the infantry to flee. A bold attack failed, and a charismatic leader was captured; the retreat of the cavalry caused the Bohemians and Hungarians to flee. Seeing that, the Moravians fled. The first remnants of the routed army showed up while the king and queen were still at lunch.

Frederick fled to the old fortress of Prague. At first, he declared that he would stay behind to join in the defense of the city, but the declaration rang hollow. With his family, and all their valuables packed in wagons, Frederick fled. As a girl Elizabeth had been forced to flee her home. Now she fled another castle, this time with an army of enemies pursuing. They were in such a rush, the story is told that, at the very last minute, a bundle of clothes tossed into the coach as it departed contained baby Rupert, who in the confusion had been left behind. But this was propaganda.

About two hundred satires and farces were published after the disastrous defeat. Rumors, taken for truth by many historians, claimed that Frederick's Order of the Garter, his cherished gift from his father-in-law King James, was found left behind in Prague. Later it turned up in the collection of the Elector of Bavaria. Interpreting a telling comment in one of Elizabeth's letters, Nadine Akkerman suggests that it may have been stolen months before the battle. Frederick became the laughingstock of Europe. Pamphlets called him "King of Snow," and broadsides caricatured him fleeing with his stockings fallen down around his ankles.

When a German song called "A True and Faithful Depiction of the Winter King" became popular, Elizabeth became known as the Winter Queen. Frederick, people sang, should be crowned king of Lapland because the winters last longer there. Frederick's supporters issued pamphlets in response, calling him the Winter Lion or, better yet, the Summer Lion.

Both armies suffered around six hundred dead in the battle, a low number of casualties. Frederick's army lost another thousand in retreat, along with over a thousand wounded. These casualties may have had different consequences with more organized leadership. The army could have lived to fight another day. Many of those who fought in the Battle of White Mountain would fight in future battles between Protestants and Catholics, but Prague was lost.

Frederick's army should never have been in the field. While his generals argued over strategy, they spurned the obvious safety of Prague. Had the army retreated inside, the Catholic League, having scarce provisions, would have been forced to retreat. But blame for the defeat must be shared with Frederick's allies. Most of the Hungarians, who had promised to join the fight, didn't show up because they were fighting imperial troops in their own country. The Dutch, whose monetary contributions helped pay for the army, had suspended payments, diverting funds to prepare for their inevitable war with Spain. The king of Denmark wanted to send troops to defend his niece Elizabeth, but his council strongly opposed the idea.

The royal retreat had to be protected not only from the pursuing enemy but also from Frederick's own mutinous troops. Even those thought to be loyal betrayed him, stealing wagons full of Elizabeth's valuables. The Count of Thurn volunteered to turn back. He would rally the rear guard and help them hold a crucial bridge.

Frederick tried to be a courageous leader, but he was visibly crestfallen. Elizabeth never lost her dignity or her poise. The baggage train was too slow. The enemy was gaining on them. Two annotations, one made in the 1800s on a letter to Elizabeth and the other in a biography of Lord Hopton published in 1668, claim that the pregnant queen climbed behind Ralph Hopton on his horse for a forty-mile ride to safer ground. Akkerman questions the story since we know a very pregnant Elizabeth had successfully hunted deer on horseback, but she points out perhaps there were no spare horses.

Everywhere the refugee Elizabeth went she impressed the people she met, noble or common. Soon she was being called the Queen of Hearts. Her grace and good nature even under such terrible circumstances led a Venetian ambassador to say that she "captivates all who have dealings with her." Aware of her nickname, heart symbols adorned her jewelry and dresses.

In Breslau Elizabeth wrote a letter to her father. Of Frederick she said, "I am resolved never to leave him for if he perishes, I too will perish with him." Frederick didn't think Breslau safe. He wrote his brother-in-law George William, the Elector of Brandenburg, not as a prince but as a husband and father, whose wife was very pregnant and had been exposed to terrible dangers during their flight from Prague. George responded that he had no castle that could offer Frederick safety from the marauding Catholic army. The humble castle Frederick requested actually belonged to George's sister and it had no provisions. The kitchen was understaffed. The bare walls, without tapestries to lessen the cold of the stones, made the castle almost unbearable in winter. Frederick did not know that the Elector of Brandenburg had received a letter from the emperor warning him not to harbor the fugitives. Fortunately, a British envoy friendly with Elizabeth intervened.

The propaganda war continued. Engravings of Elizabeth's funeral procession and of her coffin were sold by street vendors in the Spanish Netherlands. Rumors spread that she had died in childbirth. When Frederick and Elizabeth reunited, he had to break the news that two more alliances had ended. He left just days before she was to give birth. But the sequestration of women before childbirth was customary at that time.

The story that Elizabeth gave birth to her fourth son, Maurice, without a midwife, on a bed of straw, on Christmas is a taste of Protestant propaganda. Akkerman points out that the athletic queen, who was pregnant for ten years of her fifteen-year marriage, was surrounded by experienced ladies and got back on her feet quickly. Later, Elizabeth would explain in a letter that she had been thin and pale after the birth of her first child. Hunting on horseback had reinvigorated her.

Prince Maurice was born in January. His uncle George must have felt relief when the news arrived that Elizabeth had left the castle. But then she arrived at his court in Berlin. Soon Maurice was under the protective care of his uncle. Dispersing the children to different locations to live with relatives improved their chances of survival.

During their time apart, Frederick's letters to Elizabeth were not about the endless negotiations. He was pessimistic about them. The two deals being discussed stripped him of his lands and titles. Frederick wrote about tapestries and paintings. But he also asked her to choose what gold plate to pawn.

No letter survives in which Frederick told Elizabeth that he had been captured by imperial troops. We are left to wonder if he ever told her. He was known to travel near enemy lines "shaved and disguised." The soldiers who captured him thought the king of Bohemia, the father of many children, an insignificant looking youngster, so they let him go.

After five months of almost constant flight and separation, Frederick and Elizabeth met an escort of Dutch troops. The Dutch Republic welcomed the royal refugees. The Dutch, held up as the best example of rebellion against the pope and Spain, were respected for their prosperity and practical creativity, such as the use of windmills for energy, providing inspiration for radicals all over northern Europe. Without serfs on their farms or retainers in their castles, the nobles of the Netherlands provided an example of independence.

As they neared the Netherlands, the Prince of Orange and a long line of coaches containing all the Dutch nobles and foreign ambassadors met the royal refugees. When they entered The Hague, the people wept for them in the streets.

A house well stocked with provisions awaited them. Two stone lions adorned the front, a gesture to Frederick's now ironic heraldic animal, but the furniture had been rented for only three days. The Dutch expected Elizabeth to return home to her father. Frederick, they thought, would be returning to the war. But Elizabeth was to become the guest that never left. Her court in exile in the Dutch Republic lasted forty years.

For several reasons James did not want his daughter and her family to return to England. He thought they should stay among the Dutch to encourage the battle to reclaim their lands. Uncharacteristically, James asked Parliament to match his funds for an army of thirty thousand to liberate the Palatinate, but Parliament hesitated. That may have been part of the king's plan. James thought his best hopes of getting some form of restoration or at least compensation for his son-in-law were tied to ongoing negotiations with the king of Spain for the wedding of Prince Charles and Isabella. Issues concerning the Palatinate were under discussion in the framing of the marriage contract.

While the Dutch debated and worried about harboring enemies of the Holy Roman emperor, the court of Frederick and Elizabeth gathered fine furniture and other necessities. Soon lavish masques and banquets returned to the weekly itinerary, while the Palatinate burned. But Frederick and Elizabeth had to present themselves as the king and queen of Bohemia in exile or risk losing what support they still had and hoped to get. There must have been a melancholy mood among the participants, in contrast to Elizabeth's memories of joyful masques in the court of James or in Heidelberg.

Elizabeth had found Bohemia to be a backward place; she didn't like the worshipful, overawed peasantry, or the cantankerous and boisterous nobility. Surrounded now by the reverence of Dutch women, and the awe of the young, who were taken with her romantic story, her bravery, and her loyalty to her husband, Elizabeth was more comfortable than she had been in Prague.

Frederick, who had been raised with strict German formality, who expected traditional court etiquette and exquisite servility, found the casual manners of the Dutch irritating. The farmers and merchants were blunt, which to Frederick smacked of insolence. Once, while Frederick hunted, a local farmer with a pitchfork berated him for trampling his oats. Frederick politely withdrew.

But what of Bohemia? For several months the Bohemians enjoyed imperial mercy. Certain Bohemian nobles were rewarded, causing whispers of treachery. The Jesuits moved back to Prague, but the Lutherans and Calvinists were tolerated. Then without warning the emperor accused the leaders of the revolution and had them arrested. They protested their right to choose their own king and to fight for their liberty and their religion. The heads of twenty-eight Bohemian nobles decorated the Old Town Tower for ten years. Severed heads adorned the beautiful bridge across the river. Protestant nobles and people lost their privileges. Those who would not convert were banished. Two-thirds of all property exchanged hands, enriching already powerful Catholics. The Thirty Years' War had begun.

EIGHT

The Rumored Rosicrucian Maier

The conflicts of Christian politics may have been the moving forces of the time, sweeping aside the ideals of intellectuals, but among the intelligentsia at the court at Heidelberg, and in university towns, a counterculture flourished, much of which has become associated with the Rosicrucians.

As we have seen, a favorite candidate for an actual Rosicrucian has been Michael Maier. His publication of a book called *The Laws of the Fraternity of the Rosy Cross* led many to believe he was publishing in the name of the Rosicrucian order itself. But the book is a meditation on the implications of the Rosicrucian laws presented in their manifestos.

Alchemists never knew when they might be chased out of town, not only because their pursuits were often considered diabolical, but also because foul stenches wafted from their labs, and sometimes explosions. In 1596, in his late twenties, Maier had severely harmed a fellow medical student in Padua. Arrested, he was fined, but the victim refused to take the money, so fearing imprisonment, Maier fled. His alchemical experiments in his hometown attracted more gossip, but his success was limited. While he failed to achieve the great work, he did create a potent medicine he tried on himself and his family.

Though he lacked the academic degree required to practice surgery, Maier became a surgeon in 1590. Two years later we find him at the University of Frankfurt. As official *Poeta Laureatus Caesareus*, he signed his eloquent Latin verses with an anagram: Hermes Malavici. In December 1601, Maier was in Gdańsk, Poland, at the White Horse Inn, where his medical practice based on his own recipes for remedies included a dried frog soaked in vinegar. This time Maier wasn't exactly chased out of town, but he believed the stress of dealing with nosy disapproving neighbors had ruined his alchemy, so he headed for the court of the emperor Rudolf II, arriving in Prague in 1608. Melancholy about what he then considered the autumn of his years, Maier had no idea that exciting times were just around the corner.

To get the emperor's attention, Maier composed an open letter that was both an outline of his alchemical theory and a résumé, which included a story about a dove landing in Maier's mother's lap as she sat in a field three days before his birth. The dove is a common alchemical symbol of divine power in the purification process of distillation, evidence of the Holy Spirit in action. Maier humbly confessed indifference to the omen, yet clearly hoped it would impress.

It took a year but then Maier learned that Rudolf was intrigued by his alchemical knowledge and sympathetic to his struggle. To his relief Maier was appointed physician-in-ordinary to the emperor, an honorary title; he does not appear to have treated his patron. Rudolf also gave Maier the title *palatinus*. Little power came with the honor. As a Count Palatine Maier may have helped supervise the universities. He had the privilege of granting doctorates and naming poet laureates. While in Prague, Maier wrote a book about Hermes Trismegistus and another in which he claimed to reveal the alchemical meaning, the divine language of symbols, behind Egyptian hieroglyphics and ancient Greek myths.

In Prague in 1609, approaching age forty, Maier wrote an autobiographical piece, the rediscovery of which has revolutionized scholarship concerning his life. The piece was published in a book of which he had only a few copies printed. Only one original copy is known to exist today. In it he tells us that he was not a member of the Rosicrucian order.

The emperor's support only lasted two more years. When Rudolf's brother took the throne, Maier left Prague for Hessen-Kassel and the court of Moritz the Learned, publisher of the Rosicrucian manifestos. Maier had sent Moritz three manuscripts and two letters, but he received no response, probably because alchemy had to be sacrificed to the demands of navigating the political crisis that had split Germany into the Catholic League and the Protestant Union. So Maier went to England to study and translate important alchemical texts.

In London, Maier was confronted with English theatrical depictions of Germans as drunken oafs. Christmas 1611, Maier sent Prince Henry and King James clever intricate greeting cards featuring pattern poems with melodies in musical notation. The king's card featured an engraving of a rose atop a scepter, which together make a cross. Some have called it the first Christmas card. Part of the inscription read: "May the rose be joyful under thy protection."

Rumors spread that a red-haired doctor had poisoned Prince Henry. Apparently, Michael Maier was the only ginger physician anywhere near the prince, but were these suspicions disinformation? Since Maier shared many of Henry's goals and wished to cultivate his patronage, it's hard to imagine him poisoning the future monarch, at least deliberately; but there is no evidence that Maier treated Henry. Maier attended Prince Henry's funeral with Frederick and Elizabeth.

While his Paracelsus- and Kabbalah-loving alchemist astrologer colleagues back home viewed the marriage through the prism of their imaginations—and then through the books published in England, Germany, and France describing the wedding—Maier was in London for it. He wrote a wedding song in honor of the bride and groom. He observed or heard about details of the withdrawal of royal favor so soon after the ceremony. He understood that in the aftermath of Henry's death James was beginning to have doubts about the strong position he had taken under his son's influence. Soon the queen's advice would prevail, and James would become conciliatory toward the Spanish. Among early writers associated with Rosicrucianism, Maier is one of the few who advocated continued secrecy, patience, and forbearance while most beat the drums of war, denouncing the pope in anticipation of a grand Protestant alliance.

Robert Fludd is another popular candidate for an actual Rosicrucian. As W. Wynn Westcott wrote in a privately published pamphlet for members of the Societas Rosicruciana in Anglia: "Some few notable persons only appear to have had the right to function as recognized members of the Rosicrucian Colleges, for instance, Michael Maier . . . and Dr. Robert Fludd" (Westcott, 1915)

Many have argued that Fludd and Maier were friends who met when Maier was in England. They shared what Andrew Weeks, associate professor of German, calls "the passion for the intricate" (Weeks 1991). We have no evidence that they were friendly, though they had mutual friends. Nor do we have evidence, despite the claims of some authors, that Fludd visited the Palatinate or Moritz. Maier admitted to Moritz that he had read a manuscript of Fludd's, but he said nothing about knowing him. We have no evidence that one initiated the other into a Rosicrucian order. But of course, how could we when the order was secret? That is why their friendship was kept secret, to protect the order, some have argued. A paradoxical argument since both wrote about Rosicrucianism enthusiastically and publicly.

Frances Yates has argued that Maier had brought Fludd's manuscripts from England, arranging for them to be published by Thomas de Bry, who also published Maier's books. But that is speculation as we have no record of letters between them, and they never published anything about each other's books. We may presume Fludd would have wanted to know what arrangements were made for his books, though in some cases he did not pay for their publication himself. His benefactor must have been a noble with esoteric interests, but researchers haven't been able to identify him.

Maier does mention Fludd in a letter he later wrote to Moritz, but it's not the sort of communication one would expect from one initiate about another. He describes Fludd as "very insolent" because he had written that the Germans are "idle, negligent and slow" (Heisler 1989). The Germans, Maier insisted, "share the Empire and are truly in command." Maier especially resents Fludd's portrayal of the English as "good-hearted, audacious, and courageous" (Moran 1981). He promises to deliver a written whipping unless dissuaded by Moritz. The friendship of Maier and Fludd seems logical, but historians have not been able to find any solid evidence that they were friends.

Maier wrote three long Latin poems about alchemy. Writing in 1617, he says he first heard of the Rosicrucians while he was in England. That year he also published a multimedia work of art and alchemy titled *Atalanta fugiens,* which included fifty allegorical engravings, explanatory tracts, and musical compositions. Maier refused to write about any of the practical details of alchemy; he believed those secrets could only be shared personally. For Maier the great work of alchemy was the task of manifesting divine power in the mundane world. As we have seen, Maier earned a place in the history of science. Isaac Newton studied Maier, leaving eighty-eight pages of notes.

Carl Jung was fascinated by Maier's *Allegoria Bella* published in book 12 of his *Symbola aureæ mensæ duodecim nationum. Mensæ* means "table" in Latin, but also has the connotation of the altar slab, the flat stone top of a Roman Catholic altar, so the title could be translated *Symbols of the golden altar top of the twelve nations.* A blend of solar mysticism, Christian piety, and vitalism, the belief that life and consciousness are more than biology, this imaginary travelogue of a journey to find the legendary phoenix proceeds according to the stages of the alchemical process by which metals evolve. Maier searches all over Europe but can't find what he's looking for. In the Canary Islands he witnesses a royal wedding, not only an echo of the royal wedding in the famous Rosicrucian book *The Chymical Wedding of Christian Rosenkreutz* but also of Frederick and Elizabeth.

He sails to America where he hears of sages who have taught the natives to breed mules from horses and donkeys. There he plants the seed of a fruit, and when the sapling grows, he grafts it to another tree.

Among the many interesting details, factual and imaginary, in the book is his claim that in Peru could be found *aqua Americana*, which makes gold soft and yet doesn't burn.

Along the way Maier argued that the phoenix arising from the ashes of its death is not a pagan concept but a precursor of Christ and a proof of resurrection. At the Nile the anonymous narrator of Maier's travelogue finds the local people have lost their wisdom and prosperity. He searches the mouths of the Nile unsuccessfully, until he almost gives up hope, believing he may have been deceived since to the Egyptians he is a stranger and therefore not to be trusted.

At last the traveler finds the god Mercury where the local people said he couldn't be found. With instructions from Mercury, he at long last arrives at the nest of the phoenix, only to find that the bird has "gone abroad." It had flown away on a mission "as appointed arbiter between the owl and the other birds attacking her," a reference to his book *Jocus Severus*, where he compared the Rosicrucians to an owl attacked by lesser birds. The traveler returns to Europe with "nothing in his hands." Maier says the phoenix can't be seen with physical eyes, only with what he calls the "little eye of the soul" (1617). Jung thought the story tragic.

Maier identifies the alchemical *nigredo*, the burned stage or phase of putrefaction, with worldly suffering. The heart, gold, the sun itself, and the sun as deity are linked together like octaves of the same note, or something like the Golden Chain of Homer, which unites all beings in a hierarchy, from the simplest and least powerful to the omnipotent and omniscient. Gold points to God, Maier learned from the Neoplatonists. The soul, like gold in the fire, survives earthly trials.

Maier had great interest in America. His vision of a utopia in the New World inspired four of the people behind the plan for the newly founded Virginia Colony, including a committee member, a legal adviser, the treasurer, and the future treasurer.

In spring of 1618 Maier gave all eleven of his printed books as a present to Moritz. Moritz was impressed. The following year Maier was appointed doctor to Moritz and his family, official court chemist, and compiler of news and intelligence reports. He must have thought that he was sitting in the sweet spot of a wave of reform that was about to sweep across Europe. But then the Battle of White Mountain shattered that hope. Maier died in 1622; the manner of his death obscured by the fog of war. Some say he was one of many innocent victims of artillery assaults. Others claimed he had been contacted by the Rosicrucians, accepted into the order, and disappeared into another life, which they had prepared for him.

NINE

Three Little Books

Rosicrucianism began with three little books: *Fama Fraternitatis,* *Confessio Fraternitatis,* and *The Chymical Wedding.* The first, *Fama Fraternitatis Roseae Crucis oder Die Bruderschaft des Ordens der Rosenkreuzer* (A report on the brotherhood of the Rosy Cross) (1614), was probably circulating in manuscript by 1607, although John Montgomery argued that it might have been as early as 1590. It may have reached England, since Ben Jonson mentioned the Rosy Cross in a masque in 1610 four years before the *Fama* was actually published. His first and perhaps greatest comedy, *The Alchemist,* was a sharp satire that tells the story of two frauds who cheat the gullible by convincing them they are alchemists. It includes a condemnation of "the Invisible Lady styled the Magical Sister of the Rosicross" whose prophecies of wonders never came true.

Authors with complicated revelations flourished in the days of the comets. Around the time the *Fama* was passed around in manuscript, the *Aurora* by Jakob Böhme, a classic of Christian mysticism, circulated in manuscript among the same group of intellectuals. The question of when the *Fama* was written has created controversy. Nick Pelling makes a compelling argument based on the *Fama*'s reference to, as Thomas Vaughan translated it, "looking glasses of divers virtues." The microscope was invented in 1590, but the word *divers* (diverse) suggests more than one such "looking glass." The telescope was invented in 1608.

Pelling suggests plausibly that the *Fama* must have been written after that, but we can't be certain (Pelling n.d.).

Adam Haslmayr claimed to have seen a manuscript copy of the *Fama* in 1610. His statement, published in his *Answer to the Praiseworthy Brotherhood of Theosophers of Rozenkreuz*, was included in the same volume as the *Fama*. Haslmayr, his friend Karl Widemann, and Benedictus Figulus appear to have been early participants in whatever Rosicrucianism was at that time. Haslmayr's *Answer* was published in 1612, the year Rudolf II lost his power. Rudolf might have enjoyed the book. A preeminent example of bad timing in publishing, Rudolf's severely Catholic brother Matthias became Holy Roman emperor. Endorsing the Rosicrucians in print proved dangerous. Matthias condemned Haslmayr to row an oar for five years in a Genovese galley.

The manuscript of the *Fama* was supposed to have been shared only among a few friends; perhaps the author or authors couldn't imagine that many people would show interest in a concoction of righteous outrage, optimistic prognostications, bawdy jokes, Paracelsian precepts, coded messages, and satirical asides. To their surprise, what had been their creative response to English masques and theater and Italian drama had become a controversial declaration of an alternate future.

The Rosicrucians, according to the *Fama*, could make gold, but they considered it a "trivial matter." The break with imperial power had not yet occurred in the *Fama*, where the emperor received praise, but the pope only condemnation. With promises of unlimited gold, the *Fama* appears to make an effort to sway Holy Roman Emperor Rudolf II to lead the Universal Reformation himself. The Aristotelian mindset of the Catholic Church is dismissed to be replaced by the philosophy and practices of Paracelsus and his followers. The star of the show is, of course, Christian Rosenkreutz (also spelled Rosenkreuz), also known as Christian Rosy Cross or Father CRC. We can't be certain if he ever existed. Most scholars consider him a literary invention, probably a caricature of John Dee, Sir Francis Bacon, or the Polish alchemist Michael Sendivogius.

In the manifestos, CRC was a German monk of noble birth. During a pilgrimage to Jerusalem he encountered and studied alchemy, communication with nature spirits, and the secrets of the Kabbalah. He perfected his wisdom among Arabian mystics. CRC hoped to share his knowledge back home, along with the rare plants and animals he brought back with him, but European intellectuals ridiculed him. He took his wonders to other countries, where he received no better a welcome, so in 1459 he founded the Brotherhood of the Rosy Cross. The first cloister, as the *Fama* calls it, included three of his like-minded friends.

The four men invented a magical language, a magical alphabet, and the first part of the mysterious Book M, a "large dictionary" of "great wisdom" that they used daily to praise and glorify God. They constructed a new building named *Sancti spiritus* or Holy spirit and then accepted four additional brothers into the fraternity. We are told one was CRC's cousin, another a skilled painter. All but one were German bachelors sworn to virginity. When they had learned all they could together, the eight journeyed to other countries where they cured the sick, never accepting payment.

Inspired by Socrates, who said, "I know that I know nothing," CRC said, "the height of knowledge is to know nothing." CRC, according to the manifestos, died at age 106 in 1484 but predicted correctly that his tomb would be found in 1604. Inside the tomb, the *Fama* tells us, with its hermetic Pythagorean alchemical construction and adornment, his body was found still fresh, along with an ever-burning lamp, manuscripts of powerful secrets, and three books by Paracelsus. The *Fama* ends with the enticing announcement that these secrets would now be shared with the few found worthy to keep them. All one need do is casually mention interest, and the worthy would be contacted.

The *Fama* contains an evocative description of the romance of books in a passage that foreshadowed the internet: "Would it not be a precious thing if you were able to find in one book everything that has appeared in every book that has ever existed, that does exist, or will exist, everything that has been found out, and may be found out, to read, understand, and have it as your own?"

When they reconvened annually on day C at their Rosicrucian sanctuary, where exactly were they? In the twentieth century, some authors argued that the Rosicrucians, since they were ascended masters, met in a building on the astral plane. According to Manly Hall in his obscure book, coauthored with A. Russell Slagel, *The Rosicrucians and Magister Christoph Schlegel: Hermetic Roots of America,* an anonymous manuscript that was in the collection of the Philosophical Research Society titled *Rose-Croix* contains the following paragraph: "The belief of the Germans is that there are certain Protestant monks, previously of the order of Cisteau, living on a hill along the banks of the Danube, in an almost inaccessible place where they go into contemplation, practicing fasting and austerities very severe in appearance in order to establish more easily their opinions. Their principal exercise is the search for the stone which is named Philosopher's in which several estimate that they have found perfection" (Hall and Slagle 1986, 75).

Hall, who believed the manuscript might date from around 1626, added: "The unknown author then mentions a cloister which is the principal seat of their order and explains that the brethren abiding in this place are given largely to alchemy by which they restored and perpetuated their physical bodies and gained a considerable reputation as physicians and chemists. They advocated a reformation of human society for which reason they were considered dangerous to the policies of their time" (Hall and Slagle 1986, 75).

Elias Ashmole wrote down in cipher Dr. Robert Childe's claim that the Brothers R.C. lived in France in a seemingly ruined monastery at the German border seven miles from Strasbourg. Childe was among the intelligencers in the circles of John Winthrop the Younger and Samuel Hartlib. Winthrop was the great celestial intelligencer of America. Childe practiced alchemy with Winthrop in the colonies, but later back in England he specialized in medicine and the theory and practice of agriculture.

Hartlib was known as the leading intelligencer in England and Europe. His circle of knowledge seekers may have been an important step toward the establishment of the world's first academy of the sciences: the

Royal Society of London for Improving Natural Knowledge, which, in the twenty-first century, greets visitors with the sentence: "Our origins lie in a 1660 'invisible college' of natural philosophers and physicians."

Hartlib was one of a trio of philosophers who would become "both in their limited, practical aims, and their wild bloodshot mysticism, the real philosophers and the only philosophers of the English Revolution," as Hugh Trevor-Roper wrote. Comenius was also one of them. The ideal of a Universal Reformation would soon become a justification for military dictatorship, as we'll see.

As Nick Pelling in his blog *Cipher Mysteries* has pointed out, Childe's romantic Rosicrucian ruins appeared in a book published the same year as the *Fama* called *Assertio Fraternitatis*. The anonymous author claims to be an actual brother of the Rosy Cross. We know now that the book was written by the German theologian Raphael Eglinus, in his youth a student of the hermetic philosopher Giordano Bruno and an editor of one of Bruno's texts. Eglinus left us this description of Bruno's lecturing style: "off the cuff."

In 1966, Oxford University, home of the Ashmolean Museum, published a five-volume comprehensive collection of Elias Ashmole's diary entries, letters, and supporting documents. The diary entries are fascinating, providing an intimate glimpse into the life of an extraordinary collector of curiosities and knowledge, including many of the papers of John Dee. Ashmole's diary includes records of sickness and cures as correlated with medical astrology. He also wrote notes about his astrological readings for matters of business and the health of others. His services were in demand among sickly nobles. The legendary astrologer William Lilly, also an expert in medical astrology, was his close friend. The diary also includes many dreams and a riddle that promises to reveal the prime matter (Ashmole 1966).

> *Of one part of mans Frame, Six letters make ye the Name,*
> *One P: add unto them, Then change S into M:*
> *This done you do uncage, The Subject of ye Sage.*

The great British librarian Marianne Winder offered an interesting solution. The part of man's frame would be the *lumbus* or the loins. Add P and change S to M to get *plumbum* or lead. The lead of lust must be transformed into the gold of divine love.

Ashmole is best known as an early English Freemason, He did whatever he could to protect fellow astrologers from Cromwell. He cast sigils of tin, iron, and gold, corresponding to rats, lice, flies, fleas, and moles. Some writers have alleged that they rid houses of pests, but they were actually used in his cures for ailments ranging from syphilis to poor digestion. In 1663, Ashmole became one of the first Fellows of the Royal Society. In the prologue to his *Theatricum Chemicum Britannicum* (1652), he wrote that the Earl of Norfolk had been cured of leprosy by a brother RC and that Queen Elizabeth had been saved from smallpox twice by another.

But there was a darker side to Ashmole. He married two older widows for their wealth and his third wife for her connections. All three found him untrustworthy. He did not hesitate to exploit the elderly when acquiring items for his famous collections. He routinely used Masonic and other contacts for his own purposes and then ignored them when he found more useful affiliations. While the Portuguese and then the Dutch had opened the way for European profit from the sale of enslaved Africans, Ashmole was an early investor in the Royal African Company, which, with the help of the Pilgrims, brought enslaved people to America. The Royal African Company was a project of King James II, his son King Charles II, and the City of London, so it was a mainstream investment at a time when few European consciences were bothered by slavery. Not until 1834 would slavery be outlawed in the United Kingdom. It would take a civil war thirty years later for America to do the same.

Everett Bleiler (2008) has pointed out that alchemical storytelling, especially the Rosicrucian manifestos, are part of the history of science fiction. Paul Bembridge (1999, 228) describes Rosicrucianism as "an unwelcome emergence of the age-old esoteric tradition into political and cultural expression." Although the authors of the manifestos considered themselves exemplary Christians, they believed that Hermes and Plato anticipated Jesus, arguing that studying Neoplatonic and hermetic wisdom improves a student's understanding of Christianity. The same argument that got Pico della Mirandola in serious trouble a hundred years earlier. To most of their contemporaries, especially their enemies, this passion for Plato, the Neoplatonists, and the *Hermetica* suggested a dangerous resurgence of paganism.

For generations of mystical romantics, the *Fama* has been a book that seemed to have fallen from the sky, but like any book it had a specific context: the country of Hessen-Kassel ruled by Moritz the Learned, which was, as we have seen, a destination for occult studies, alchemy, and the hermetic arts that surpassed even Emperor Rudolf's Prague.

◄○►

Moritz, Landgrave of Hessen-Kassel was an accomplished musician and composer, founder of Germany's oldest, still active, wild animal park and patron to English theatrical players and strolling musicians. He found nothing in his devotion to Calvinism that prevented him from studying hermetic philosophy or keeping a gaggle of alchemists. Moritz's court printer published the *Fama*. Why did Moritz support the printing of such a volatile declaration when he considered his own position precarious? Rivals outside his borders and inside threatened his reign and his country. Did he hope the trumpet call of the *Fama* would inspire his own people? Did he think it might transform him from an obscure pawn to a fervent leader for reform? And why did a member of Moritz's court write a tract suggesting that the headquarters of the Rosicrucians was near Hessen-Kassel?

The *Fama* may be comparable to a late twentieth-century zine. The creation of a group of friends whose contributions reflected various levels of involvement and intent: a pooling of ideas. Moritz became known as the one who sponsored this anonymous announcement of a cultural and political revolution some thought was imminent.

But there is no evidence that the publication of the *Fama* by Moritz's printer was ever approved by Andreae or anyone from the Tubingen circle. Susanna Åkerman has pointed out the strong possibility that Andreae's early retreat from the Rosicrucian controversy may have been his reaction to having his writing commandeered by instigators with a political agenda that would start the Thirty Years' War. The *Fama's* hermetic cry in the wilderness was transformed into propaganda. Moritz seems to have been one of the early converts to the mistaken idea that a war against the Holy Roman Empire would mean the liberation of the world. Moritz had been involved in diplomacy with Henry IV of France before the Protestant champion's assassination.

By 1619, Moritz's dream of a golden age, whether as public relations campaign, sincere enthusiasm, or political maneuver, faded as the first tremors of the Thirty Years' War disrupted Europe. The war would destroy Moritz's country and force his abdication. In 1619, Michael Maier left the court of Moritz the Learned for reasons unknown.

To understand the *Fama* it's helpful to keep in mind that Europe was buzzing about Trajano Boccalini's famous satire *The Parnassus News* (1612). The introduction to the first edition of the *Fama* was "The General and Universal Reformation of the Entire World," chapter seventy-seven of *The Parnassus News*. It's a satire on Boccalini's eminent contemporaries. It includes a scene where the wise men of Olympus compose a manifesto of reform that actually doesn't reform anything. It fixes the price of cabbage and delivers lengthy self-congratulatory praise. Boccalini was appointed governor of Benevento by Pope Gregory XIII, but his misbehavior caused the pope to order him back to Rome. This gave Boccalini more time to work on his hilarious book, which would make its targets so angry Boccalini had to leave Rome, never to return.

Packaging a satire with a Rosicrucian manifesto could be perceived as undermining it, unless the *Fama* was also satirical. Writers including Julianus de Campus suggested that the Rosicrucians deliberately placed a light satire in front of their serious manifesto so as to weed out those who couldn't see the difference. Perhaps they were thought to belong together as works of social criticism.

Michael Maier claimed that *The General and Universal Reformation* was bound with the *Fama* by accident. He pointed out that many publishers made such illogical pairings. Also, putting a lighthearted work in front of a more serious one was customary. The next edition of the *Fama* did not include *The General and Universal Reformation*. But the third edition included *The General and Universal Reformation* at the back of the book. A new preface claimed that the *Confessio* had cleared up the confusion caused by people who did not understand the real message of the *Fama*. But the last of these earliest printings omitted *The General and Universal Reformation* again, replacing it with the story of a Rosicrucian who was arrested for practicing black magic because he cured a sick woman and took no payment.

The *Fama* asserts the existence of an ultimate book of total revelation called M, not written in any ordinary language but in the language of being, the language of the very existence of things, the language of the inner workings of the visible and invisible universe. Paracelsus was not a Rosicrucian, the *Fama* stipulates, but he did derive his wisdom from glimpses of M. Maier called M "the book of the world (*liber mundi*), or the book of natural magic" (Tilton 2002). French occultists of the nineteenth century, beginning with Éliphas Lévi, argued that the Book M was the tarot when understood as a symbolic system derived from the Kabbalah. Lévi claimed that all the knowledge in the world can be found in the tarot but only after devoted study and meditation.

What began as a privately circulated underground creation within three years produced seven reprints and countless manuscript copies. Over four hundred books and pamphlets about the Rosicrucians were published between 1614 and 1623. Readers overreacted. For example, in imitation of the Jesuits, who conform to the habits of the places their missions take them, the Rosicrucians were described as invisible, but people took the metaphor literally, believing that Rosicrucians could disappear at will.

The manifestos helped inspire and inform Francis Bacon's classic *New Atlantis* (1626). However, Bacon warned readers that he considered: "the ancient opinion that man was microcosmus . . . fantastically strained by Paracelsus" (Bacon 1915). Descartes went to Germany looking for Rosicrucians. Ben Jonson made fun of the people who hoped to be contacted by the secret society of the "brethren of Rosy Cross." Isaac Newton wrote notes in the margin of his copy of the *Fama*, dismissing the story of CRC as a fraud. Catholic priests preached against "rosycross wolves."

Claiming to clarify the confusion caused by the *Fama*, the *Confessio* or *Confession of the Rosy Cross* was published several times in 1615 in Latin and German. The Latin first edition, bound with a German translation, also republished the *Fama*.

The second edition began with "Brief Consideration of the Secret Philosophy," an amalgam of John Dee's *Monas Hieroglyphica* and the Emerald Tablet of Hermes, by Philip à Gabella, a pseudonym. Since the end of the world was near, the book argued, now was the time for a general reformation.

Nick Pelling points out that the *Confessio* advises us to give up vanities that cloud understanding, mentioning specifically "vain Epicycles, and Excentrick Astronomical Circles." Pelling takes this as a reference to Kepler's *Astronomia nova* (1609), a compelling argument that the *Confessio* could have been written no earlier.

In its second paragraph, the *Confessio* reaffirms Rosicrucian loyalty to the Holy Roman emperor while making the enemy clear (in my own translation): "we condemn the East and the West [Islam and the pope] blasphemers against our Lord Jesus Christ, and offer and present with good will to the chief ruler of the Roman Empire our prayers, secrets, and great treasures of gold" (Philalethes 1652). In case there's any doubt, the *Confessio* later adds: "many godly people have secretly and very desperately fought the Pope's tyranny," adding: "his final fall is delayed, and kept for our times, when he will be scratched to pieces with nails" (Philalethes 1652). The nails mentioned here are likely a reference to the one Luther used to nail his ninety-five theses to the church door and the nails of the cross. The Rosicrucians considered themselves devout Christians. Anyone who wishes to learn the Rosicrucian secrets, the *Confessio* says, should carefully study the Holy Bible.

What are we to make of the following passage (Philalethes 1652), which certainly resembles science-fiction fantasy? Was it the revelation and promise of superior powers attainable by worthy humans? Or is it an allegory of enlightenment and the existence of the eternal soul? Or a joke intended to alarm the superstitious?

> Would it not be a precious thing, to always live so, as if you lived from the beginning of the world, and will live to its end? How excellent to dwell in one place, yet neither the people who dwell beyond the River Ganges in India can hide anything from you, nor those in Peru who might seek to keep secrets from you. How precious to read only one book to understand and remember all that was in all other books that have ever been, are now, or will ever be. How pleasant to sing drawing not stones and rocks but pearls and jewels, instead of wild animals, spirits, and instead of moving hellish Pluto, move the mighty princes of the world.

The Rosicrucians also enjoy divine protection: "God surrounds us with clouds, so that no violence can be done to we his servants. We can be seen and known only by the eyes of an eagle" (Philalethes 1652).

The *Confessio* acknowledges the success of the *Fama* but points out that its meaning requires superior intelligence to understand. "Although the *Fama* is given in five languages," the *Confessio* declares, "and is manifested to everyone, yet we do very well know that unlearned and gross wits will not understand it."

The political agenda appears with a proclamation of the scheme hatching among radicals to place Frederick on the throne of Bohemia as a first step toward making him the first Protestant Holy Roman emperor and leader of the holy war against the Roman Catholic Church that would at last defeat the pope: "our treasures shall remain untouched and unstirred, until the Lion arrives, who will ask them for his use, and employ them to confirm and establish his kingdom." As we have seen, Frederick's heraldic symbol was a lion.

The idea that the world was ending soon and that before its end God would restore the lost language of Adam seems to have been sincerely held (Philalethes 1652):

> We must observe well, and make it known to all, that God has certainly granted to the world before the end, which will happen soon, such truth, light, life, and glory, as the first man Adam had, which he lost in Paradise, after which he and his descendants were driven out to live in misery. Therefore let us cease all slavery, fraud, lies, and darkness, which little by little, with the great world's revolving, have crept into all arts, works, and governments of men.

Is this a metaphor? Would natural philosophy, officially dismissed as the occult but to some degree viewing itself as science, not only restore the language of Adam but also end the world, literally or metaphorically, by inaugurating a new society?

The *Confessio* clarifies: "Yea, the Lord God has already sent certain messengers to testify his will. They are the new stars which do appear and are seen in the firmament in Serpentario and Cygno, which signify and make themselves known to everyone" (Philalethes 1652). Later in the *Confessio* the phrase "alteration of government" (DeVries 2021) makes explicit the political dimension of the Rosicrucian agenda.

According to astrologers of the day, the great conjunction of Mercury, Jupiter, and Saturn in Sagittarius on December 23, 1603, signified the beginning of a new age. The configuration, they said, had only occurred twice before, once at the birth of Jesus and then at the birth of Charlemagne. Catholics took these predictions as proof that they would soon defeat and eliminate all heretics, including the Protestants of Germany, France, and England. Protestants believed the opposite, of course, that they would finally triumph against Rome, Madrid, and Vienna. Two novas, which appeared to be new stars, added to the excitement. Galileo thought a new day was dawning, and it was.

Astronomy, geography, physics, and mathematics were transforming the intellectual standards of Europe.

Kabbalah, Neoplatonism, Paracelsus, and the hermetic doctrines of signatures and sympathies seemed to reveal the secret language that explained a Rosicrucian's ability to predict the future by reading nature, a power reminiscent of Daoist (Taoist) ideas about the use of oracles like the YiJing (I Ching) to predict outcomes by studying natural patterns. "These characters and letters," the *Confessio* declares, "as God has here and there incorporated them in the Holy Scriptures, the Bible, so has he imprinted them in all animals. Like the mathematician and astronomer who foresee eclipses long before they happen, so we may foresee the darkness concealing the Church, and how long it will last."

The *Fama* and *Confessio* were taken very seriously by Catholics and Protestants alike. Christian Gilbert de Spaignart, a prominent theologian, even warned European royalty to beware the Rosicrucians: "Take heed all you princes, authorities, captains and soldiers, to the regard in which you are held by this fraternity, [to them] you are but mere tyrants, thieves and robbers!" (Penman 2009).

—◄o►—

In his masterpiece *The Consolation of Philosophy* (532 CE), Boethius wrote chapters in verse he called songs, including a song called "Orpheus and Eurydice," in which the plot's turning points are similar to that of *The Chymical Wedding of Christian Rosenkreutz*, published more than a thousand years later in 1616.

Having spent over thirty years collecting and copying unpublished works by Paracelsus, Karl Widemann, a physician and esoteric manuscript and book collector, preserved much of the work of Paracelsus for future generations. At the court of Rudolf II, Widemann had been secretary to Edward Kelley, John Dee's collaborator in alchemy and angelic communication. In 1604, Widemann wrote about his friend and one-time roommate Johannes Valentinus Andreae: "He has the Alchemical

Wedding." So this book was known in manuscript form before its publication.

Andreae was nineteen years old when he wrote *The Chymical Wedding*. It's probable that he received comments from friends and mentors he let read the manuscript. He edited a new draft before allowing it to be published in 1616. Written in imitation of English drama and masque, though it shows more Italian influence than English, *The Chymical Wedding* is hard to describe. Novelist and screenwriter John Crowley considers *The Chymical Wedding* the first science-fiction novel. Frances Yates wrote that "it ranks almost as a third Rosicrucian manifesto—the third item in the series which launched the Rosicrucian furore" (Yates 1975a, 68). "Often looked upon as the third Rosicrucian manifesto," agrees Adam McLean, a Scottish writer on alchemical texts and symbolism. He also points out that *The Chymical Wedding* has "an entirely different tone from the other Rosicrucian documents and addresses itself to inner transformation rather than the outer transformation of society and religion heralded in the *Fama* and *Confessio*" (quoted in Willard 2017, 130).

Thomas Willard, a leading scholar on the subject of Father CRC and *The Chymical Wedding*, describes it as a "satiric dream vision." He writes: "I have argued that the author, Johann Valentin Andreae, regarded it as a satire (German *Posse* or *Spott*; Latin *ludibrium*), and particularly as the sort of intellectual *jeu d'esprit* called Menippean satire" (Willard 2017, 130). Popular in ancient Rome, Menippean satire is known for cynical wit, exaggerated humor, and dreamlike disregard for the laws of nature—a genre as skeptical of tradition as it is of politics and humanity. A comparatively recent example is *The Hitchhiker's Guide to the Galaxy*.

The Christian Rosy Cross of the *Fama* is quite different from the one in *The Chymical Wedding*. The only difference in their names is the umlaut over the letter *u* in the latter. Umlaut CRC is an old man as disinterested in the world as young CRC was interested. On an evening just before Easter, old CRC sits in a hut meditating and praying. Almost the narrator, certainly a commentator, he's presented with ambivalence. Is he a holy monk or a selfish fool? The wedding of the title is more than simple matrimony; the word in German at the time carried connotations of the alchemical marriage between sun and moon, the result of transmutation, union with divine consciousness. Much of the plot is drawn from Boccaccio's *Amorous Vision* (1343) and *Love's Labor* (1336). Boccaccio was one of the first great authors and poets of Italy, a friend of the great poet, scholar, and pioneer humanist Petrarch, and the first to collect and publish the biographies of great women.

The Chymical Wedding contains erotic stories, dreams, gory alchemical allegories, and number and word puzzles. One of the puzzles reveals that the young woman who takes over the adventure is named Alchimia or Alchemy. Another puzzle can be solved two ways. One gives the alleged birth date of CRC, the other Andreae's birth date, perhaps a claim to ownership of not only *The Chymical Wedding* but all three Rosy Cross manifestos.

The action of *The Chymical Wedding* begins with a joke. Old CRC sits in his hut, perhaps a satirical nod to his hermetic tomb in the *Fama*. The Roman goddess of rumor, known to the ancient Greeks as the goddess of fame, Fama herself, her wings covered with eyes (a nod to the Roman poet Virgil's portrayal of her), enters carrying a large horn and a bundle of messages. Fama prods the oblivious old man, startling him.

The comedy continues when, after she gives him a message, as she flies away, she blows her horn, deafening him. The message is an invitation to a royal wedding with a warning that anyone unworthy who attempts to attend will suffer. The letter bears the Hieroglyphic Monad of John Dee, but the symbol had other meanings, too. Some took it to represent Paracelsus. Others claimed it had always represented Hermes Trismegistus. Astrologers noted that in their shorthand it indicated Mercury in Aries. Alchemists recognized it as the sigil of Mercury and a symbol for the source of life.

After an ordeal by nightmare, CRC sets out the next day. He wears clothes that represent the coat of arms of Andreae's family. Could this be Andreae's claim to authorship of the anonymous book, or it just another red herring by the actual author or authors?

In a castle, in a great hall full of very important people bragging to each other about achievements, like seeing Plato's forms, counting atoms, and perpetual motion, CRC witnesses more slapstick when a liar says he can actually see the invisible servants managing the feast and so gets a slap in the face from an invisible hand, another satirical nod at the Rosicrucians.

The play turns bawdy when a depressed CRC laments his lost youth, and the young woman, who has been his guide throughout the story, commenting along the way, laughs at him for his lust. She winks at the reader: "What do you think?" she asks. "If I slept with him tonight, he'd be more cheerful tomorrow." Even CRC laughs. Then follows another mathematical puzzle, but this one based on a sexy arrangement of her maidens and the candidates for initiation. They sit in a circle while she counts by sevens, leaving to chance who will pair off, like an early alchemical game of spin the bottle. By the time the narrative reaches the description of a nude female, the goddess Venus sprawled on a bed before CRC, it becomes clear that one of the book's attractions was the erotic content.

For spying on naked Venus, CRC is sentenced to become a lowly gatekeeper at the castle, instead of a guest of the royal couple. Here we can perhaps glimpse Andreae's own story as he retreated from his radical adolescent ideas, which however humorous and satirical nevertheless contained sincere utopian and hermetic themes and a revolutionary political intent.

During a time when women were disempowered and had few legal protections, the women in the *Chymical Wedding* are unusual because they are powerful. Andreae claimed to have written the *Chymical Wedding* as a satire on alchemy when he was sixteen years old. He dismissed *it* as a *ludibrium*. *Ludibrium* derives from the Latin *ludus*, meaning "a trivial toy or fun game unworthy of respect." Perhaps the best translation is "prank," though plaything, lampoon, and farce have been offered. The point is that the *Chymical Wedding* is playful.

Inspired by the simultaneous obscurity and great influence of the Rosicrucians, the Nobel prize–nominated Argentinian writer Jorge Luis Borges wrote the classic short story "Tlön, Uqbar, Orbis Tertius," which mentions Andreae: "Valentin Andrea. . . . I knew that it was the name of a German theologian who, at the beginning of the seventeenth century described the imaginary community of Rosae Crucis—the community which was later founded by others in imitation of the one he had preconceived" (1962, 29).

In another paragraph Borges described the Rosicrucians: "The elaborate story began one night in Lucerne or London, in the early seventeenth century. A benevolent secret society . . . came together to invent a country. The first tentative plan gave prominence to 'hermetic studies,' philanthropy, and the cabala. Andrea's curious book dates from that first period. At the end of some years of conventicles and premature syntheses, they realized that a single generation was not long enough in which to define a country. They resolved that each one of the master-scholars involved should elect a disciple to carry on the work" (1962, 39).

When Borges wrote "The metaphysicians of Tlön are not looking for truth or even an approximation to it: they are after a kind of amazement. They consider metaphysics a branch of fantastic literature" (1962, 34), was he offering his own definition of Andreae's *ludibrium*? This fascination of Borges inspired Umberto Eco to explore the Rosicrucian mystery in his own writing (Ketzan 2019).

The author of the *Confessio* writes in chapter 12: "For conclusion of our Confession we must earnestly admonish you, that you cast away, if not all yet most of the worthless books of pseudo chemists, who think it a joke to apply the Most Holy Trinity to vain things, or to deceive men with monstrous symbols and enigmas, or to profit by the curiosity of the credulous" (Philalethes 1652). The author of the *Fama* condemns "ungodly and accursed gold making." Andreae's father wasted his fortune and died young, chasing gold in an alchemy lab.

Instead of supernatural initiates of malevolent or benevolent secret societies, perhaps the Rosicrucians were something closer to intelligencers, counterculture catalysts like the English romantic poets, the Surrealists, the beat poets, the Situationists, and the flower children, They are perhaps most comparable to the abolitionist New England Transcendentalists who flourished two hundred years later in America. All of these were the sort who got called bohemians by people who had no idea where the name came from.

The influence of theater on Andreae's youth has been traced to touring English minstrels and theater companies, while other scholars have suggested Italian mystery plays. Andreae and his friends were inspired by the bawdy humor and sarcastic social criticism of British comedy. For example, when the young woman guiding CRC delivers an aside to the reader that the old man would cheer up if she slept with him, she breaks the fourth wall with a wink. As Åkerman writes: "English stage settings had already been shown to have influenced Andreae's youthful plays . . ." (1998, 69).

The *Fama* may not be a holy relic of a mystic cult of ascended masters but instead the work of a brainy nineteen-year-old attending Tübingen University, who is inspired by English and Italian theater, but also Paracelsus and Boccalini, and who is encouraged and perhaps assisted by friends like the Paracelsian physician and lawyer Tobias Hess and a law professor at Tübingen, Christoph Besold, a German jurist who later converted to Catholicism. Besold was a close friend of Kepler. When Kepler's seventy-three-year-old mother Katharina was put on trial as a witch, she was kept in chains for fourteen months. Besold helped Kepler gain her acquittal.

Tobias Hess had been influenced by Simon Studion, who died in 1605. Studion wrote an almost two-thousand-page unpublished book of predictions that circulated in manuscript around 1604 called the *Naometria*. The predictions, which include the fall of the papacy, with the crucifixion of the pope in 1620, are based on numerology and include numerous references to roses. Hess and his student Andreae were members of a Society Naometria in Tübingen. And yet John Montgomery

argued that Andreae could not have been one of the Rosicrucian founders because in his youth he had tried to convince his friends to reject
Studion. Since the Rosicrucians and Studion shared so many opinions
in common, Montgomery thought Andreae a devout Lutheran and
nothing more. Studion was one of many writers in the 1590s using rose
and lion symbology, astrology, and the medium of prophecy to imagine
a world without a pope. Tobias Hess corresponded with Simon Studion
in 1597. Both men were certain that soon the papacy would fall.

Hess claimed that as a child he had seen a lion in a vision. The
lion had ordered him to write down what he saw and heard. His letter
describing the event survives. The lion explained that he had come to
punish sins. An eagle, representing the Roman Catholic Church, lost its
wings. The manifestos and Hess's interrogation documents agreed: after
120 years the lion would defeat the eagle, and the last pope would fall.

Andreae referred to the so-called Tübingen Circle as a society, but
we have no evidence that he meant an organized fraternity rather than a
gathering of friends with similar interests and an enthusiasm for reform.
As Christopher McIntosh wrote: "Andreae and his friends felt that the
time was ripe for a new age. European civilization had reached a critical
point. The Reformation had failed to bring about the hoped for spiritual renewal, Europe was bitterly divided into Catholic and Protestant,
science and religion were drifting apart—it was obvious that something
had gone wrong. So Andreae and his friends decided to express their
vision for Europe in the form of an imaginary brotherhood, which they
hoped would in due course attract people and so turn into a real brotherhood. As we have seen, they skillfully wrapped this all up in a mystery
and dropped this mystery into the collective mind of the age through
the manifestos" (White 1999, 250).

In the days before the arrival of Elizabeth, Andreae used the library
at Heidelberg, becoming friendly with one of Frederick's librarians,
himself a book collector. Was Andreae caught up in the fervor of the
royal wedding that seemed to bring the dream of a Protestant Holy
Roman emperor one step closer? He had already been disillusioned by

the unauthorized use of the manifestos as propaganda and by the widespread overreaction to them. Perhaps he still hoped that a Protestant emperor might succeed where the manifestos had failed.

Emblem books were very popular in those days. They involved a language of symbols common to all Europe that Andreae used with great fluency. Did Andreae try to destroy the myth he helped create because the reaction to it had revealed how few were ready for such lofty considerations as the Universal Reformation? Was Andreae covering his tracks or merely adding to the fun when in 1617 he attacked Rosicrucianism in print, satirizing it in his book *Tower of Babel*, published in his own name? A satirical collection of seventy-five allegorical characters, each with a unique opinion about the Rosicrucians, this cathartic book described the leading overreactors that disillusioned Andreae, including young nonconformists, pious fools, opportunistic pseudoscientists, false prophets, self-righteous fanatics, and aristocratic connoisseurs of art.

From 1613 to 1620, the area around the Palatinate was a hotbed of radical publishing, including a book titled *Sisters of the Rosy Cross; or, Short Discovery of these Ladies, and what Religion, Knowledge of Divine and Natural Things, Trades and Arts, Medicines, &c., may be found therein* (1620), first translated from German into English by Russell Yoder in 2024. In the section "Sisters' Art of Flying," the Sisters of the Rosy Cross claim that they teach "the right and certain art of flying, which we benefit from in our women's lodge of the sisters of the Rose-colored Cross." They boast that "we can make a person fly from a low place to a higher one." Lest we take this literally, the punch line is delivered: "That's because we have a number of wings ready, and we don't want the least of these to be: 1. Religion and justice, 2. Love of God and neighbor, 3. Prudence and fortitude," and thirteen others, including "be a shepherd and not a wolf," make it clear that what appeared at first to be a coven of witches with flying ointment was really a pious Protestant metaphor. They also claim to have the secret of desalinating water for drinking and cooking, having made sweet water from seawater. Was this a literal claim or another alchemical allegory?

Later in life, in the autobiography he submitted as part of the requirements for becoming what amounted to a Lutheran bishop, Andreae wrote that he laughed at the *Fama* and the *Confessio* and had nothing but contempt for novelty seekers and the people suckered by them. But what did he mean by that? He didn't say he didn't write the books. Was he laughing because he was in on the prank? Or was he looking back with disdain at his own behavior?

As we have seen, Andreae began distancing himself from the Rosicrucian fervor he helped create long before disaster struck. But Andreae's retreat from controversy didn't save him from the forces the manifestos helped unleash. During the Thirty Years' War, he suffered through the destruction of two households. He had to hide in the woods from marauding soldiers. An organizer of charities and a prolific writer, later in life he became spiritual adviser to Antonia the Learned, a royal princess, and well-respected scholar of the Kabbalah. Called "the Minerva of Württemberg," she was well known for her generous acts of charity and her restorations of churches destroyed by war. She commissioned an altar painting she designed that captured her understanding of the journey of the soul, now known as the Kabbalistic Lehrtafel (teaching painting) of Princess Antonia. The intricate, brightly colored masterpiece decorates the royal chapel at a favorite holiday retreat. At her request, her heart is said to have been buried behind the painting.

In 1887, an anonymous book by "a student of occultism" was published called *An Adventure among the Rosicrucians*. Since it was copyrighted by esoteric author Franz Hartmann, he was thought to be the author. In 1910, Hartmann republished the book as *Among the Adepts*. In his introduction, he clarified that a friend had given him the notes that became the book. Later the theory gained traction that the true author was Madame Blavatsky. It's a novel but also an encyclopedia of esoteric theories and experiences and a poignant search for control in a world of illusions. Characters include the Water Queen and a dwarf with the power to read minds.

Whoever the author was, he or she wrote that "the name 'Rosicrucian

Order,' or the 'Order of the Golden and Rosy Cross' . . . is a comparatively modern invention, and was first used by *Johann Valentin Andreae*,
who invented the story of the knight *Christian Rosencreuz* for the same
purpose as *Cervantes* invented his *Don Quichote de la Mancha*, namely,
for the purpose of ridiculing the would-be Adepts, reformers, and gold-
makers of his age, when he wrote his celebrated 'Fama Fraternitatis'"
(Student 1887, 39).

That Andreae wrote these three little books that have cast such long
shadows is far from certain. Richard Kienast argues that his philological
analysis comparing the *Fama*, the *Confessio,* and the *Chymical Wedding*
proves that Andreae may have written the *Chymical Wedding* but not
the other two. He thinks Christoph Besold wrote them. Andreae wrote
in a letter to Besold: "Many people I owe very little, few a lot, you everything" (DeVries 2021). Besold's library of thousands of works was as
impressive as his education. In 1624 Besold wrote in his copy of the
Fama: "autorem suspicor J.V.A." He suspected that Johann Valentin
Andreae wrote the *Fama*.

Both Montgomery and Frances Yates doubted Andreae's authorship.
Yates suggested the possibility that Andreae's friend Joachim Jungius
authored the books. Jungius, a professor of medicine and a leading philosopher of the time, contributed to the development of mathematics,
the birth of early science, and various improvements in essential crafts
such as weaving and knitting.

Though Andreae claimed to have "always laughed at the
Rosicrucian fable" there are similarities between the *Fama* and
Confessio and Andreae's other writing. *Fama* and *Confessio* and his
later books, including *Christianopolis* and *Image of a Christian Society,*
propose model Christian communities. The description of Damcar,
the city in the east where Father CRC was initiated, is similar to
Andreae's depiction of *Christianopolis*. Scholars are certain that the
book *Sheath of the Sword of the Spirit* (1616) by Tobias Hess was actually written by Andreae, which he admitted in his autobiography.
Composed of eight hundred aphorisms, it included many sentences

from Andreae's published and unpublished works, including twenty-eight from *Confessio*.

Even as a precocious child Andreae had written comedies and utopias. Andreae's father was a clergyman who practiced alchemy, and his mother was appointed court apothecary in Tübingen. With their shared interests, his mother and father were themselves a kind of alchemical wedding.

Christopher McIntosh sums it up: "Andreae and his friends thus created a potent mixture of symbols that, when it was made public, created an enormous resonance. And very quickly things took a turn that Andreae himself found alarming. What he had intended as a symbolic and somewhat playful message to bring about a renewal of Christianity had been taken literally and turned into the great furor that we know about—which is why later in his life he backed away from the whole enterprise" (White 1999, 253).

Many years after the three little books were published, Johann Arndt claimed that Andreae had confessed to him that he was one of those behind the Rosicrucian controversy. Arndt is remembered as the father of Pietism and a devout Lutheran, but he was also an alchemist. Rumored to have succeeded in his quest for the philosopher's stone, he described it as being of the same spiritual substance as Christ, that substance being the essence of all living things. To achieve it, an alchemist must become pure, surrendering "what is owed to Adam" (DeVries 2021).

Arndt anonymously praised Khunrath's *Amphitheater*, but he was overt about his interest in Neoplatonism, Gnosticism, hermeticism, and what Paracelsus called theosophy. Paracelsus believed that God rules creation with the help of spirits, both astral and divine. The signatures of these spirits can be found everywhere in the world. The signatures are seeds that can be purified. Andreae's *Christianopolis* was dedicated to Arndt.

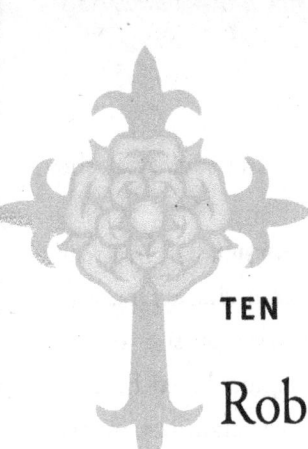

TEN

Robert Fludd in the Twilight of the Renaissance

The 1782 German translation of Fludd's *Tractatus apologeticus integritatem Societatis de Rosea Cruce* (Treatise to defend the integrity of the Society of the Rosy Cross), includes a note by the translator Adam Booz that describes how magnetic electrum (a gold and silver alloy) absorbing moon beams created starry flowers that dissolved back into the water from which they arose. In the sunlight they would appear again, blossoming with an overwhelming glory. According to the *Hamburg Correspondent* in 1776, many nobles had witnessed a demonstration of the astonishing flowers.

Adam Booz also included an astrological chart of the Universal Reformation cast for December 20, 1603, when the great conjunction of Jupiter and Saturn in Sagittarius occurred. Other astrologers gave December 23, but modern calculations indicate the correct date would have been December 17. For seventeen years, enthusiasm for the universal reformation grew, but then the general public lost interest. Early Rosicrucian scholars wondered why. But Frances Yates and others have shown how the political misfortunes of Frederick and Elizabeth shattered the Rosicrucian dream of an esoterically inclined Protestant Holy Roman emperor.

Though he was a doctor and friend to King James I and King Charles I, perhaps Robert Fludd's greatest fame is Dan Brown's inclusion of him in the list of grand masters of the secret society at the heart of his novel *The Da Vinci Code*.

His contemporaries considered Fludd a leading physician. The great playwright Ben Jonson, despite his comical Rosicrucian characters, was one of his patients. Fludd was one of the better-known scientists of his day. For generations, enthusiasts of metaphysical religion listed him as one of the most likely candidates for a genuine Rosicrucian, but in his unpublished *A Philosophical Key*, Fludd had included an oath in which he denied being a member of the order.

In 1598, newly graduated from Oxford, Fludd traveled to Paris, Rome, and other cities in Italy, France, Germany, and Spain as a tutor but also as a student. He met Paracelsian physicians and Jesuits in the mountains between France and Spain who taught him techniques of theurgy, the art of attuning to communion with the divine as documented by the Neoplatonist Iamblichus. The earlier Neoplatonists such as Plotinus had emphasized the contemplative side of salvation. They taught that remembering our true selves leads to enlightenment and liberation. Iamblichus thought only divine grace can free a soul from ignorance and forgetfulness. The right use of imagination can create a connection with the divine. But that communication is nothing less than the grace of the gods.

In 1604, back in England, Fludd returned to Oxford to earn his medical degrees. Fludd reports that as a university student he was already so good at astrology one of his professors interrupted his studies before an exam and insisted he cast his horoscope to reveal who had robbed him.

A lifelong celibate, proud of his virginity, Fludd never married. He believed that sexual desire was the cause of the fall from paradise. By denying his sexuality, he hoped to achieve the vision of Eden. By age forty, in 1614, Fludd was a respected doctor in London, successful enough to have a full-time secretary and an apothecary on his premises. An experienced alchemical experimenter, Fludd had more than two decades of philosophical writing in manuscript, but he had never been in print. The Rosicrucian manifestos and the reaction to them started Fludd on a publishing career, some of which he came to regret. He exemplifies the way the Rosicrucian manifestos inspired authors who had been at best isolated in small groups to come forth into the light in defense of ideas much like their own.

As a practitioner of Paracelsian medicine, Fludd must have been thrilled when the *Fama*, with its appreciation of Paracelsus, first arrived in England. In 1610 he saw it in manuscript. Five years later he read the *Confessio*. Seeing the witless overreaction to the manifestos and the shoddy and partisan criticisms of a fraternity of devoted hermetic Paracelsians, whose goals he shared, in 1616 Fludd published *A Brief Apology, washing away cleansing the stain of suspicion and infamy applied to the Fraternity of the Rosy Cross with, as it were, a Fludd of truth.* He defended not only the Rosicrucians but also the Kabbalah and astrology in a book full of longing for educational reform and for a renaissance in research and philosophy. A year later he published the expanded edition bound with an open letter to the Rosicrucians, requesting consideration for membership in their order.

His defense of the Rosicrucians wasn't the only book Fludd published in 1617. Using a pseudonym he penned a brief work about resurrection, 126 pages with ten mentions of the Rosicrucians, and dedicated to the Brothers R.C. The year 1617 also saw the publication of the first volume, in two books, of Fludd's masterpiece *The History of the Macrocosm and Microcosm*, which he audaciously dedicated to King James without asking permission to do so first.

Fludd had just received the honor of becoming a Censor of the College of Physicians, making him one of the examiners who decided which candidates should be eligible. He was also experimenting with steel making. Complaints against him had already been filed by the holders of England's steel patents. James had been told that Fludd, alleged to be an "unchaste" defender of the Rosicrucians, had dedicated his book of dubious philosophy to the king without the king's consent. James summoned Fludd to explain himself. Fludd explained himself so well James became his lifelong patron, even helping him with his patent problem, once the Privy Council discovered that Fludd made better steel than the patent owners.

James encouraged Fludd to present a digest of his defense, which became his next book: *Brief Declaration to James I*. Here, Fludd denies that the Rosicrucians are heretics: they are soundly Lutheran, acceptable to many Calvinists, and therefore clearly Protestant. Fludd lived the life of a decent Anglican. He insists that far from being unchaste, he is a forty-year-old virgin. As for dedicating his history to James, Fludd explained that his agent wanted to dedicate the book to the Landgrave of Hesse, but Johann Theodor de Bry the publisher and also Hieronymous Gallerus the printer wanted to dedicate the book to Frederick. Fludd chose James as the only polite way to avoid a dispute. William Huffman argues that Fludd's agent who wanted to dedicate the book to the Landgrave of Hesse was Michael Maier, whose own books were dedicated to the Landgrave of Hesse.

The first half of Fludd's *History of the Macrocosm and the Microcosm* rests on a foundation of Pythagorean geometry. But the second half has shifted to a framework drawn from the Kabbalah. Why were the two volumes in four books of Fludd's *History of the Macrocosm and the Microcosm* published in Germany instead of England? Fludd blamed it on the extra expense of the high-quality copper plates. De Bry was the most skilled and far cheaper than English printers. After joining an expedition to North America, de Bry's father had engraved depictions of life among indigenous Americans that became popular.

Fludd recorded his delight that the publisher returned forty pounds of the fee and included sixteen free copies. Volume one of the cosmic history was published in 1617 in Oppenheim in the Palatinate, while Frederick and Elizabeth ruled in Heidelberg. But volume two had to wait for de Bry's escape to Frankfurt in 1620, after Spanish troops invaded Oppenheim.

Andreae lampooned people who bragged about "counting atoms" and "seeing the ideas of Plato." Fludd was the penultimate example of the type, but *The Chymical Wedding* was published a year before *History of the Macrocosm and Microcosm*. Fludd's monumental history included the art of memory, astrology, cosmology, biology, anatomy, geometry, medicine, philosophy, the art of war, meteorology, perspective in art, geomancy, arithmetic, and music.

Fludd's writing is a rich amalgam of Pythagorean theory and Christian Kabbalah. He read Plato and the Neoplatonists, especially that master of metaphysical complexity, Proclus. Fludd explores the numerical basis of the universe and the importance of mathematics, geometry, and music to understanding nature. Renaissance interpretations of the writings attributed to Hermes Trismegistus inspired Fludd to apply the theory of signatures and correspondences to his understanding of the relationship between the microcosm and the macrocosm.

In the fifteenth century, when Cosimo de' Medici heard that a copy of the *Hermetica* had been found, he ordered Marsilio Ficino to stop his eagerly awaited translation of Plato to translate the hermetic scriptures first. Ficino, and everyone else at the time who cared about such matters, believed that the *Hermetica* preserved the spiritual wisdom of ancient Egypt. As old or older than even the writing of Moses, the *Hermetica* offered a philosophy of sufficient antiquity and profundity to pose a challenge to the Catholic claim on truth.

Then in 1614, classical scholar Isaac Casaubon analyzed the *Hermetica* linguistically, arriving at a date of third or fourth century CE and an origin in the Neoplatonist school. Fludd either never heard of Casaubon's discovery or he ignored it. He continued to write about the *Hermetica* as if they were ancient Egyptian texts, which discredited him in the eyes of future generations of intellectuals.

Fludd's theories evolved. In one of his earliest books, he argues that God manifested the universe through the act of viewing. Lightning, Fludd thought, was the direct expression of the will of God. Perhaps influenced by Khunrath, he believed that divine fire created everything, even darkness. He thought the sun the living Christ in his true angelic form. Some of his theories were based on experiments gone wrong, such as his experiments with wheat where contamination from contact with the air, a concept unknown during his time, misled him to believe he had witnessed spontaneous generation of living worms from inert matter.

Fludd was capable of building practical contraptions. He designed various mechanical innovations, including a perpetual motion machine to grind grain that would run on water and then pump the water back into a supply tank to recycle it. William Harvey's discovery of the anatomy and physiology of the circulatory system was inspired by his friend Fludd's theory five years earlier that the life force circulates through the heart to the rest of the body. Fludd was the first to defend Harvey's theory in print. Fludd's experiments and mechanical inventions, practically outsider art during his lifetime, resembled the activities and practices of the Royal Society a generation later.

Fludd believed music began with the creation of Earth, the lowest note, so he composed counterpoint bass first with the other melodic parts built on top of it. He considered the universe a vast musical instrument with the sun at the center of the nexus of consciousness and form or, as modern physics says, in the balance between fusion and entropy.

As Roseen H. Giles has written, Fludd's speculative music "retained the notions of *musica mundana*, the inaudible music of the spheres, and *musica humana*, the analogous proportion and harmony of the human body. These ideas derive primarily from Boethius's treatise, De institutione musica, of the sixth century" (2016, 32). Fludd wrote (Godwin 1979, 14):

In all realms of creation there are beings: angels in the empyrean world; stars, planets and demons in the ethereal, and the elemental world of men, plants and minerals. All these creatures partake of God's light in measure according to their place on the hierarchy. But there is one level in particular which, though not at the top of the hierarchy, is nevertheless particularly favoured by God. This is the Sun, which is placed at the crucial midpoint of the chain of being, where spirit and matter are in perfect equity and balance.

Fludd believed music was a spirit of living air. A spirit with the power to nourish souls and heal bodies and minds. Music was achieved by understanding the relationship between Apollo and Saturn, or melody and rhythm.

His book *The Temple of Music* concludes with the details of his invention, a mechanical psaltery (or zither) with which a host could delight dinner guests with slow courtly music and sprightly galliards. He claims he built a similar one for King James, much to the delight of the court musicians. His design was simple, no real breakthrough in technology; he merely applied mechanization where it had not been applied before.

Fludd was not only a musical theorist but also an active musician and composer. He returned to music often, to help his readers visualize his theories. He imagined a two-octave, one-stringed musical instrument, known as the Fludd monochord or celestial monochord, as an illustration or metaphor for how divine light manifests the material world. Every human being is a monochord with a spiritual octave and a material octave. If we stay focused on the notes of a lower vibration, we stumble into temptations of the flesh and other evils. If we rise to the vibrations of the spiritual octave, heaven is ours. Fludd's octaves are a theory of frequencies, with eternal life at a higher frequency than physical life on Earth. They were also his map for the soul's descent from "higher spheres" and its return there "after death, when the ties of the body, the meanest of all places, have been dissolved" (Giles 2016).

The celestial monochord is an elaboration of Pythagoras's discovery of the ratios of harmony or sympathetic resonance. When one vibrating string vibrates another string of the same tuning, or a guitar chord vibrates a drumhead, we call it sympathetic resonance. Fludd considered sympathetic resonance an example of the way thought occurs and how different organs of the body communicate and regulate. "But, good God," Fludd wrote, "what is this when compared with that deep and true music of the wise, whereby the proportions of natural things are investigated, the harmonical concord and the qualities of the whole world are revealed, by which also connected things are bound together, peace established between conflicting elements, and whereby each star is perpetually suspended in its appointed place by its weight and strength, and by the harmony of its lucent spirit" (Waite 1887, 29).

Fludd commented on his illustration of the monochord, in Peter Ammon's translation (1967, 209):

> In this picture we see the miraculous harmony in which the two extremes, the most valuable and the meanest, are chained together and are in harmony; we see how the intermediary world spirit, the vehicle of the souls, is the tie which links the two extremes in joyful harmony and we see how God is the player of musica humana, the player of the string of the monochord, the inner principle which, from the centre of the whole, creates the consonant effects of life in the microcosm. The string which by its vibration spreads the luminous effect of the Inspirer through macrocosm and microcosm as accents and sounds of love, as it were, is the luminous spirit which participates in the two extremes and which joins them together.

While art lovers and students of metaphysics and the history of metaphysical religion have always prized the amazing copperplate engravings in his books, most scholars have dismissed the accompanying textual content as deluded speculation. *The Temple of Music,* a section of his encyclopedic extravaganza, was dismissed by scholars over the years as the work of a crank, a throwback to a less rational time, unworthy of serious attention. One writer suggested that Fludd had painted himself into a corner: he had intended to write a tract on each liberal art but got stuck writing about music, a subject about which he apparently knew little.

Recently, Peter Hauge has provided a more nuanced look at *The Temple of Music.* Omissions dismissed as ignorance he shows may have been deliberate. Hauge also points out that "Book one, dealing with the ancient history of music, etymology, the 'working of music on body and soul' and the sense of hearing, is clearly based on Marsilio Ficino's writings and commentaries to the Latin translation of Plato's works.

At times, Fludd even copies verbatim from Ficino, though without acknowledging the author" (Hauge 2008). Another obvious influence Hauge uncovers is the occult philosophy of Agrippa. Fludd received Ficino's ideas mostly by way of Agrippa, whose classic *De Occulta Philosophia* was influenced by Ficino. Agrippa may have been an inspiration for Fludd's monochord, since in *De Occulta Philosophia* Agrippa compared the great chain of being to a taut string.

The rather plain depiction of a majestic but severe-looking temple that illustrates *The Temple of Music* is actually a mnemonic device: the drawing illustrates the theories that take many pages to explain. For Fludd, music, like alchemy, reveals the spectrum from dark to light and facilitates the evolution from impurity to purity.

While it remains a beautiful metaphor, Fludd's celestial monochord was inaccurate, as Kepler pointed out. For example, the F natural should be F sharp for the semitones to work, a mistake Fludd corrected with a new monochord illustration in his response to Kepler. Nobel Prize-winning quantum physicist Wolfgang Pauli admitted his preoccupation with the idea, saying, "I carry both Kepler and Fludd within myself" (Roth 2021).

The music section is full of mistakes, but most of them appear to be printer's errors. Although music historians of his and later generations have dismissed Fludd as a hermetic "charlatan" who had nothing useful or original to offer, more recent scholarship proves he was aware of the musical standards of his day but chose to follow his own muse. As Giles wrote: "It is fitting then to see Fludd as the last of the humanists, simultaneously signaling the end of the Renaissance and demonstrating that occult philosophy and Ficinian medicine continued well into the seventeenth century" (2016).

Pamphlet wars dominate Fludd's later publications as he engaged in spirited printed debates with luminaries like Kepler and Marin Mersenne, one of the fathers of the mechanistic philosophy at the root of modern materialism, who called Fludd an "evil magician, a doctor and propagator of foul and horrendous magic, a heretical magician." He wondered how and why King James could allow "such a man to live and write in his Kingdom."

Kepler dismissed Fludd's theory of harmony as mere imagery. In response, Fludd criticized the use of mathematics to understand music, claiming it revealed only "shadows" and gave people the idea that music, a mystery understood by physics, had been explained: "the ordinary mathematicians deal with the shadows of quantities, the chemists and hermeticists, however, grasp the true essence of natural things" (Giles 2016, 154).

As Peter Ammann (1967) wrote: "Kepler rejects the mystique of numbers because those numbers are abstract and of no use in mathematical arguments, whereas Fludd calls the numbers of vulgar mathematics abstract, because they only measure the accidental quantities of things which are close to the sense, but which in reality are mere shadows."

That same year, 1631, Fludd got himself into a controversy that ruined his reputation. Until then he had prospered. Charles I granted Fludd and his heirs a manor house and "associated outbuilding and property" in Suffolk for an unspecified service that probably had to do with a cure, or perhaps in appreciation of his astounding attempt to capture all knowledge in his books. But then a country clergyman named William Foster wrote a book called *A Sponge to Wipe Away the Weapon-salve,* and in the middle of the night, knowingly or unknowingly in homage to Luther, nailed two copies of its title page to Fludd's front door. He agreed that the cure was magical but denounced it as demonic. It appeared nowhere in scripture, and no known natural law could explain why it should work. Then Foster dismissed Paracelsus as "a man of base and wicked life and conversation" (Giles 2016). The weapon-salve, he concluded, was witchcraft.

Fludd and many other physicians of the time believed that by sympathetic resonance a doctor could treat the blood on a blade to heal the wound it caused, even if the wounded man wasn't present. In a text perhaps falsely attributed to Paracelsus, a gruesome recipe is given. Moss from a skull or bone from a corpse left in the open air, a man's blood and fat, and rose and linseed oil, among other ingredients, are mashed by mortar into an ointment. After dipping a stick in the blood of the wound, one was to let it dry and then dip it in the ointment. Every morning the wound was to be washed with the patient's own urine and then bound up in fresh rolled linen. A cure was guaranteed, even if the patient was "ten miles away" and even if the patient was a horse.

Fludd responded to Foster with *Doctor Fludds Answer unto M. Foster; or, the Squeesing of Parson Fosters Sponge, ordained by him for the wiping away of the Weapon-Salve. Wherein the Sponge-bearers immodest carriage and behaviour towards his bretheren is detected; the bitter flames of his slanderous reports, are by the sharpe vineger of Truth corrected and quite extinguished: and lastly, the vertuous validity of his Sponge, in wiping away of the Weapon-Salve, is crushed out and cleane abolished* (1631). Fludd begins by pointing out that Foster is a humble parson with no experience of the matter. Next, he makes fun of his poor grammar. He dismisses Foster's argument that the salve is witchcraft by pointing out most forms of current medical practice couldn't be found in the Bible. But the bulk of Fludd's argument is an exposition of what he called theo-philosophy.

Fludd argues that spirit circulates life force through the bloodstream, and therefore blood retains something of a man's spirit in it. He compares the process to "the wise spider" who repairs her damaged web. He compares this power of the spiritual life force to the way sunbeams give life to plants. Magnetism is the secret of the salve: the magnetism of microcosm and macrocosm, of being born from the cosmos and so sharing every element with everything else in the cosmos—the wisdom and power of as above, so below. For this reason, to Fludd, Jesus, as the soul of the sun, as the Word, as the kabbalistic Chochmah, was the ultimate healing force.

But doubts were being raised not only about the weapon-salve but about many other core beliefs cherished by the Renaissance. Fludd also engaged in a seventeenth-century pamphlet war with Marin Mersenne, the French Jesuit theologian and mathematician sometimes called the father of the science of acoustics. Mersenne dismissed as mere poetry Fludd's theory that the harmony of spheres is the real structure and resonance of the cosmos. Fludd is not the voice of reason or revelation but of demonology. In his defense, Fludd appeals to the Neoplatonic philosopher beloved by ceremonial magicians, Iamblichus, who said music helps the soul remember the divine harmony it knew. Fludd also debated a lesser-known author's argument that the philosopher's stone should be understood as allegory and not taken literally.

In 1636, Daniel Sennert, a respected doctor and alchemist, entered the weapon-salve debate that Fludd had been fighting now for five years, pointing out that from his experience there didn't really seem to be any connection between healing and the salve. Yes, some people healed, but many didn't. The wounds probably healed naturally. What if different weapons caused different wounds? Would all the weapons need to be treated? If one wasn't, would that wound never heal? If the salve had the spirit of life, why not use it on the wound? His defense of the weapon-salve ultimately made Fludd look ridiculous to the next generation of doctors, scientists, and historians.

In 1623, Mersenne published *Quaestiones in Genesis*, his influential dismissal of Agrippa, Ficino, his friend Pico, and the other masters of the hermetic tradition, most of all Fludd. Thirteen years later, Mersenne published *Harmonie Universelle* in which he critiqued the idea that musical ratios have any relation to planetary orbits. Music is not magical, Mersenne declared, its fascination is merely the natural effect of motion on the ears and nerves.

Mersenne and Kepler exemplified the way in which Fludd provided opposition against which science defined itself. Fludd had lived in a world where God was immanent everywhere, in each atom and in the very glory of the light and warmth of the sun. Mersenne may have described the physics of music, but *Harmonie Universelle* had a chapter on the theology of music. Ironically, both Fludd and Mersenne helped to open the door to a world in which their treasured but opposed spiritual beliefs would be subverted by science.

Mersenne believed the Rosicrucians were evil, from the ambitions of Frederick and his supporters to the undeniable failure of the Protestant prophets and the poverty of alchemical pamphlet writers who had claimed they had wealth and power. Their Paracelsian recipes were nothing more than black magic. Though Mersenne defined himself in opposition to Fludd, they both represented an ideology-driven approach to what would become science. Mersenne's apprentice, Descartes, would set the stage for what we today call the scientific method.

Fludd's erroneous celestial monochord would live on, mostly appearing uncredited, although occasionally attributed to "the Rosicrucian Fludd." It appeared, for example, in the work of midcentury Los Angeles Christian mystic and *New Age Bible Interpretation* author Corinne Heline, as a symbol for the chakras or energy centers of the human body.

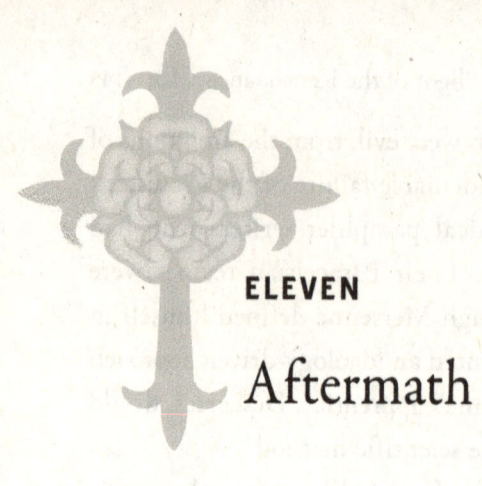

ELEVEN

Aftermath

In 1621 the printing presses of Heidelberg, which had produced so many Rosicrucian-inspired works, were turned to other uses as the Spanish and Austrian occupiers printed pamphlets with titles like "Warning against the Rosicrucian Vermin."

The following year, while Holy Roman Emperor Ferdinand II celebrated his marriage to Empress Eleanor Gonzaga, a famous beauty, his army was agitated by a rumor that Frederick had arrived in the rebel camp. Noticing the strong reaction, Count Mansfeld, leader of the remnants of Frederick's forces, urged the dejected monarch to join them. On the way there, while passing through Paris, Frederick bought Elizabeth little gifts. After one of his visits, she had gotten pregnant and was about to give birth again.

Frederick rejoined his forces in the Palatinate and called for the Protestant Union to send their army to fight the Catholic League, but his plea was ignored. Small victories soon gave way to big defeats. Then the banks of the Rhine overflowed, causing floods that brought even more misery to areas devastated by disease and war. As we have seen, Frederick established a Palatinate Court in exile in the Netherlands. When Emperor Ferdinand questioned the legitimacy of the Protestant Union, the German princes finally realized they would have to fight. Elizabeth's uncle, the king of Denmark, provided six thousand men specifically to fight for the restoration of the Palatinate, but Frederick's military fortunes depended on unreliable allies.

Among the few Frederick could count on was Christian of Brunswick. Despite his superior rank, even though he detested Mansfeld's tactics, Christian subordinated himself so he could serve Frederick. Christian's motto, written on his flag, was "God's friend, enemy to priesthood." For generations the Habsburgs had been pushing their borders into his family lands. As a cavalry commander Christian earned a reputation for cruelty to Catholics, who called him *der Tolle* (the Insane). The stories may have been propaganda, but atrocities were committed by both sides during the Thirty Years' War.

Christian declared his love for Elizabeth according to the traditions of chivalry, having taken an oath to serve her even at the cost of his life. James had the king of Denmark send another twenty-two hundred soldiers for Christian to command. The following year, Christian's courage and stubbornness helped Frederick achieve an important victory against the Spanish army, though it cost Christian most of his infantry and the loss of an arm. But for the first time since his ill-fated journey to Bohemia, Frederick slept in Heidelberg Castle.

The victory didn't last long. Soon Heidelberg was under siege. When the Protestant army finally united, it retreated from Heidelberg, which fell to the army of the Catholic League in September. Boots trampled what was left of the beautiful garden of love, and the mechanical wonders, abhorred as works of witchcraft, were destroyed. The legendary library of the Palatinate was packed up by Maximilian of Bavaria and shipped to the pope as a gift with gratitude for the money he provided to make the campaign possible. This proved fortunate since the contents of the library would have almost certainly been destroyed as battles repeatedly devastated the area. The despondent Frederick wrote to Elizabeth: "Voila, my poor Heidelberg is taken. They have used all sorts of cruelties, pillaged the entire town, burnt all the suburbs which were the chief beauty of the place" (Akkerman 2015, 297). When Frederick came home a few months later he was so haggard Elizabeth fainted when she saw him.

In 1623 the emperor announced that Frederick's treason meant he had forfeited all lands, rights, and privileges, which were now formally given to Maximilian of Bavaria. Frederick became so depressed he announced he couldn't endure anymore and disappeared for several days. Elizabeth feared that he was throwing himself into a hopeless battle, but Frederick, she was informed, had taken a tour of local art museums. His gloom only deepened when for the first time their newborn child didn't survive.

In the spring of that year, Elizabeth's brother Charles pursued a harebrained scheme with Lord Admiral George Villiers, First Lord Buckingham, such a favorite of King James that scholars have speculated that they were lovers. Marriage negotiations having dragged on, the two decided to go to Spain themselves, disguised in ridiculous fake beards, despite the great danger. They intended to complete the deal and bring Isabella home, perhaps in imitation of James, who had sailed to Oslo to wed Anne.

The Spanish presumed on the enthusiasm of the Prince of Wales, making a condition of the marriage agreement that Charles eventually convert to Catholicism. With the heir to the English throne somewhere between a guest and a prisoner at the Spanish court, and a tempting target for enemies when he embarked for home, James let it be known that if anything happened to his son, he would make arrangements to have Elizabeth declared his successor.

Neither Spain nor the Vatican wanted a second Queen Elizabeth, especially one married to the deposed king of Bohemia. Negotiations were brought to a standstill. Charles refused to convert. He wanted his sister and brother-in-law returned to power in the Palatinate. The Spanish insisted that such a complicated process would take years not months. After all, they were at war with his sister. As the prospect for a successful match dwindled, and it became clear that the British people did not wish to have their future king marry a Spanish Catholic, James began negotiations on behalf of his grandson Frederick Henry, without permission from Frederick and Elizabeth. When they heard about the negotiations, they demanded the condition that the Palatinate be restored to Frederick. One of Frederick's biographers reports that Elizabeth sent Francis Nethersole, her secretary of foreign affairs, to tell

Charles that he must not marry if the Palatinate was not part of the deal and to make clear that there would be no match for her own son, whatever King James might have proposed. But Nethersole arrived too late. He met Charles and Buckingham on the road headed for home.

Buckingham's strangely crass behavior, including insults like not removing his hat and going about partially undressed, had so offended the Spanish court that one of the king's ministers was overheard saying he'd rather throw Isabella in a well than agree to the match. Buckingham was an impeccably polished courtier. Had he deliberately acted the fool at the command of his king? A very unhappy Charles returned to England without his intended bride. As we have seen, Isabella eventually married Rudolf II's younger brother Albrecht VII, Archduke of Austria.

On a hot summer morning that same year, Paris woke up to find handwritten posters all over the city. One declared: "We, the deputies of our chief college of the Brethren of the Rosy Cross now visiting, visible and invisible, in this town—we will transform all those who seek to join our society from visible beings into invisible, and from invisible to visible, and they shall travel to any foreign country they desire—so that we may liberate our fellow men from folly and destruction" (Waite 1887, 388). Another poster declared that thirty-six Rosicrucians had arrived like beams of light to a meeting where they decided to send six of their number to represent them in Paris, with both endless wealth and invincible eloquence. The intention seemed to be an improvement of society for everyone, but Parisians panicked. Wild accusations flew that the Rosicrucians had magical powers provided by the devil.

Even the respectable journal *French Mercury* hyperventilated during that hot summer of fear, reporting that thirty-six Rosicrucian agents were terrorizing Lyon, moving anywhere and disappearing at will, and meeting with demons. Pundits predicted deaths of innocents. The frenzy of witch trials now turned its attention to the Rosicrucians. Every morning Paris woke up wondering if there would be a new message.

Descartes, returning to France from the war, and known to have traveled to Germany, was accused of being a Rosicrucian. His friends enjoyed his explanation that he could not be a Rosicrucian because he was visible. His Jesuit mentor Mersenne intervened to vouch for him. The Rosicrucian accusation didn't come out of nowhere. Descartes was a close friend of Johann Faulhaber, a mathematics professor who dedicated his book *Mysterium Arithmeticum* (1615) to the "most enlightened and famous Brothers R.C." Descartes met Comenius in Holland and corresponded with members of Samuel Hartlib's circle, including Theodore Haak, a refugee from the heart of Rosicrucian enthusiasm and devastation, the Palatinate.

Eventually, a popular writer dismissed the Rosicrucian posters as a hoax, and the population of Paris relaxed. But what was the intention of the hoax? To defraud the gullible? To frighten the superstitious? To inspire reform? Or was it just a prank? No one knows. Meanwhile, writing under a pseudonym, probably in response to these events, Frederick's chaplain Scultetus condemned the Rosicrucian movement. Over three centuries later, the Rosicrucian poster controversy inspired Guy Debord and the Situationist Internationale to use posters and wall paintings as protest art and social criticism, to encourage the student demonstrations of May 1968.

In his essay "The Situationists as Rosicrucians" Luther Blissett (1995) pointed out that a brief account of the Rosicrucians by Andreae from his utopia *Christianopolis* "could just as well describe SI [Situationist International] in the late sixties." Andreae had written: "A certain Fraternity, in my opinion a joke but according to theologians a serious matter—promised the greatest and most unusual things, even those things which men generally want, it added also the exceptional hope of the correction of the present corrupted state of affairs—. What a confusion among men followed the report of the thing, what an unrest and commotion of impostors and swindlers—" (Blissett 1995).

At the end of January 1624, the Council of Holland detained an alleged brother of the Rose Cross newly arrived from Paris. After studying the problem, the theological faculty of Leiden University reported that they were convinced Rosicrucians existed, and they named one, the master painter Johannes van der Beeck. A libertine as devoted to alcohol as to obscenity, Beeck was convicted of blasphemy and heresy. Most of his paintings were burned because as an admitted Rosicrucian he had all but confessed to atheism and Satanism. This doesn't sound like Father CRC's idea of Rosicrucianism, but could perhaps represent the kind of hotheads who claimed membership in the secret order to aggrandize themselves, intimidate enemies, or gain favors.

Amid all the chaos of their exile, Elizabeth found time to assist in the education of her daughters, teaching them the six languages that she knew. Except for martial arts, her daughters received the same education as her sons did.

In 1624, King James, venerable but feeble, talked to Parliament about the Palatinate. He said he had hoped to be remembered for the peace he had kept all his reign, but now he could not die without first seeing his daughter's rights restored. A plan was floated to send fifty English and twenty Dutch ships to attack vital Spanish targets under the flag of the queen of Bohemia. Parliament voted three hundred thousand pounds to pay for war, but the preparations proceeded slowly. A year later, a plan that involved Christian, Mansfeld, and the king of Denmark failed when Christian, tasked with rescuing the Rhineland, suffered a fever and died. According to the Catholic pamphlets, he was eaten from the inside by a giant worm, like King Herod.

Elizabeth found herself accused of conspiracy. She and Buckingham had schemed to prevent Charles from getting married to the Infanta or anyone else. Since he would have no heir, Elizabeth would surely succeed her sickly little brother. In return Buckingham's daughter would marry one of Elizabeth's sons. The Spanish were especially keen to promote that conspiracy theory. The Spanish ambassador alleged that James had been threatened that if he did not go to war against Spain, he would be removed by Parliament and Elizabeth would be placed on the throne. Elizabeth wrote to her father denying all accusations. But as Nadine Akkerman points out, portraits of Elizabeth's son and Buckingham's daughter had been exchanged.

In April of 1625, King James died. Mary, Queen of Scots, Elizabeth's grandmother, owned six long pearl necklaces with twenty-five pearls as big as nutmegs and seven large single pearls for earrings and dress ornaments. Queen Elizabeth I inherited them when she sentenced Mary to death. When James died, the pearls were given to his daughter. The Armada portrait of Queen Elizabeth I made the pearls famous. Her namesake also had her portrait painted wearing them.

The court under James had become infamous for its sarcasm as much as its debauchery, or so we are told. Stories about a drunken King James lecherously petting a favorite young man or slobbering a joke had helped give more momentum to the Puritan movement, whether these rumors were true or not. The queen's all-night parties were as notorious as they were expensive. Courtiers gossiped that the king had fewer dalliances with young men than did his wife, and darker rumors were whispered that certain Stuart royal babies had died in infancy for reasons having more to do with who fathered them than health problems. The queen was even accused of incest with her brother. However, we are left to contemplate again the influence of propaganda on historians as no evidence of her supposedly numerous and scandalous affairs has been found.

The diplomats of the Palatinate and their allies urged English politicians to make war on the Habsburgs. If the new king of England committed to his sister's cause, an alliance could be built between the British, Danish, Dutch, and Swedish, possibly including France, Savoy, and Venice. Charles agreed, but the full coalition never united behind the British. Those who did had their own ends in mind. As the war expanded into northern Germany, the Palatinate became less important. Denmark's defeat in 1626 and England's in 1629 punctuated a series of military and political debacles that left Frederick as helpless as ever. Meanwhile, the Holy Roman Emperor Ferdinand II mandated conversion to Catholicism, and harsh punishments for those who refused to be saved.

Frances Yates argues persuasively that Comenius was in Prague during the Bohemian Revolt. In his book *The Labyrinth of the World and the Paradise of the Heart*, a masterpiece of Czech literature written in 1623 but published in 1631, Comenius describes the destruction of a king very like Frederick. A royal throne "suddenly shook, broke into bits, and fell to the ground." As the people led a new king to the throne, "they joyously declared that things would now be different from what they had been before." Talk of "the common welfare" encourages Comenius to contribute "a nail or two to strengthen the new throne." But his royal enemy with his army thrashed "the whole crowd, till they fled and many even lost their necks" (Comenius 1901, 196).

In this book Comenius captured the state of mind of European intellectuals at the beginning of the Thirty Years' War. He inverts utopia, presenting a symbolic city where the arts and sciences lead nowhere and all knowledge is questionable. He tells the story of the Rosicrucian crisis. Its arrival he compares to the sound of a trumpet in the marketplace. A rider appears to tell the gathered philosophers that hidden sages are about to reveal themselves. These adepts have lived hundreds of years. They know how to prolong life, heal sickness, make gold, and talk with each other even when they are a thousand miles apart. Then the messenger vanishes.

Comenius says most of the learned men were frightened by the news. But some rejoiced. They looked forward to "several hundred years without sickness or gray hair" and pitied their ancestors for having to live in a world without the superior knowledge that was about to be revealed. But others thought the message obscure and doubtful. Some dismissed the messenger as a liar and fraud. If such reforms existed for so long, why wait to reveal them?

As we have seen, then began the mass publishing of hundreds of Rosicrucian-related books and pamphlets. Comenius tells us some authors claimed membership in the fraternity with pseudonyms such as "the youngest of the Brothers of R.C.". Sincere seekers petitioned the invisible masters. Feeling joy, they waited to hear from the Rosicrucians. But when no answer came, they were reduced to grief or outrage. What was worse? To have been found wanting and been ignored, or to have fallen for a ridiculous joke? Disbelievers laughed at them. Some published pamphlets attacking the Rosicrucians as real but evil, a threat to all. Others produced pamphlets that dismissed the Rosicrucians as a fairy tale. For twenty years Rosicrucian books and pamphlets kept printers busy.

Comenius himself wrote a letter asking to be allowed to become a member of the Rosicrucian fraternity, and he was wise enough to send it to Andreae, who responded with a Latin pun: "We are a very few men of good standing, who came together after the mockery (*ludibrium*) of the vain report (*fama*)" (De Vries 2021).

By 1626 mass witch trials were executing women in parts of Germany where war and plague had reduced people to superstitious paranoia. Comenius visited The Hague, bringing Frederick an illustrated manuscript of Christopher Kotter's most recent prophecies. Kotter, like his brethren in the Bohemian clergy, suffered persecution and oppression after the defeat at White Mountain, but his vision of Frederick's future had not changed: "Frederick, Palatine of the Rhine, is by God crowned King. Frederick, Palatine of the Rhine, King of Bohemia, crowned by God, the supreme King of all Kings, who in the year 1620 fell in to danger, but will again recover all and far greater riches and glory" (Yates 1975a, 158).

Kotter had visions of angels: young men without wings in long robes. In the visions Frederick appeared as a lion. In one vision, he is a four-headed lion, representing the Palatinate, Bohemia, the Netherlands, and England. A lion standing on the moon promised that Frederick's fortunes, which had waned, would like the moon wax again to full brightness. Sitting under a tree with two angels, Kotter was shown a golden glowing lion strutting, while another lion attacked a snake. The chopped pieces of the snake appeared in the sky; an obscure presentiment of Ben Franklin's famous cartoon of the American colonies as a snake in pieces captioned "Join or Die." Kotter also saw three angels holding their hands protectively around a miniature lion. These visions, enigmatic as Michael Maier's alchemical emblems, impressed Frederick even less than the prophecy he had heard in person before his total defeat. But Comenius published them, along with prophecies by Christina Poniatovia, in his book on the legitimacy of modern prophecy, *Lux in tenebris* or *Light in Darkness* (1657).

Comenius was celebrated for going beyond the utopias of Francis Bacon and Tommaso Campanella. *New Atlantis* and *City of the Sun* were evocative myths but impractical guides to real-world challenges. Comenius distilled the idea of Universal Reformation into some practical suggestions. First, he wanted to establish universal education for men and women. Not everyone would become a scholar, but everyone would know how to write and do math. Today, it's hard to imagine how radical that idea was in the seventeenth century, especially the education of all women and of the indigenous people of all continents.

Second, Comenius proposed that books be compiled that would contain all the information anyone could need; "the condensed essence of all knowledge" must be given to everyone. Three books would be written collaboratively. *Pansophia* (All Wisdom) would reveal the metaphysics of the structure of the soul and the world as designed by the deity. *Panhistoria* (All History) would reveal the secrets of all the specific arts and sciences, all crafts, and other aspects of life. *Pandogmatica* (All Dogma) would contain all theories about human life and activity and whether they proved to be true or false.

Third, a universal language must be collaboratively created. And finally, from all the nations across the globe, the best minds must cooperate for the betterment of the world, their organization to be known as the College of Light, where a new generation of innovators would be educated. While none of these suggestions were realized, they did inspire cooperation and faith in science. Andreae and Comenius remained friends, comparing notes on utopias.

The year 1626 ended with terrible losses. Christian of Brunswick, still only in his twenties, died after a long illness. Parliament fell into disagreement with the new king, and money for the war to restore the Palatinate dried up. Charles had to pawn the family silver. The next year, 1627, began with another disaster: Mansfeld, who had long been suffering serious illnesses, finally succumbed to them. He had been for the most part loyal to Elizabeth's cause.

Frederick focused on domestic improvements for his large family. Receiving English and Dutch donations to build an Italianate palazzo of many windows, he exasperated his benefactors with his expenditures. He built gardens for his wife, less lavish than the lost gardens of Heidelberg.

As Akkerman writes: "The eleven years she and Frederick spent in exile had transformed The Hague, their place of residence and the centre of the Dutch government, into a rich cultural capital. Their patronage and influence was instrumental in changing it into a fertile environment for all sorts of courtly activities, a place where the elite . . . enjoyed a life filled with tournaments, tilting, art, plays, masques, ballets, and other musical performances" (2011, 48). But Elizabeth was also in communication with military commanders. She used her connections to get information for them about the movements of ships and troops, even offering her own suggestions as to what strategies they should employ.

In 1628, after getting England into a war with France, Buckingham first lost his astrologer, whose demise came at the hands of a mob. Not long after, Buckingham himself was assassinated by one of his own soldiers. Though Elizabeth had often been exasperated by his actions, she mourned the loss of a friend who had strongly supported her cause.

In January 1629, Frederick took his eldest son, sixteen-year-old Frederick Henry, to see the Spanish treasure ships recently captured by the Dutch West India Company. Elizabeth had invested in the venture. Negotiations were underway to arrange a marriage for Frederick Henry with a daughter of Holy Roman Emperor Ferdinand II. It would seem that father and son spontaneously decided to visit the ships, as no provisions for a suitable boat had been made. Instead, they boarded a small barge that was carrying beer barrels. On a treacherous body of water notorious for sandbars, possibly in the fog of late afternoon, a collision with a bigger barge capsized them. Most of those onboard drowned in the icy water, including Frederick Henry. His body was found the next day, fully frozen, one hand grasping the mast. Frederick was badly injured. Another Henry whom Elizabeth loved dearly had died too young. The shock, those closest to Elizabeth said, almost killed her.

That summer Frederick, still recovering, rejoined the army of the Prince of Orange. Elizabeth was never told the doctor's opinion that her husband would not live long. He was well enough before he left to have fathered their twelfth child, Sophie, whose name was picked out of a hat.

Sophie later joked that her mother preferred "the sight of her monkeys and dogs to that of her children" (Akkerman 2021). The 2011 update of the *Oxford Dictionary of National Biography*, not getting the joke, says condescendingly of Elizabeth that she showed "greater concern for her even more numerous pet monkeys and dogs." Repeated by generations of historians, the story lacks the context provided by Akkerman in 2021. It's a good example of the way historians can misrepresent their subjects. To own a menagerie in those days required great wealth. Elizabeth received rare pets as gifts from allies and admirers. Her menagerie was a symbol of her power. Also, as many parents still do, Elizabeth referred to her children affectionately as her monkeys.

The tone of the quote that supposedly supports Oxford's view can't be understood until we know that it came from a satire Sophie wrote about her family. Yet, in a letter written in invisible ink to the master of her household, Elizabeth described Sophie as an untrustworthy hypocrite. Sophie grew up to enjoy a happy marriage; she became the mother of the king of England and the great-grandmother of numerous kings. Through her, Ben Jonson's prophecy about Elizabeth becoming the mother of nations came true.

In 1630 Frederick formally apologized and admitted he had been wrong to take the crown of Bohemia, but the negotiations as usual bore no fruit. On July 4 of that same year, King Gustav Adolf brought his army from Sweden to fight for the Protestant cause. The following year France's Cardinal Richelieu signed a treaty with Maximilian of Bavaria, placing the upper Palatinate and its electoral power under the guardianship of France. Alarmed by the growing power of the Catholic League, France would soon enter the war on the Protestant side.

With a huge army, including Italian mercenaries who called him the Golden King, Gustav proved himself an exceptional leader. But as we shall see, his reputation may have resulted from the Holy Roman emperor's lack of faith in his finest general.

Elizabeth asked Charles to declare war on her enemies, but like his father, Charles valued peace with Spain. Perhaps in imitation of his father, he did allow seven thousand troops under a Scottish general to join the Swedish army, but the general paid for the campaign out of his own pocket. The Lion of the North wanted twenty-five thousand English soldiers and the promise to keep them provided with supplies for four years. Gustav was planning an extended war against the Habsburgs.

Frederick knew that he might never return to his family. He delayed his departure to join Gustav in the field so that he could be at the christening of his newborn son. Frederick and Elizabeth continued their habit of naming their boys after the royal their fate depended on at the time of birth: Gustavus Adolphus was their thirteenth child. Frederick sold plate and redeemed investments he had made by selling a town they still owned to provide Elizabeth with liquid assets. He compiled an inventory of their belongings. He wrote a letter to his brother-in-law King Charles, entrusting Elizabeth and their children to his care.

On February 11, exactly nineteen years after he had enjoyed the fireworks provided by King James to celebrate his wedding, Frederick met Gustav in a newly liberated town of the Palatinate. Frederick expected to raise an army and lead it to battle beside Gustav. Though Gustav had been told that Frederick was a failure, and he could see he was worn out, he called him brother and treated him with all the courtesy due a king. The people of the Palatinate, the survivors, greeted their returned ruler with sincere joy. But he was not allowed to raise an army. Frederick wrote to Elizabeth that Gustav was making proposals that would have left Frederick nothing.

As the campaign continued, Gustav killed the grand commander of the imperial army. By May, the Swedes were feasting in the castle of Maximilian of Bavaria, who had finally reaped the rewards of his disloyalty to his cousin Frederick. It only remained to liberate Heidelberg and two other towns of the lower Palatinate from the Spanish army. Frederick wanted to command troops in the battle for his former capital. Gustav refused, insisting instead that he be nothing more than a volunteer. The German princes were unhappy about the Swedish army on their territory. With Frederick riding at his side, Gustav would seem less of a threat.

Frederick wrote to Elizabeth twice a week. In every letter he wrote about wanting to be by her side. He began his letters: "Dearest heart." He called her his "soul's star." When she offered to send him her small inheritance at last given to her by Charles, he wrote back: "I would wish you to have this inheritance and invest it, and thereby pay off your debts bit by bit, wanting nothing from you but that you love me always as much as I love you" (Akkerman 2021).

His letters to her include descriptions of the hairdos, dresses, and wigs of German noblewomen, alongside news from the armies, and complaints of boredom and irritation at having been reduced to nothing more than a figurehead. Thirteen miniature portraits, one for each child, were painted by Alexander Cooper, tokens of love Elizabeth mailed in letters to Frederick. In turn he commissioned precious agate cameo busts based on the portraits.

The year 1632, which had begun with such promise when the Swedish army liberated most of northern Europe, ended in tragedy for Elizabeth. Frederick had been sick for three years, ever since he tried to save his son in the icy polluted water. In October, Frederick suffered a high fever. He didn't want to alarm Elizabeth, since her brother Henry had died of an October fever almost two decades earlier. In his last letter to her, he wrote that he would soon be on his way to bring her with him to Germany. He would die content if he could see her one more time.

In November, Gustav was killed during his victorious battle to drive the Catholic army out of Saxony. Two weeks later, Frederick slipped into a delirium. He died of plague, a few days before another Swedish victory, which liberated the Palatinate. As in life, Frederick's embalmed body became a vagabond. His internal organs were said to have been buried at the Katharinenkirche in Oppenheim. History lost track of his embalmed body, which disappeared on its way to his final resting place. By then, the Palatinate's population had been reduced by 75 percent. New prophets emerged to predict the arrival of a lion who would reform the world. The years of war ahead would end not with the victories of the Lion of the North but with a treaty signed by leaders who at last had come to understand that, after so much carnage, Europe needed peace.

Elizabeth wrote about her reaction to the news of Frederick's death: "It was the first time that ever I was frighted, for it struck me as colde as ice and could neither crie nor speak nor eat nor drink nor sleep for three days" (Akkerman 2021). From that day until her death, Elizabeth's glamorous gowns were the color of mourning. Akkerman's research reveals that the black velvet that draped the walls, beds, and furniture cost a thousand pounds sterling. In London a rumor spread that she had died of grief.

For more than two months after Frederick's death, her letters were written for her by others. When she returned, her notes were short. The seal on them was black, as was the floss. She preferred paper with black edges. To a kinsman she wrote: "I know not what to say more to you, you having lost a dear friend and I the best husband in the world, I shall never take any more contentment in this world, having lost all in him." To her brother she wrote, "the most wretched creature that ever lived in this world, and this I shall ever be, having lost the best friend that I ever had." To a female friend she confided her assumption of new political responsibilities: "I have little time left to write to my private friends, I think you would never have thought that I should become a stateswoman, which of all things I have ever hated, but my infinite loss of my dear husband forced me" (Akkerman 2021, 280).

Elizabeth had always been an avid letter writer. She kept her pen in an enameled gold inkstand. She wrote and received letters in English, Latin, Dutch, French, and cipher. She could even imitate the writing of others when necessary. Because the English crown monitored the postal service, the Bohemian court in exile sent their mail unregistered by way of Antwerp and Brussels, through a clandestine message-smuggling service run by spies in service of Alexandrine, a postmistress with the official sanction of the Habsburgs, whose principal loyalty seemed to have been to making money. Not only did Elizabeth have to fear that her letters would fall into the hands of her imperial enemy, but also that Swedish spies might seize them, as they already had, to her embarrassment, since her candid opinion in a letter had differed from her official stance.

The British and Swedes argued over the Palatinate. The Swedes demanded a large payment for liberating it. Many of the towns, and all the most strategically important areas, would remain under Swedish control. They were too vulnerable to counterattack to be left in the hands of less-experienced fighters. At least Heidelberg was in friendly hands again. Elizabeth hoped her brother Charles would help, perhaps even send soldiers to defend the Palatinate. But he wanted nothing to do with the Swedes. Then in September 1634, the imperial army inflicted a devastating defeat on the Swedish army. Soon Heidelberg was lost again and was even more badly damaged when reconquered by the French.

Ironically, Albrecht von Wallenstein, the emperor's finest general, perhaps more responsible than anyone for the Catholic military victories that doomed Frederick, was born in Bohemia to a poor but noble Protestant family. There he married a rich widow, inheriting her wealth when she died young. He earned the emperor's respect as a mercenary raising troops and fighting on behalf of the empire against the Republic of Venice. He was in command at the Battle of White Mountain. After further victories, he became an imperial count Palatine, buying many estates that had belonged to Protestant Bohemian nobles.

Wallenstein's military prowess made him one of the wealthiest men in Europe. By 1630 the emperor began to fear him, so the generalissimo was relieved of duty. His equally famous replacement lost battle after battle against Gustav, making the Golden King seem invincible. So the emperor turned to Wallenstein again, not only to take command but also to raise another army and to loan the money needed to pay for it all. Wallenstein agreed, but only if allowed to keep the spoils of war, making himself even richer.

Wallenstein defeated Gustav in two successive battles, and then as we have seen, Gustav was killed during a victory. After a series of losses that left them depleted and demoralized, the Swedes were driven back to the north. More victories made it seem that Wallenstein was poised to conquer all Europe for the pope and the emperor.

Could Wallenstein's victories be the result of his deep interest in horoscopes? When Wallenstein was a young noble in Prague, Kepler had cast his first astrological chart, predicting that he would fight many battles and win most. Wallenstein appears to have used astrology to help him in the timing and strategy of his warfare.

The leading general of the empire could see how weary Europe was of war, disease, and starvation. He began a complicated process of peace negotiations. He knew he had many enemies by then, on both sides of the Catholic-Protestant divide. The damage done and the abuse committed by his armies were blamed on him. He knew the emperor didn't trust him. But he did not know that a secret court convened by imperial command had found him guilty of treason. If he wasn't planning to take the imperial throne, he must be conspiring to join the Protestant cause.

After a public announcement of the warrant for his arrest alive or dead, Wallenstein turned to his army expecting them to choose him over the emperor. They did not. With his officers and most trusted soldiers, about a hundred men, he retreated in the hopes of meeting up with the Swedes, to whom he would offer his services. But his officers were slaughtered while at feast. Wallenstein, asleep in a bedroom, woke up to an Irish captain shouting at him. The survivor of so many campaigns, who had become so sick he had to be carried to battles in a wagon, but who had usually won them nonetheless, stood without weapons or armor. He died run through by a spear. The emperor handsomely rewarded the assassin, relieved to be rid of his most successful general.

By the 1630s, portraits of Frederick and Elizabeth as the king and queen of Bohemia were among those commonly on display at traveling entertainments for the common folk of Europe. The romance of their story and the distant memory of their glamorous wedding made them popular figures in the public imagination.

TWELVE

Fall of the Queen of Hearts, Rise of Prince Rupert of the Rhine

In the spring of 1633, Elizabeth's eldest sons, sixteen-year-old Charles Louis and thirteen-year-old Prince Rupert, joined the army of the Prince of Orange. Rupert was already a skilled swordsman and was making a study of the late king of Sweden's successful cavalry tactics. When Charles Louis turned eighteen in 1635, with seventy noblemen at his side, he visited his cousin King Charles to petition for the restoration of what was his birthright.

Hearing positive reports from across the channel, Elizabeth ignored her trepidation about Prince Rupert's unpredictable and sometimes impertinent charm, sending him to join his brother. To her surprise, Charles and the English court found Rupert enchanting. A plan was hatched for Rupert to colonize Madagascar and become its first viceroy. Elizabeth put an end to it with several letters. She compared it to some scheme of Don Quixote, and she speculated that the Spanish may have come up with the idea as a way of getting rid of Rupert.

The princes enjoyed celebrations organized by Elizabeth's supporters, but their pleas for help in the war to regain their lands produced only renewed diplomatic negotiations with the emperor. Charles refused to allow his cousins to go home. He didn't want them to ruin the negotiations by going off to war. But in May of the following year, diplomacy failed when the emperor offered Charles Louis the Lower but not the Upper Palatinate and an older, unattractive Habsburg princess to marry. Charles let his nephews go home. At least he had completed a treaty with Richelieu, who promised that France would not make peace with the empire until the Palatinate was restored.

In January 1637, King Charles agreed to lend his nephew a fleet and allowed him to raise troops. By the autumn of 1638, Charles Louis had four thousand soldiers. The newly elected Emperor Ferdinand III, son of Ferdinand II, was the living embodiment of the fear shared by all Protestants, and by some Catholics, that the Habsburgs had made the empire their family inheritance. Ferdinand III declared the Upper Palatinate the property of Maximilian of Bavaria. The only recourse was war.

Elizabeth spent a fortune to help pay for an army for Charles Louis, but she was shrewd. For an amount less than she would receive from it in yearly income, she bought a small town to house the new Palatinate army. Her sons Charles and Rupert were experienced soldiers for their ages. Two veteran generals were sent with them. Perhaps because these generals actually owed their allegiance to the Swedes, they made decisions based on what would be advantageous for the Swedish army, and the result was a battle with a superior force of the imperial army that ended in another disastrous defeat. Rupert was captured. Elizabeth lost her town.

Bernard of Saxe-Weimar was a skilled general with a powerful army. He expressed interest in contracting a marriage agreement with Elizabeth, Princess Palatine, eldest daughter of Frederick and Elizabeth. The king of Poland had sought the same, but mother did not approve, not only because he was Catholic but also because he insisted on his right to have mistresses. For Bernard she gave her approval. Unfortunately, he died in the war. Elizabeth maneuvered to place his army under the command of the new Elector Palatine Charles Louis. But Richelieu apparently found out about the plan. The French captured Charles Louis as he traveled to his army. He was imprisoned for seven months to keep him out of trouble.

Rupert lost three years of his youth in a lonely room heavily guarded. He concentrated on drawing and limning, and quickly mastered Dürer's theory of perspective. England's ambassador to Austria gave Rupert a gift, a white standard poodle puppy. Rupert named the dog Boy (Boye in the English of the time). Rupert also tamed a hare that slept on his bed.

Emperor Ferdinand III's brother Archduke Leopold decided to meet the imprisoned prince. Charmed by Rupert, he convinced the emperor to allow the prisoner to visit nearby nobles, with whom he could enjoy playing handball and riding horses. In 1641, Rupert was released upon the condition that he never take up arms against the empire again. Rupert visited the emperor to formally kiss his hand. Ferdinand III was so impressed, he offered to forego the customary ransom if Rupert would live under his roof in Vienna. Elizabeth allegedly declared that she would sooner strangle her son.

In August of 1642, Rupert and his brother Maurice set sail for England. It's a small irony of history that the manifestos, which as we have seen were partially inspired by touring English and/or Italian actors, inspired Cromwell, the dictator whose Parliament shut down all the theaters in England that year. A Parliamentary cruiser fired on the princes, but they escaped to join King Charles at Nottingham. Charles made Rupert his General of the Horse. Royalists adored him as much as the Puritans hated him. Soon he gained the reputation of being "shot free": however dangerous the risks he took, bullets never hit him.

By October the Royalists enjoyed a series of successes thanks to Rupert. He moved his troops so swiftly they were called a "flying army." He seemed to be many places at once: recruiting, strategizing, besieging, launching surprise attacks. The Puritans called him the Robber Prince, the Mad Cavalier, the Diabolical Cavalier, the Ravenous Vulture, and the Bloody Prince. Cromwell condemned him as "a man that hath had his hands in the blood of many innocent people in England" (Akkerman 2021). Accused of "barbarousness and inhumanity" in his treatment of women and children, Rupert responded with a printed declaration of his innocence.

Stories were told that Rupert moved among the Puritans in disguise— unlikely, given that he was six foot four when the average height was five foot eight. Boye was accused of being Rupert's familiar or a witch. The "divill dog" (Akkerman 2021) had supernatural powers, including invisibility, prophecy, and the power of magically protecting his master from harm. Puritan propaganda reported that the poodle fed on human flesh.

Rupert's other favorite pet was the appropriately named She Monkey, who wore a coat tailored for her and was said, like Boye, to accompany Rupert into battle. She too had a pamphlet written about her, becoming among the earliest celebrity animals in the United Kingdom. Puritan writers described her with a relish for obscenity. Rather than common beliefs, these seem to have been attempts to label the Royalist cause satanic.

In response to this slander against Boye, Rupert's army honored the dog by kneeling and drinking to his good health, and satirists wrote pamphlets lampooning the superstitious Puritans by ascribing all sorts of outrageous powers to the poodle, including catching bullets. A satirical tell-all portrayed the Puritans as shivering in terror when faced by the wizard Prince Rupert and his witch dog.

The Puritans celebrated when Boye, tied up in camp for his own safety, worked his way free and was killed in battle on his way to his master's side. Rupert lost that battle. He escaped capture by hiding in a bean field. The defeat consolidated the power of Parliament. Cromwell's New Modelled Army was about to be born.

Having intercepted some letters between Rupert and his mother, Parliament responded by cutting off Elizabeth's thousand-pounds-a-month allowance, which she had relied on for years. By 1644, Elizabeth no longer enjoyed good health; she suffered a chronic cough. She spent most of the year writing letters to Parliament haggling for her money. Yet her court in exile remained a fascinating salon where astronomy and politics were discussed with equal relish.

The following year Rupert was forced to surrender the city of Bristol. King Charles was so angry he accused Rupert, who demanded a court martial. Rumors that Rupert might become the new king of England had caused Charles to distrust his nephew. Exonerated of all blame by the court martial, his uncle publicly declared him not guilty.

Elizabeth's life next became the stuff of soap operas. A younger son, Edward, handsome but poor, was swept off his feet by an older woman, the daughter of a wealthy duke, who seduced him into not only marriage but conversion to the Catholic faith. Elizabeth was distraught. She announced in a letter to Charles Louis that she wanted to die.

While her celibacy was unquestioned, Elizabeth was friendly with a French gentleman. She treated him with such familiarity that gossips started a scandal suggesting he was involved not only with Elizabeth but with Princess Louise, one of her daughters. Eighteen-year-old Prince Philip felt it his duty to defend the honor of his mother and sister. His eldest sister, Princess Elisabeth, had written Descartes after being inspired by his early books. They exchanged letters about his theories and about the human passions in the hopes of helping her to calm her brother down. But Philip stabbed the Frenchman to death in the street one night, and then fled to another country. Princess Elisabeth begged her mother to forgive Philip so earnestly that the unforgiving Elizabeth sent her away to live with relatives in Brandenburg. He was never brought to justice for his crime. He died in battle four years later.

Meanwhile, Rupert, still trying to help his uncle, worked on plans for the monarch to escape to Europe. The king had decided to disguise himself. He would surrender to the Scots and hopefully play them against Parliament. At this point, all parties expected Charles to remain king of England. The argument was over money and policy. Rupert insisted on going with his uncle, but Charles explained to him that at six foot four inches, Rupert would be a dead giveaway. Instead, he gave his nephew command of a Royalist fleet. But the Scots had more in common with Cromwell than with King Charles. For one hundred thousand pounds sterling (almost twenty million dollars today) and promises of future payments, the Scots gave the grandson of Mary, Queen of Scots to Parliament.

As negotiations continued, Charles was moved to different locations, sometimes at his own suggestion. He escaped from one castle, but he chose the wrong refuge and was kept prisoner there. That didn't stop him from continuing negotiations. When he agreed to establish Presbyterianism throughout his realm for three years, the Scottish army invaded England on his behalf. The Second Civil War began in May 1648. Oliver Cromwell's New Modelled Army demonstrated its superiority by repeatedly winning battles, although Rupert continued to harass them with his daring cavalry tactics. Cromwell suppressed the Royalist uprising with brutal efficiency. Charles offered negotiations again. Parliament voted to negotiate with him. But Cromwell had other ideas. He considered Charles a tyrant, and he wasn't too keen on the idea of kings in general. Having engineered what amounted to a military takeover of the government, Cromwell took control of the fate of the king.

In 1648, theaters were demolished in England. To watch a show meant risking a fine. Charles was found "guilty of all the treasons, murders, rapines, burnings, spoils, desolations, damages and mischiefs to this nation, acted and committed in the said wars, or occasioned thereby." Around 6 percent of the population of Great Britain had died in the wars, and as far as Cromwell was concerned, the king was to blame. He had placed his personal interests over the good of the people, and that was treason. Charles claimed that as a divinely appointed king, the Parliamentary court had no right to judge him. He said, "no earthly power can justly call me (who am your King) in question as a delinquent. . . . the authority of obedience unto Kings is clearly warranted, and strictly commanded in both the Old and New Testament" (Sanderson 1658, 1130).

On January 30, 1649, King Charles I walked out of the Banqueting House where Elizabeth's private wedding ceremony had taken place. A crowd gaped at the dignified monarch, who wore all black, his blue Order of the Garter sash, and two shirts, so no one would see him shiver in the cold morning and mistake it for fear. Ranks of soldiers surrounded the black scaffold where the executioner waited with his axe. The boy who had been so sickly few thought he would live had grown up to become king. He had made the mistake of trying to turn back the clock to the divine right of kings. At his signal the axe struck his head from his body with one stroke. No one ever took credit for the deed. The executioner held the head up for the crowd to see, then tossed it to the soldiers. They dipped their handkerchiefs in the royal blood, and many took keepsakes of hair they pulled from his head. The king's head was exhibited but sewn back on his body for the funeral. Cromwell was said to have visited the king's coffin where he was heard to mutter about "cruel necessity."

Soon a book came out that purported to be a collection of the late king's meditations about the decisions he had made. He presented himself as a martyr for the true Christian faith and for his people. The book was so popular that songs were written so the illiterate could hear the best parts. Parliament responded by shutting down publishers and book merchants and unleashing a wave of its own propaganda—books and pamphlets justifying the murder of the king.

Elizabeth had a mourning ring made to remember her younger brother by. Under a crowned skull and crossbones, it bore the initials C.R. It contained a lock of his hair. She wore it the rest of her life. Much has been made of that C.R. as in Father CRC, but it simply stands for Charles Rex, *rex* meaning "king" in Latin.

Rupert took his twenty-eight ships and his brother Maurice to Kinsale in County Cork on the southern coast of Ireland. From that base he attacked Cromwell's ships and supported what was left of the Royalist army. Parliament sent its main fleet to blockade Rupert's ships. Rupert took advantage of the opportunity to repair and improve his fleet. But crossing through Ireland, leaving devastation in his wake, Cromwell defeated the Royalists. Royalist garrisons melted away in fear of his brutality. When bad weather scattered the blockade ships, Rupert and Maurice took to the open sea. By then they only had sailors for seven ships; the rest had deserted rather than face

Cromwell. Rupert sailed for Portugal. But the fleet that Parliament sent to blockade him soon followed. Rupert and Maurice escaped to the Mediterranean.

That year Charles Louis, Elector Palatine, regained his titles, rights, and the lower Palatinate under the Peace of Westphalia. The Upper Palatinate became part of Bavaria, the elector of which now enjoyed the powers and title of First Elector of the Empire. Charles Louis was given a new eighth electorate, with less power and privilege than the others. He returned to devastated Heidelberg.

When his younger sister Sophie visited Charles Louis and his bride, Charlotte Elizabeth, she was shocked when her unhappy sister-in-law confided that she had been forced into the marriage. Yet the couple knelt and embraced and kissed ostentatiously, as if performing a pantomime of the love between Frederick and Elizabeth. Sophie commented on her sister-in-law's strange habit of dyeing her eyebrows black despite her light blonde hair.

As mentioned earlier, Princess Elisabeth was friends with Descartes. Her fate was tied to the "three Olympian dreams," as their dreamer called them. An angel appeared to Descartes in these dreams. Descartes, then a teenage soldier, witnessed the angel's proclamation that nature would be conquered by measure and number.

The letters of Descartes and Elisabeth became a book. She engaged him in dialogues that helped the father of modern philosophy formulate his ideas. He dedicated his books *Principles of Philosophy* (1647) and *The Passions of the Soul* (1649) to her. Scholar Susanna Åkerman wrote in *Rose Cross over the Baltic*: "Numerous indications are that Descartes' final choice to become a professional mathematician was influenced by Rosicrucian readings" (Åkerman 1998). Even the family chaplain was enthusiastic about the philosophy of Descartes, which soon became popular among the Dutch nobles of the Hague.

Young Elisabeth's letters to Descartes complain of the melancholy details of her life. She must calm her younger brothers though she doesn't understand the treaty they are so angry about. Another sister falls deathly ill. Elisabeth became even more depressed when Descartes died in 1650. Eventually, she retired to a Protestant convent, where she became abbess, dedicating her meditations to God. Nadine Akkerman affirms her status as "a great female philosopher."

That same year of 1650, hermetic and alchemical circles in England were thrilled when John Everard published the first English translation of the *Divine Pymander*. Like Robert Fludd, Everard either ignored or had never heard of Casaubon's discovery that the *Hermetica* were most likely Neoplatonic forgeries actually dating from around the third or fourth century. The first sentence of Everard's introduction proclaims: "This book may justly challenge the first place for antiquity, from all the books in the world, being written some hundreds of years before Moses." The argument for the antiquity of the *Hermetica* would be recast by modern academia. While it may have been written down by the Neoplatonic school, many of the underlying ideas do appear to have come from ancient Egypt. Like the *Hymns of Orpheus*, also written during the twilight of paganism, it's an attempt to preserve the wisdom without completely giving away the secrets.

By 1650, Elizabeth faced such dire circumstances that her ledger shows debts to people like her portrait painter Gerard van Honthorst. In 2023 dollars, Honthorst lent Elizabeth about $360,000 for bread and nearly a million dollars for meat. When a close friend died, she couldn't afford to have a mourning dress made. Two years earlier as part of the Peace of Westphalia, Ferdinand III had granted her a huge settlement, but Charles Louis refused to let her have the money. He needed it to rebuild Heidelberg.

Elizabeth's communications with her eldest son Charles Louis became little more than financial arguments. Charles Louis wanted his mother to join him in Heidelberg; one household would be cheaper than two. But Elizabeth didn't want to go back to Heidelberg. Perhaps she didn't want to disturb her beautiful memories of the place during a happier time. She was forced to pawn Frederick's engagement ring. Sophie joked that all they had to eat were jewels. Elizabeth wrote Charles Louis demanding immediate funds to save priceless family heirlooms whose pawn repayments had come due, including a diamond necklace of cinquefoils and lover's knots given to Queen Elizabeth I by her alleged lover Robert Dudley and a "great table diamond" that had belonged to her brother, the long-lost Prince Henry Stuart.

Rupert and Maurice became pirates. Rupert's ship was named *Constant Reformation*. During a terrible storm his ship sprang a leak. The ship's log records the loyalty Rupert earned from his men: "The Princes endeavored to speak one to another, but the hideous noise of the winds and seas overnoised their voices—. His men, seeing supplications would not prevail launched the lifeboat and by force put him into it, desiring him at parting to remember they died his true servants" (Ross 1979, 125).

In March of 1652, off the west coast of Africa, Maurice captured an English ship and named it the *Defiance*. With their remaining four ships, the brothers sailed to the West Indies but were caught in a hurricane near the Virgin Islands. Only Rupert's flagship survived. The grief-stricken Elizabeth was tormented for years by rumors that Maurice still lived: a prisoner of the Spanish kept in Algiers or spotted in some faraway port. Finally, in 1664 Spanish fishermen found wreckage from the *Defiance* on a beach in Puerto Rico.

By the 1650s to call someone a Rosicrucian was an insult meaning they had lost touch with reality, that they couldn't be counted on because they had filled their heads with superstitions. The flood of pamphlets had dwindled to an occasional curiosity. The three little books and the controversy they caused had been all but forgotten except among a few enthusiasts, some of whom, such as John Winthrop the Younger, put Rosicrucian principles to work. As we have seen, Winthrop was a founder of Connecticut, yet an obscure Welsh poet and alchemist named Thomas Vaughan had more influence on how Rosicrucianism evolved mythologically.

Using the pen name Anthroposophus, Vaughan wrote a book called *Anthroposophia Theomagia*. His better-known pseudonym was Eugenius Philalathes. He claimed to be not the translator but the publisher, in the sense of making public the first English translations of the

Fama and *Confessio* in 1652, for which he wrote a lengthy preface. He declared he was not a Rosicrucian and admitted he didn't "much desire their acquaintance." But he also argued that they were good Protestants and "true Philosophers."

Vaughan explains the invisibility of the Rosicrucians by referring to a passage written by the first-century Greek philosopher Apollonius, who described the lives of the Brahmin sages of India: "And now let us see what kind of Habitation they had, and how much a parallel it is to that place or dwelling of R. C. . . . . The Wise-men (saith Apollonius) dwelt on a little Hill, or Mount, and on the Hill there rested always a Cloud, in which the Indians housed themselves . . . and here did they render themselves visible or invisible, at their own will and discretion. This Secret of Invisibility . . . the Fraternity of R. C. can move in this white Mist" (Vaughan 1919, 354). Vaughan's description of hidden masters helped inspire the mythology of the ascended masters of Theosophy and the secret chiefs of the Hermetic Order of the Golden Dawn.

As R.A. Gilbert wrote: "By the end of the 18th century the introduction of 'Secret Chiefs' was a masterstroke permitting the most outrageous claims to be made which could be neither proved nor disproved. English Rosicrucianism was said to encompass Dr. Dee, Robert Fludd, John Heydon, Thomas Vaughan, William Backhouse and Elias Ashmole— indeed anyone who had an interest or skill in mathematics, natural science, astronomy, astrology, or alchemy" (Gilbert and Hamil 2009, xix).

Vaughan also helped establish the hermetic lineage we know today, going all the way back to what he called: "the Ancient real Theosophy of the Hebrews and Egyptians." Esoteric authors like Madame Blavatsky, Alexander Wilder, W. Wynn Westcott, Manly P. Hall, H. Spencer Lewis and many others have reiterated this family tree. I've written elsewhere of Vaughan's alchemical experiments with his lab partner and wife, Rebecca, his poignant reaction to her death, and his experience of her guidance from beyond.*

---

*See *American Metaphysical Religion* (Inner Traditions: 2023), 181.

In 1653, the year Ferdinand IV inherited the imperial throne, Charles Louis, after allowing only shipments of corn and wine to reach his mother, at last convinced her to join his household in Heidelberg. Plans were made. Once the word got out, bills amounting to what would be millions in today's dollars came due. Elizabeth wrote that she had nothing to eat and emphasized this was not hyperbole. No one in The Hague would extend her credit. "I shall have no meat, bread or candles." She refused to leave until her debt had been settled. Negotiations commenced, and various deals were proposed and rejected by one party or another. Elizabeth's robust health began to fail. She suffered indigestion and a painful case of shingles. One of her hands began to tremble.

Meanwhile, in England, Cromwell laid the foundations for what would eventually become the Industrial Revolution. He modernized at home while supporting embattled Protestants in Europe. When the Duke of Savoy and the Spanish army attacked the peaceful shepherds of Rora in northern Italy, Cromwell sent guns and volunteers. Cromwell allowed Jews to return to England in 1656 after a banishment of over three hundred and fifty years. He knew they could help move Europe's financial center from Amsterdam to London. As a Puritan, Cromwell believed that the Second Coming would happen when the Jews regained the Holy Land and that God chose the English to make that happen. To this day, many American evangelicals believe that God intends them to support Israel and restore the Temple of the Mount to hasten the Second Coming.

In his groundbreaking and controversial study of the poet Andrew Marvell, Paul Bembridge (1999) argues persuasively but controversially that Cromwell and the two great poets who worked in his government, Andrew Marvell and John Milton, were influenced by Rosicrucian ideas. He reveals themes and imagery drawn from the Rosicrucian manifestos in the works of both poets. For example, we find in the first edition of Marvell's *Miscellaneous Poems* at the bottom of page 5 the enigmatic inscription "C. Ros.," which Bembridge considers a subtle Rosicrucian reference.

In his essay "Three Foreigners and the Philosophy of the English Revolution," Hugh Trevor-Roper wrote: "through twenty years of what Cromwell called 'blood and confusion,'" the revolution's leaders "were led on by a vision of society which they hoped somehow at the end of it, to attain: a vision, moreover, made vivid to them by three philosophers, none of whom was English" (1960). All three of those philosophers had a deep and abiding interest in Rosicrucianism, and all three of them had been part of Elizabeth Stuart's circle.

When Milton gave Satan that legendary line: "Better to reign in Hell, than serve in Heav'n," he gave counterculture a motto. Hadn't the Rosicrucian manifestos promised a world without a pope? That was Cromwell's goal, too. And if Europe couldn't be purified, at least the New World could be consecrated to this vision of a Puritan country free from the clutches of the Roman Catholic Church and the hereditary Holy Roman Empire.

As Cromwell demonstrates, countercultures can evolve into dominator cultures if they become popular enough to facilitate the radical changes they believe inevitable. The Rosicrucian ideal of a universal reformation inspired by esoteric wisdom and a yearning for independence begat an autocracy. In this way an idealistic rebel can become what Winston Churchill called Cromwell: "a military dictator." But then the prince of peace, who said "if anyone slaps you on the right cheek, turn to them the other also," became the god of empires sustained by the armies of tyrants.

Around 1655, as Cromwell suffered health problems and other troubles, Elizabeth relished the details. In letters, she allowed her spite full expression. When Cromwell died in the fall of 1658, she wrote that he had "lived with the curse of all good people" (Akkerman 2021).

Two years later Charles II was invited back to England to fill the void left by Cromwell's death. Cromwell had been king in all but formal title, and he received the funeral of a monarch, but Elizabeth thought of him as the Beast from Revelation. The charming young king was a relief to commoners and nobles alike. Before departing for England, he stopped at The Hague. Elizabeth had lived for forty years in the city that now turned to celebration in anticipation of the arrival of the new king of England.

Throughout the festivities, Elizabeth was given the honor of sitting at her nephew's right hand. The dignitaries of England paid their respects. The arch wit of England, Samuel Pepys, wrote of the faded Winter Queen: "a very debonair, but plain lady." Her blonde hair was gray now. She had few jewels to lend her glamor. She reported that Charles II treated her more as a mother than aunt. He also promised to talk to Parliament about paying off her immense debt. Recognizing the service of Prince Rupert, he asked Elizabeth to extend to Rupert an invitation to return to England. Only Charles Louis rained on Elizabeth's parade, complaining that the new king snubbed him by not visiting Heidelberg.

Charles Louis tried to make his restored principality a showplace of liberal ideas. He developed Heidelberg University into a premier institution of learning. To the horror of his mother, he even renounced his wife and married a woman below his rank, one of her ladies-in-waiting. If such behavior wasn't enough of a shock, the last of Elizabeth's children to remain home with her, Princess Louise, unmarried at age thirty-six, ran off to join a Catholic convent.

As the huge crowd that came to witness his departure cheered, King Charles II was rowed out to his ship with Elizabeth at his side. "We have him!" the English sailors cried. "God Bless King Charles!" It's hard to imagine what emotions Elizabeth must have felt at that moment as she watched her nephew sail away. So many of her friends were going home. Alone in the quiet of The Hague, her health having improved, she longed to return to England. She decided to attend the coronation. She made arrangements with friends. The French ambassador would loan her his coach. An old friend would shelter her at his own expense. But just as she prepared to leave, having packed her baggage and said her good-byes, a messenger arrived from King Charles II asking her to postpone her visit. She exchanged letters with Prince Rupert, who also urged her to wait, but she decided to go to England for her nephew's coronation anyway.

In the spring of 1613, when sixteen-year-old Elizabeth's barge had floated down the Thames as she began her life with her husband, crowds cheered and cannons fired salutes. Now almost fifty years later in 1661, she returned with about two dozen servants. King Charles II easily forgave his aunt, the only surviving elder of his immediate family. He acted as her escort, taking her to grand events every week. A constant stream of important visitors treated her with the utmost courtesy and respect.

Elizabeth intended to live out the rest of her life in England. She sent for her remaining possessions but then found out that not only had they been held up, but that debtors were demanding immediate payment, accusing her of trying to sneak away. She was especially angered by the realization that this crisis had been provoked by Charles Louis, who invoked his right to check her shipments for any possessions that might be his, thereby tipping off her creditors.

No longer famous as the Winter Queen or Queen of Hearts, the Bohemian tragedy long forgotten, she was beloved as the mother of the dashing hero Prince Rupert of the Rhine. Charles granted her a thousand pounds a month for life. In a more forgiving mood, she reconciled with her Catholic children, writing her son in Paris requesting he find some nice lace for her so she could keep up with the latest fashions in London. Her daughters were envious of her glamorous new lifestyle.

Rupert and his cousin the king of England became close friends, famed for their feats of feasting and "wenching," as well as their scientific curiosity and appreciation of art and theater. Prince Rupert, like Charles II, had such a keen interest in alchemical experimentation that they both had well-equipped laboratories, but Rupert was less likely to be making gold than a new kind of gunpowder. He invented a new brass alloy. He improved the mezzotint process, the art of engraving using halftone copperplates. He devised a "handgun with rotating barrels," and a gun that fired multiple rounds at high speed. He improved the design of surgical tools, and he invented a way to permanently stain marble with color. Rupert became the third founding member of the Royal Society.

In January 1662, Elizabeth moved into a modest manor house. A cold she had was at first exacerbated by the move but then seemed to subside. But by February 10, she coughed up blood. The king of England came to her bedside. She died on February 13, 1662, at age sixty-five, a few hours before what would have been her forty-ninth wedding anniversary. King Charles II did not attend her state funeral at Westminster Abbey. Of the six children who outlived her only Prince Rupert joined the torchlit procession by barge up the Thames on the night of February 17.

She was buried in the vault of her grandmother, Mary, Queen of Scots, alongside her brother Henry Frederick and eventually her son Rupert, as well as others from the same family tree, including twenty-nine infant children of later royals. As Akkerman writes, Elizabeth "died with many wishing she had reigned as Queen of England" (2021, 14). As I write this, the death of Queen Elizabeth II has captivated the world's attention. Although a member of the Windsor family, she was also descended from the Stuarts on both sides, including the exiled queen of Bohemia.

The death of the Queen of Hearts inspired no commemorative poems about her passing, though her wedding had been celebrated by Shakespeare and Donne. She who had been the beauty at the eye of the storm that was the Thirty Years' War, the abandoned daughter, the beloved wife, the devoted widow, had outlived her symbolic value. In her the nostalgia for the Elizabethan golden age came to life again but perished. Yet Merlin's prediction at the masque that celebrated her wedding, Donne's comparison of Frederick and Elizabeth to phoenixes, and even Kotter's prediction of world domination came true in a subtle way. As we have seen, Elizabeth's youngest daughter gave birth to a king of England. By 1938 Elizabeth, by way of Sophie, was the mother of descendants that included the ruling monarchs of Denmark, Italy, Greece, the Netherlands, Sweden, Norway, Romania, Belgium, and Bulgaria.

-◄O►-

In December of 1662, Samuel Butler became the hit humorist of London when he published his poem *Hudibras* in installments. It went through nine editions in its first year. *Hudibras* ridiculed Cromwell and his pleasure-hating followers as Rosicrucian knights, a fraternity of Don Quixotes. King Charles II found it delightful. Butler describes his Rosicrucian hero (Butler 1854):

> *Deep-sighted in Intelligences,*
> *Ideas, Atoms, Influences,*
> *And much of Terra Incognita,*
> *Th' Intelligible world could say:*
> *A deep occult Philosopher,*
> *As learned as the Wild Irish are,*
> *or Sir Agrippa, for profound*
> *And solid lying much renowned:*
> *He Anthroposophus, and Fludd,*
> *and Jacob Boehme understood;*
> *Knew many an Amulet and Charm,*
> *That would do neither good nor harm:*
> *In Rosy Crucian Lore learned . . .*
> *He understood the speech of Birds.*

Of Rosicrucians in general, Butler (1854) wrote:

> *As Rosicrucian virtuosos*
> *Can see with ears, and hear with noses;*
> *And when they neither see nor hear,*
> *Have more than both supply'd by fear*
> *That makes 'em in the dark see visions,*
> *And hag themselves with apparitions—*

While London laughed at the Rosicrucian preoccupations of Cromwell and Marvell, what must Prince Rupert have thought? It must have struck him as strange, since his parents had been the object of Rosicrucian hopes when he was born in Bohemia. Did he wonder how the Rosicrucians who had hoped to see his father elected the first Protestant Holy Roman emperor had become the Rosicrucians who beheaded his uncle? There certainly seemed to be quite a difference between the British Rosicrucians and the German Rosicrucians who had inspired them.

Rupert turned his attention to the New World. "Our Dear and Entirely Beloved Cousin" was only one of the honors conferred on Prince Rupert by the king. He held the titles Count Palatine of the Rhine, Earl of Holderness, Duke of Bavaria, Duke of Cumberland, and first governor of Hudson's Bay Company, a position he held for twelve years. Rupert's Land, a vast territory in Canada that once comprised modern-day Quebec, Ontario, Manitoba, Saskatchewan, Alberta, and the Northwest Territories, was named in his honor, as was the Canadian port city of Prince Rupert, British Columbia.

After a visit from King Charles II during which drunken courtiers trashed Rupert's lab, the hero became reclusive. He preferred to spend his time alone with his experiments and studies. A "faithful great black dog" (Akkerman 2021), his inseparable companion, accompanied him on his solitary evening walks. Locals thought him a wizard and the dog his familiar.

The last fourteen years of his life he lived happily with the legendary actress Peg Hughes, the first female to play Shakespeare's Desdemona. But his lifelong aversion to marriage persisted. They had a daughter named Ruperta Hughes. Rupert died at age sixty-two, leaving his wealth to be split between Peg and Ruperta. Sophie suspected that Rupert had left their mother's jewels to Peg and that she had lost them gambling, but no one is sure what happened to them. We do know that another legendary stage actress Nell Gwynn, the favorite mistress of the "merry monarch" Charles II and a great bawdy wit of her day, bought a necklace that Frederick had given Elizabeth.

In the twenty-first century, a role-playing game from the United Kingdom called Clockwork and Chivalry is described on its website as follows: "As Oliver Cromwell and his gigantic clockwork war machines fight against the cavalier-alchemists of Prince Rupert, ordinary folk struggle for survival, split into a myriad political and religious factions" (Scott 1900). A twenty-first-century blog devoted to Rupert dubbed him "His Royal Hotness."

Prince Rupert is notable for many reasons, but he earned infamy as well. Perhaps of all the reasons for his infamy, the most disturbing is that he was at the vanguard of the rush among the European elites into the profitable business of trafficking human beings. Traveling in Africa hoping to find gold on the river Gambia, Rupert established a British monopoly on the sale of enslaved Africans. The dashing Prince Rupert of the Rhine was the driving force behind, the main investor in, and the governor of the Royal African Company. As the active partner, Rupert can be thought of as the man who established the "Great Evil," as Lincoln called it, at the heart of America's Civil War.

THIRTEEN

Rosicrucian Reflections

Under Westminster Abbey, in a neglected vault, lies what looks like a tribal fetish, the wooden effigy of Henry Frederick, Prince of Wales. The torso lacks arms, the head is long gone, the clothes stolen centuries ago, but the beautifully carved legs of an athlete remain. A surviving print of Henry's hearse shows the missing head with handsome lifelike features. Henry's effigy may be the ultimate relic of the Rosicrucian dream at the dawn of the seventeenth century. Had he lived to lead the war he envisioned against the Holy Roman Empire, the Rosicrucians may have had their Hermetic Champion.

In 1694, the German mystic Johannes Kelpius and his followers crossed the Atlantic and arrived in a new town called Philadelphia. In the scenic Wissahickon wilderness, they established their community, Woman of the Wilderness. The telescopes they set atop their tallest building provide early evidence of astronomy in America, but they were seeking heavenly signs of the end of the world. They brought with them a melange of Rosicrucianism, German pietism, the theosophies of Paracelsus and Böhme, and an early manuscript of a book that wouldn't be published for a hundred years: *The Secret Symbols of the Rosicrucians.*

After Kelpius died, a new mystical leader arrived from Germany. Conrad Beissel founded the Ephrata Cloister, where he and other leading members of the community slept in caves like biblical hermits. Beissel used strict diet, moral codes, and endless practice to make his choir worthy of the music of heaven. Those who heard it, even sophisticated travelers from Europe with a love of opera, described it as the most beautiful music they had ever heard. Kelpius and Beissel have sometimes been credited with bringing Rosicrucianism to America, but as we have seen, John Winthrop the Younger had devoted himself to Rosicrucian ideals in the Connecticut Colony a generation earlier.

The Habsburg victory at the Battle of White Mountain gave the Catholic imperial family three hundred years of dominion over what would become Czechoslovakia. Prague, the city of alchemists and Rosicrucians, would become the hometown of Kafka, who captured in his writing the nightmarish bureaucracy of the sunset of the Habsburg dynasty. World War I finally broke the imperial grip, but first the Nazis and then the Red Army invaded. The USSR held on for fifty years.

When American poet Allen Ginsberg visited Prague in 1965, he was elected King of May for the May Day parade by the students of the University of Prague. Three years later, the Soviet Union crushed the revolt that had become known as the Prague Spring. Finally, in 1989, the Velvet Revolution, also called the Gentle Revolution, liberated the people of what had once been called Bohemia.

At the sunset of the Renaissance and the dawn of what would become modern science, Rosicrucianism combined the mystical metaphysics of the Renaissance with science's confidence in the human ability to learn and nature's readiness to be understood. Radical politics and apocalyptic pietism coexisted for a moment in the atmosphere of enthusiasm for experiments and discovery. Ironically, Rosicrucianism also helped open the door to materialism and scientism. Before long, natural philosophers would leave behind first alchemy and astrology and then the soul, the afterlife, and the gods and would become known as scientists.

But the romance of the secret order of the Rosy Cross would enchant artists and esotericists for centuries, from English romantic poet Percy Bysshe Shelley's undergrad gothic horror novel *St. Irvyne; or, The Rosicrucian: A Romance*, written in 1810, to the three illustrious members of Joséphin Péladan's turn-of-the-twentieth-century Salon de la Rose + Croix: composers Claude Debussy and Erik Satie and the symbolist painter Gustave Moreau.

The Rosicrucian myth and the myth makers themselves have been transformed in the mirrors of generations of historians and enthusiasts. Rogue scholars have argued that Johann Valentin Andreae became the leader of a secret society originally founded by the great medieval writer Agrippa. Others claim a direct teacher-to-student lineage all the way back to ancient Egypt. These scholars consider Andreae's own written dismissals of Agrippa, along with his ridicule of Rosicrucian literature, disinformation.

"Who but a Rosicrucian could explain the Rosicrucian mysteries?" Lord Bulwer-Lytton wrote over two hundred years after the manifestos were published. His classic metaphysical novel *Zanoni* not only inspired the dramatic ending of the more famous novel by his friend Charles Dickens, *A Tale of Two Cities,* but also exemplified the supernatural version of the Rosicrucian story (Bulwer-Lytton 1842, vi):

With that the old gentleman condescended to enter into a very interesting, and, as it seemed to me, a very erudite relation, of the tenets of the Rosicrucians, some of whom, he asserted, still existed, and still prosecuted, in august secrecy, their profound researches into natural science and occult philosophy.

"But this fraternity," said he, "however respectable and virtuous, —virtuous I say, for no monastic order is more severe in the practice of moral precepts, or more ardent in Christian faith, —this fraternity is but a branch of others yet more transcendent in the powers they have obtained, and yet more illustrious in their origin. Are you acquainted with the Platonists?"

"I have occasionally lost my way in their labyrinth," said I. "Faith, they are rather difficult gentlemen to understand."

"Yet their knottiest problems have never yet been published. Their sublimest works are in manuscript, and constitute the initiatory learning, not only of the Rosicrucians, but of the nobler brotherhoods I have referred to. More solemn and sublime still is the knowledge to be gleaned from the elder Pythagoreans, and the immortal masterpieces of Apollonius."

"Apollonius, the imposter of Tyanea! are his writings extant?"

"Imposter!" cried my host; "Apollonius an imposter!"

"I beg your pardon; I did not know he was a friend of yours; and if you vouch for his character, I will believe him to have been a very respectable man, who only spoke the truth when he boasted of his power to be in two places at the same time."

"Is that so difficult?" said the old gentleman; "if so, you have never dreamed!"

The Rosicrucians in *Zanoni* traffic with salamanders, sylphs, and gnomes, creatures of another order than human, elementals inhabiting fire, air, water, and earth. Since in Galatians chapter 3 and Colossians chapter 2 the devil employs elementals as his agents, Rosicrucians have been dismissed as satanists by some Catholic and evangelical writers who didn't realize *Zanoni* is fictional.

Today, elementals are categorized as quaint folktales, a chapter in the menagerie of imaginary creatures. Yet Terence McKenna reported how the drug DMT, which he compared to ceremonial magick, opened a world of elves to his perception. Why do people have identical hallucinations under high doses of tryptamines? How can two or more people at the same time see the same hallucination? Are the reports of Agrippa and so many others fantasy or fraud? Or do they represent encounters with dimensions human beings as yet have been unable to understand?

Perhaps *Zanoni* inspired Thomas De Quincey to investigate the Rosicrucian controversy. De Quincey is best known for having written the first drug confession book in English: *Confessions of an English Opium Eater* (1821). His essay "Historico-cultural inquiry into the origin of the Rosicrucians and Free-masons" first appeared in the January 1824 issue of *The London Magazine*. His insights are well worth sharing.

De Quincey began by rightly reminding us: "We must not forget, however, that the Rosicrucian and Masonic orders were not originally at all points what they now are" (1824). He found no evidence of organized Rosicrucian or Masonic activities earlier than the manifestos: "In general, then, I affirm as a fact established upon historical research that, before the beginning of the seventeenth century, no traces are to be met with of the Rosicrucian or Masonic orders. And I challenge any antiquarian to contradict me. Of course, I do not speak of individual and insulated Adepts, Cabbalists, Theosophists, etc., who doubtless existed much earlier. Nay, I do not deny that in elder writings mention is made of the rose and the cross as symbols of Alchemy and Cabbalism," but none of those meet De Quincey's criteria for a functioning group of masons or rosicrucians (1824).

De Quincey believed Andreae wrote all three manifestos: "From a close review of his life and opinions, I am not only satisfied that Andreae wrote the three works which laid the foundation of Rosicrucianism, but I see clearly why he wrote them. The evils of Germany were then enormous; and the necessity of some great reform was universally admitted. As a young man without experience, Andrea imagined that this reform would be easily accomplished" (1824).

De Quincey found no reason to believe that the *Fama* was to be taken as a factual account of history (1824):

As to the Fama, which properly contains the pretended history of the order, it teems with internal arguments against itself. The House of the Holy Ghost exists for two centuries, and is seen by nobody. Father Rosycross dies, and none of the order even knew where he is buried; and yet afterwards it appears that eight brothers witnessed his death and his burial. He builds himself a magnificent sepulcher, with elaborate symbolic decorations; and yet for 120 years it remains undiscovered. The society offers its treasures and its mysteries to the world; and yet no reference to place or person is assigned to direct the inquiries of applicants.

De Quincey quotes the mathematical genius and philosopher Gottfried Leibnitz, who was influenced by Rosicrucian ideas, to support his position regarding the events described in the manifestos: "The philosopher Leibnitz wrote: 'des Freres de la Croix de la Rose est une pure invention de quelque personne ingenieuse' [the Brothers of the Cross of the Rose is a pure invention of some ingenious person]" (1824).

De Quincey analyzes how, from his perspective, the other two manifestos are responses to the overreaction of the public to the first. But these efforts to correct course fail because they are all taken literally. He reminds us that Rosicrucianism became a popular hustle: "Many vile impostors arose, who gave themselves out for members of the Rosicrucian order; and upon the credit which they thus obtained for a season, cheated numbers of their money by alchemy— or of their health by panaceas" (1824).

De Quincey's insight into the moment that Rosicrucianism was commandeered, in a way that would happen again throughout its history, captures the self-identification as Rosicrucian that is at the heart of its independence but also of its deceptiveness. De Quincey wrote (1824):

[Of] the conduct of the Paracelsists. With frantic eagerness they had sought to press into the imaginary order: but, finding themselves lamentably repulsed in all their efforts, at length they paused; and, turning suddenly round, they said to one another—'What need to court this perverse order any longer? We are ourselves Rosicrucians as to all the essential marks laid down in the three books. We also are holy persons of great knowledge; we also make gold, or shall make it: we also, no doubt, give us but time, shall reform the world: external ceremonies are nothing: substantially it is clear that we are the Rosicrucian order.' Upon this they went on in numerous books and pamphlets to assert that they were the identical order instituted by Father Rosycross and described in the Fama Fraternitatis. The public mind was now perfectly distracted; no man knew what to think; and the uproar became greater than ever.

De Quincey was convinced, as many others have been, that after its failure in Germany Rosicrucianism evolved into Speculative Masonry (1824):

> I shall now undertake to prove that Rosicrucianism was trans-planted to England, where it flourished under a new name, under which name it has been since re-exported to us in common with the other countries of Christendom. For I affirm, as the main thesis of my concluding labours, THAT FREE-MASONRY is NEITHER MORE NOR LESS THAN ROSICRUCIANISM AS MODIFIED BY THOSE WHO TRANSPLANTED IT TO ENGLAND.

Unfortunately, his argument presents Robert Fludd as the princi-pal founder of Masonry, and further that "his friend" Michael Maier initiated him into Rosicrucianism. De Quincy tells us that Maier "was intimate with Fludd during his stay in England, and corresponded with him after he left it" (1824). However, as we have seen, no solid evidence has been found that Fludd and Maier met in England, or that they corresponded with each other, or that they were Rosicrucians, or that Fludd founded Freemasonry.

Anacalypsis by Godfrey Higgins (1874, 301), a great work of imagi-nation masquerading as scholarship, yet filled with intriguing historical gems, contains this confident statement:

> The Rosicrucians of Germany are quite ignorant of their origin; but, by tradition, they suppose themselves descendants of the ancient Egyptians, Chaldeans, Magi, and Gymnosophists [the Hindu yogis encountered by Alexander in India]—. They had the name of *illuminati*, from their claiming to possess certain secret knowledge, and, from their secrecy, they are also called *invisible brothers*. They use as a mark of distinction or monogram the three letters. F.R.C., which probably means *Fratres Rosi Crucis*. Luther took for his coat of arms, a cross rising from a rose.

Higgins further obscures the matter by declaring he had been offered admittance into the Rosicrucian Order without clarifying that the order was Masonic or the invention of Masons. As Westcott wrote: "The Societas Rosicruciana in Scotia, as well as the Societas Rosicruciana in the U.S.A. were branches from the same Rosicrucian source and sprang from a rejuvenation by Frater Robert Wentworth Little of that lapsed Rosicrucian College in England which is mentioned by Higgins" (1915, 18).

Joscelyn Godwin in his *The Theosophical Enlightenment* (1994) suggests Higgins was referring to the Golden and Rosy Cross, an eighteenth-century German order founded by Hermann Fictuld, an alchemist and Freemason. It attracted European aristocrats from England to Russia with splendid rituals and practical alchemy. The hierarchy of the order from novice to adept and beyond was adopted by the Hermetic Order of the Golden Dawn.

Self-proclaimed Rosicrucian Paschal Beverly Randolph's work was a root from which both American Rosicrucianism and the Hermetic Brotherhood of Luxor blossomed. Randolph later confessed he had claimed to be a Rosicrucian because due to his color he was not taken seriously when he presented his ideas as his own.

Madame Blavatsky of the Theosophical Society, William Wynn Westcott of the Golden Dawn, the founders of public Rosicrucian orders like Max Heindel and H. Spencer Lewis, esoteric historians like Manly Palmer Hall, and academics like Frances Yates all added mythologizing elements that brought the Rosicrucian legend to life again, more science fiction than ever. The more extreme examples of the trend include on the list of Rosicrucian adepts Abraham Lincoln and Napoleon, and such examples can be found all the way back to a book titled *Echo of the Divinely Illuminated Fraternity of the Admirable Order of the R.C.* published in 1615 where we are told that "Adam was the first Rosicrucian."

Éliphas Lévi claimed that Dante's *Divine Comedy*, with the rose on a cross at the center of heaven, and the *Romance of the Rose* itself "are two opposite forms of a single work—initiation by independence of spirit, satire on all contemporary institutions and an allegorical formula of the grand secrets of the Brotherhood of the Rosy Cross" (Lévi 1913, 260). Manly P. Hall and others have pointed to the satirical allegory *The Golden Ass* by Apuleius as an early example of the rose symbol. After having been turned into a donkey, the protagonist suffers all sorts of hilarious and bawdy predicaments to be saved by a vision of Isis. Isis directs him to eat the roses consecrated to her. The priests try to intervene, but the donkey is made human again. This transformation from ass to spiritually aware human being became a symbol of alchemical transmutation and universal reformation.

Lévi exemplified the poetic use of metaphor in writing about the Rosicrucians that, when taken literally, gives rise to myths about superhumans having mystical meetings in the pyramids (Waite 1924, 358):

[I]f anyone asked openly who were those Brothers of the Rosy Cross, an unknown personage would perchance take the inquirer apart, and say to him gravely: 'Predestined to the reformation which must take place speedily in the whole universe, the Rosicrucians are depositaries of supreme wisdom, and as undisturbed possessors of all gifts of Nature, they can dispense these at pleasure. In whatsoever place they may be, they know all things which are going on in the rest of the world better than if they were present amongst them; they are superior to hunger and thirst and have neither age nor disease to fear. They can command the most powerful spirits and genii. God has covered them with a cloud to protect them from their enemies, and they cannot be seen except by their own consent—had anyone eyes more piercing than those of the eagle. Their general assemblies are held in the pyramids of Egypt; but, even as the rock whence issued the spring of Moses, these pyramids proceed with them into the desert and will follow them until they enter the Promised Land.

How does Lévi know that "the Comte de Saint-Germain was . . . the natural or adopted son of a Rosicrucian"? And what exactly does he mean by a Rosicrucian? According to Lévi, Saint-Germain was born in Bohemia. Was his father then a member of the loose-knit community of hermetically inclined political reformers inspired by the *Fama* and *Confessio*? Lévi says Saint-Germain's father was the real person behind the fictional character Comte de Gabalis, or Count of the Kabbalah, the hero of a book that some consider a Rosicrucian classic but Lévi thought a scathing satire. Robert Ambelain in his book *Templiers et Rose-Croix* (1955) claims that Lévi was initiated into the Rosicrucian order on his trip to London in 1853, but if so, wasn't this most likely a Masonic or self-proclaimed order?

A good example of a self-proclaimed Rosicrucian Order began with the publication by Paul Sédir in 1910 of *Histoire des Rose Croix*. Sédir included this provocative passage: "To avoid omitting anything, we should mention here a manifestation of a very elevated Rosicrucian center, the F.T.L., whose recruitment methods and the center itself have never been described. We know that this society began to spread around 1898 and we suppose that the neophytes are put in touch with the members of the order in a way like that described in the Rosicrucian posters posted in Paris in 1623" (1910, 50).

Pierre Geyraud, researching secret societies in Paris twenty years later, located the F.T.L. and discovered the founder was none other than Paul Sédir. Of these self-proclaimed orders, Joscelyn Godwin commented: "the Fraternity of the Rosy Cross appears to have had at least as many 'Grand Masters' as rank-and-file members!" (1994, 130).

Éliphas Lévi's keen critical eye recognized many similarities between Protestantism and Islam. Both reject depictions of deity as idolatry, and both renounce the splendor and spectacle of the Catholic Church. While Catholic salvation requires the blessings of priests, Protestants and Muslims are responsible for their own redemptions. Islam celebrated and furthered mathematics and science, while the Catholic Church vilified them. Appreciation of nature and of equality was to be found in

Islam and among the Rosicrucians. Lévi points to the Islamic influence on the Templars and on Christian Rosenkreutz. Important authors of the esoteric tradition such as Iamblichus and Agrippa were preserved in Islamic libraries. However, when the *Fama* and the *Confessio* "condemn the East and the West" they are dismissing Islam along with the Roman Catholic Church.

Many scholars of the time believed that Rosicrucian "secret chiefs" were the guiding lights of Freemasonry. Robert Fludd was proposed as one of the Rosicrucians who may have been a founder of Masonry. Obviously Rosicrucian ideas deeply influenced Freemasonry. By the end of the eighteenth century, two Rosicrucian Masonic rites evolved: the Rectified Scottish Rite of Central Europe and the Ancient and Accepted Scottish Rite of France whose initiates of the eighteenth degree were given the title Knight of the Rose Cross. As for the history of Freemasonry, including its alleged direct connections with early Rosicrucianism, in his *The Muses Threnodie; or Mirthful Mournings on the Death of Mr. Gall,* Henry Adamson (1774) dubbed it "the happiest of all hunting grounds for the light-headed, the fanciful, the altogether unscholarly and the lunatic fringe of the British Museum Reading Room."

The temptation to find cause and effect in the decline of the Rosicrucian movement in Germany around the time that Speculative Masonry developed in England and Scotland lacks evidence. Perhaps Masonic references to Rosicrucianism encouraged the idea. For example, the Order of the Golden and Rosy Cross of the mid-eighteenth century was inspired by the first wave of Rosicrucian events but was the creation of a Freemason. The tendency toward elitism of the Golden and Rosy Cross culminated at the end of the eighteenth century when Prussia was dominated by two members of the order who had mentored King Frederick William II. These men were notorious for censorship and other authoritarian tactics they used to control religion in Prussia. They contributed to the still-extant myth that the Rosicrucians are a dominator elite, a vision far from that of Andreae and his friends.

–◄o►–

In Germany, the extraordinary writer, social reformer, educator, architect, healer, and occultist Rudolf Steiner's Anthroposophical Society considered itself, as he put it: "under the sign of Christian Rosenkreutz and the cultural impulse of Rosicrucianism" (2006).

Two well-known societies evolved in America: the Rosicrucian Order AMORC (Ancient Mystical Order of the Rosy Cross) in Pennsylvania, led by H. Spencer Lewis, and Max Heindel's Rosicrucian Fellowship in California. Pekka Ervast founded the Finnish Rosy Cross. These groups are still active. Antti Savinainen has called the philosophy of these and related organizations Rosicrucian Theosophy. The Theosophical Society influenced them all, and their founders, except Lewis, had been members.

Manly Palmer Hall included this statement in *The Secret Teachings of All Ages*: "Another version has it that a mysterious school, resembling in general principles the Rosicrucian Fraternity, which calls itself 'The Bohemian Brothers,' still maintains its individuality in the Schwarzwald (Black Forest) of Germany" (2009, 451).

Hall's personal copy of A. E. Waite's *The Brotherhood of the Rosy Cross,* contains some notes in Hall's hand in pencil on the endsheet. He criticizes Waite for arguing from conclusions instead of toward them. Hall may have contributed more myth than fact in his wonderful storytelling about the Rosicrucians. For example, influenced by the highly questionable self-proclaimed Rosicrucian author John Heydon, the young Hall suggested Rosicrucian masters have the powers of Madame Blavatsky's mahatmas and other "ascended masters," such as the alchemical saint Elias the Artist.

In his essay "Elias the Artist," available at the Francis Bacon Research Trust website, Peter Dawkins makes a strong argument that both Elias and Father CRC were used in reference to Francis Bacon. This is not to say that these names represented myths created to honor Bacon, but they were applied to him as an example of what the names designated: a fountain of wisdom in human form. One of the first two elected secretaries of the Royal Society, John Wilkins, hinted rather boldly at this identification in his book *Mathematical Magick*: "Such a lamp is likewise related to be seen in the sepulchre of Francis Rosicross, as is more largely expressed in the Confession of that fraternity" (Dawkins 2015).

John Heydon's alleged powers of prediction attracted attention. He was said to have foretold the death of Cromwell. In his books he plagiarized Bacon, Elias Ashmole, and Thomas Vaughan, among others. In his book *A Voyage to the Land of the Rosicrucians*, he took Bacon's *New Atlantis*, changed very little, and suggested that he had actually visited the place and that he had been chosen to return as a representative of the order. We have no evidence for Heydon's claims that he visited Spain, the Middle East, and Turkey, but we do have evidence that he was arrested four times, twice for debt and twice for suspicion of treason. MacGregor Mathers thought Heydon was more than a fraud, but Elias Ashmole called him "an ignoramus and a cheate" (Lambert 2010).

◄〇►

In the vault of the Philosophical Research Society during the years when its founder Manly Palmer Hall wrote books in an office a few steps away, one of the treasures that caught my eye was a row of more than a dozen books in dark red bindings with gilt letters stamped on their spines: the Bacstrom manuscripts.

Dr. Sigismund Bacstrom was probably the most well traveled of all alchemists. His job as ship's doctor took him to Iceland, Greenland, China, West Africa, Jamaica, Cape Horn, the Virgin Islands, and the Island of Vancouver, where he made paintings of indigenous people and their canoes as an artist of the early maritime fur trade. Two years later in 1794, Bacstrom is nearer to East Africa than India when he visits the Island of Mauritius. There he meets Comte de Chazal, a student of alchemy, astronomy, philosophy, and the occult.

A. E. Waite (1924) wrote: "My conclusion is that the Comte de Chazal belonged to a branch of the Order which is not to be identified with the Golden and Rosy Cross, as the latter existed in 1777; its root may perhaps be referable to the system of which Sigmund Richter became the spokesman in his work on the Philosophical Stone, or to some still earlier development." In other words, Rosicrucian orders were attempted with varying degrees of success in a variety of places. De Chazal was said to be ninety-six years old, although more recent research suggests he was thirty years younger. In the wake of mysterious documents discussed by Waite, the idea circulated that de Chazal accomplished the philosopher's stone and had become immortal.

Bacstrom claimed that de Chazal had powers of clairvoyance. Waite wrote: "Though resident at the time in Mauritius he was cognizant of all that took place in Paris during the horrors of the French Revolution, including the execution of the French King and Queen, while all communication was suspended between France, Mauritius and the adjacent island of Bourbon. He kept a journal of that which he saw or learned, and its accuracy was verified twelve months after when news from Europe was brought by an American ship" (1924, 537).

The complex challenges of studying the history of Rosicrucianism are made obvious by the story of Bacstrom and de Chazal. Are we to take everyone at their word? For example, Riki Armstrong (n.d.) has suggested that Bacstrom may have forged the Rosicrucian diploma, and told stories of a man he heard about when he was in Mauritius, but never met, in the hope of finding support for his alchemical experiments back home in London. On the other hand, Waite thinks Bacstrom is sincere.

Because Bacstrom was a devoted student of alchemy familiar with the classics, and because he had both studied and experimented, de Chazal, who had been seeking the man who would replace him as specified by Rosicrucian laws, initiated Bacstrom into the order. The Bacstrom Rosicrucian Diploma is written in the flowing script of a good scribe, with Hebrew words including YHVH well wrought, and an enigmatic seal at the end that looks like an early painting of a chakra. Next to it is written: the Seal of the Red Stone.

One of the order's rules sets it apart from others of its kind at the time: its readiness to accept women (Waite 1887):

> And, as there is no distinction of sexes in the spiritual world, neither amongst the blessed Angels nor among the rational immortal spirits of the Human race; and as we have had women . . . believed to have been all possessors of the Great Work. . . . And moreover as redemption was manifested to mankind by means of a woman the Blessed Virgin, and as salvation, which is of infinitely more value than our whole Art, is granted to the female sex as well as to the male, our Society does not exclude a worthy woman from being initiated, God himself not having excluded women from partaking of every spiritual felicity in the next life. We will not hesitate to receive a worthy woman into our Society as a member apprentice, (and even as a practical member or master if she does possess our work practically and has herself accomplished it), provided she is found . . . to be sober, pious, discreet, prudent, not loquacious, but reserved, of an upright mind and blameless conduct, and withall desirous of knowledge.

Several of the other rules are militantly anticlerical, forbidding building chapels or churches, and members are to provide no salary to priests, who were already too "proud and insolent" (MacLean 1979).

When Bacstrom returned to London he found an anonymous patron who provided him with the materials, space, and equipment he needed to pursue alchemy. As we shall see, a possible candidate for his benefactor is Frederick Hockley, the Rosicrucian seer. But Bacstrom's good luck didn't last. The French Revolution had repercussions in London and Bacstrom was forced to return to the sea. Having been a prisoner of mutiny and of capture by an enemy nation, it's hard to imagine that he was eager to board a ship again.

Waite summarizes Bacstrom's stories about de Chazal. "He is

described as the most learned as well as the most opulent man in the island, his landed estate and other property being worth three million Spanish *piastres*, though he followed no profession or business. He is said to have educated a hundred orphan girls and to have provided them with marriage dowries totaling another million *piastres*. His more private charities were also very numerous." But de Chazal's wealth didn't come from gold making: "As to the source of his revenues, he received annually considerable sums from Bordeaux" (Waite 1924, 571).

In 1961 Hamilton-Jones suggested that the mysterious comte who had initiated the Comte de Chazal must be the Comte de St. Germain, to whom he dedicates his book *Bacstrom's Alchemical Anthology* (Hamilton-Jones 1960). This put Bacstrom in the direct lineage of the most famous of the immortals of western esotericism, but on the most circumstantial evidence, that St. Germain was in Paris around the time de Chazal claimed to have been initiated there.

In the late 1800s Frederick Hockley wrote in a note to a colleague: "Dr. Sigismund Bacstrom died very poor but still to the day of his death engaged on the Great Work. . . . Bacstrom was the author . . . of my 17 vols of Hermetic Science" (Gilbert and Hamil 2009, 66). With Hockley's keen interest in alchemy and Rosicrucianism and his connections with wealthy fellow Freemasons with similar interests, he may have been Bacstrom's patron.

So what exactly is Bacstrom? He has a diploma that says he's a Rosicrucian. But what does that mean? That he was a member of the same order that Andreae allegedly belonged to? But it seems more likely that he was a human being like the author and readers of this book. A person curious about ways to improve life, to gain health and wealth, to be a blessing to family, friends, and community. Bacstrom is proof that two hundred years after the manifestos were published they continued to inspire small groups and individuals, though the goal of universal reformation appears to have been left behind in devotion to alchemy. Some like Bacstrom would follow to the bitter end the same alchemical dream that Andreae's father had chased to an early death.

◄o►

Did the rumored powers of yogis evolve into tales of ascended masters? Or are a few evolved human beings, more spiritual than material, always discreetly with us? Ascended masters, Rosicrucian and otherwise, are offered up to encourage human evolution, as the ideal of wisdom and power that can be achieved by spiritual dedication and examples of the true creative potential of the soul. Or by imagining them with these powers do we dehumanize them and ourselves?

The night I completed the research for this book, I had a dream about a gray-haired woman who was a Rosicrucian. She critiqued my practice. She advised focusing on techniques of regeneration and pointed out that too much attention was being given to the physical, when the spiritual is the true source of renewal, vitality, and strength. Depending on the context of a life, this dream could be taken in different ways.

If this happened in London during the heyday of the Golden Dawn, I might have believed that I had been telepathically contacted by a true Rosicrucian secret teacher, perhaps Anna Sprengel herself. As a theosophist in late nineteenth-century New York, I might have been convinced that I had been contacted on the astral plane by an ascended master. If I were a Catholic, the dream might seem angelic or demonic. In 1900 Vienna, Freud might have described it as wish fulfillment. His student Jung may have described it as an encounter with the archetype of a Rosicrucian. Skeptics might dismiss the dream as short-term memories triggered by neurons firing randomly during REM sleep. Or perhaps a real Rosicrucian paid me a visit to reward the sincerity of my scholarship.

Anyone who has spent time around an enlightened human being recognizes the strange experiences they inspire, from flurries of synchronicities to inexplicable knowledge of what cannot be known by conventional means. The subtle gravity of a life well lived is tangible in the presence of a great soul. A cooperating collective of more or less enlightened human beings is certainly no mere myth or fable. History proves the pattern by which a small group of forward-thinking pioneers can open the way for the dawn of a new culture.

Yet we cannot be entirely certain about history. Secrecy and censorship, but also the loss of documentation to deterioration and destruction, leave us with only a partial view. Tantalizing unexplained historical anomalies abound. Manly Hall reported a peculiar one he found in the 1660 edition of *The Anatomy of Melancholy* (Hall 2009, CXLIII):

> This volume first appeared in 1621 from the pen of Democritus junior, who was afterwards identified as Robert Burton, who, in turn, was a suspected intimate of Sir Francis Bacon. One reference archly suggests that at the time of publishing *The Anatomy of Melancholy* in 1621 the founder of the Fraternity of R.C. was still alive. This statement—concealed from general recognition by its textual involvement—has escaped the notice of most students of Rosicrucianism. In the same work there also appears a short footnote of stupendous import. It contains merely the words: 'Joh. Valent. Andreas, Lord Verulam.' This single line definitely relates Johann Valentin Andreæ to Sir Francis Bacon, who was Lord Verulam, and by its punctuation intimates that they are one and the same individual.

Burton reports that "the renewer of all arts and sciences, reformer of the world" is "now living," according to a Paracelsian doctor named Montanus who died in 1604 (Burton 1927, 100). But Bacon was born twenty-five years before Andreae, and both men lived productive and well-documented lives. The mysterious footnote could have been nothing more than an error.

Robert Burton wrote about the Rosicrucians: "We had need of some general visitor in our age, that should reform what is amiss; a just army of Rosy-cross men, for they will amend all matters (they say) religion, policy, manners, with arts, sciences, &c." (Burton 1927, 89).

Though it can be hard to tell because of his facetious wit, Burton seems to have been sincere when he describes the Rosicrucians as "that omniscient, only wise fraternity of the Rosicrucians, those great theologians, politicians, philosophers, physicians, philologers, artists, &c." (Burton 1927, 100).

In 1660, the Royal Society was established. The man who is supposed to have first brought the key participants together was Theodore Haak, Comenius's representative in England. Haak studied at Oxford and Cambridge. As Christopher McIntosh showed in his introduction to *The Rosicrucians,* Heinrich Himmler, leader of the SS, commissioned Hans Schick, a German scholar, to write a book about Rosicrucian origins. Schick had access to requisitioned records previously unavailable. Published in 1942 at the height of World War II, his book *The Older Rosicrucianism* alleged that Haak was a Rosicrucian, but we have no evidence that he was.

Schick saw Comenius as Andreae's disciple. Schick wrote: "We have in him not only the middleman between the father of Rosicrucian thought, J. V. Andreae, and those who stood as godparents at the birth of English Freemasonry, such as Hartlib, Dury and others, but also the bridge from Rosicrucian ideology to organized Freemasonry in general. He received the torch from Andreae and carried it to the British Isles" (McIntosh 1998, 43). But as we have seen, the connection between the early Rosicrucians and the beginning of Freemasonry lacks evidencee.

If the author of the Rosicrucian manifestos was a precocious teen whose hoax helped start the Thirty Years' War, the fact that on the one hand he has been effaced and replaced by a crew of invisible telepaths, and that on the other he is accused as one of the dreaded and malevolent Illuminati, would only have confirmed his deep disappointment at the public reaction.

In a letter to a friend, Andreae talked about giving Tobias Hess authorship of one of his own works. Hess died in 1614. As Andreae continued writing, Hess became his Rosicrucian facade, a way to deflect attention from himself and his own actions and opinions. The Hess of Andreae's later works is not Tobias Hess, his friend, but a pseudonym. Hess had been an alchemical compatriot of Andreae's father. He is said to have cured the injured knee of Andreae's sister. Twenty years younger than Hess, Andreae found in him a father, a friend, a teacher, and a model of piety.

Academic authorities threatened by the success of Hess's Paracelsian cures denounced them as dangerous. In 1599 they accused him of being a fraud. A formal warning was issued to his students, but the authorities took no legal action. Ten years later his cures were again described as dangerous, since he had no degree in medicine. Worse, he wasn't practicing medicine at all. His techniques were magic, blasphemy, and the work of the devil. As we have seen, the last of the earliest editions of the *Fama* included an introduction about a Rosicrucian who had cured a woman but was arrested for black magic, the misfortune of Tobias Hess. Andreae, it would seem, defended his friend in print.

The utopian classic Andreae wrote a few years later, *Christianopolis* (1619), presented key principles of the Rosicrucian manifestos as a strict Christian socialism where art and science thrive, with freedom of religion and respect for all races. There isn't a single mention of a rose in the book. In his introduction Andreae doubted the existence of an actual Rosicrucian fraternity but credited the *Fama* for inspiring him to imagine a Christian utopia.

Bacon called his *New Atlantis* a fable. Later Rosy Cross enthusiasts would christen America as New Atlantis, the ultimate political and spiritual experiment, the result of generations of planning by esoteric masters. But Andreae wrote fables, fables that were taken literally. Borges saw in Andreae a kindred spirit because both were master fabulists. Rosicrucianism is indeed a magical mirror, reflecting the preoccupations of the viewer, but then all histories mirror the historian.

Fables may be thought of as child's play, but they can be very powerful. As Andrew Weeks writes, "even if it was only a phantom, the Rosicrucian Brotherhood furnished the scattered circles of dissenters and seekers with powerful slogans, symbols, appealing myths of organization, and a fabled tradition" (Weeks 1991, 101).

When Manly Hall and I were friends, I was bold enough to ask what he really thought of the Rosicrucians. Hall responded that he wished he hadn't written so much about initiates with superpowers because metaphors are misunderstood by sincere people seeking exotic experiences or short cuts. Approaching the end of his long life, he told me that he preferred to think of the Rosicrucians as the dedicated people in every generation who devote themselves to bettering our world as servants of divine love.

Judging from his own writing in books like *Christianopolis* and the *Tower of Babel,* the reaction to the three little books deeply disappointed Andreae. From those who accused the Rosicrucians of being evil to those who made spectacles of themselves demanding membership, everyone had missed the point. The three little books were meant to inspire people to contribute to the Universal Reformation by reforming their own corners of the universe.

By that definition, those who were inspired to emulate the Rosicrucians they admired but never met, people like John Winthrop the Younger, are the real Rosicrucians. Applying Rosicrucian principles in everyday life, Winthrop learned to heal the sick. He encouraged experimentation, made improvements in mechanical understanding, protected the weak, tried to organize a gathering of scholars called the College of Light, taught tolerance, and cultivated an eagerness to discover and apply the secrets of nature for the common good. Winthrop may be an example of the result the author or authors of the three little books had hoped for when they wrote them.

FOURTEEN

The Phoenix of Counterculture

Fans may find it a curious experience watching Terence McKenna in his Mystic Fire video collaboration *The Alchemical Dream: Rebirth of the Great Work*. Dressed up in Elizabethan costume, he strolls the streets of Prague in the role of John Dee. The Copernicus of Consciousness, as the *Village Voice* referred to McKenna, called Frederick V "a great hero of mine" and added that he "should be a great hero to all freaks in Germany and everywhere" (McKenna 1996).

McKenna's version of events was greatly influenced by the work of Frances Yates. In his "Beyond the Yates Paradigm: The Study of Western Esotericism between Counterculture and New Complexity" (2001) and in his *Rejected Knowledge in Western Culture* (2012), Wouter Hanegraaff examines Yates's vision of a hermetic conspiracy for liberty and science that has charmed many but finds no solid evidence for it.

This is how Hanegraaff explains the Yates paradigm (2001, 17):

So in Yates' writings we have, firstly, the picture of the 'Hermetic Tradition' as a quasi-autonomous counterculture of magic and mysticism, pitted against the dominant powers of church and rationality; and secondly, we have a modernist set of assumptions about science and progress, which underlies her presentation of this Hermetic Tradition. The combination of these two results in a 'grand narrative' about hermeticism, which I will refer to as the 'Yates paradigm'.

This paradigm may be presented explicitly or assumed implicitly, and it can be encountered in diluted versions with or without mention of Frances Yates.

The truth about Frederick is probably somewhere in between the alchemical monarch of Yates and the stubborn bumbler described by Catholic historians who viewed the Rosicrucian counterculture occurring around the wedding of Frederick and Elizabeth as an opportunistic infection rather than a universal reformation.

McKenna drew a parallel between those times and ours. He longed for visionary communities to infiltrate society. The artists, astrologers, alchemists, philosophers, mathematicians, politicians, patrons, writers, engineers, and publishers of the Bohemian Revolt shocked and inspired Europe with their diagrams of enlightenment, their mechanical statues, and their hermetic weddings and Rosicrucian initiates. We can do the same, McKenna tells us, "find the others and then you will know what to do." He adds: "Find the others and then using this technology which was designed to keep track of us, to pick our pockets, and to sell us junk we don't want, use this technology to produce art, massive amounts of subversive art" (McKenna 1996).

In her important book *Reformation, Revolution, Renovation: The Roots and Reception of the Rosicrucian Call for General Reform*, scholar Lyke de Vries presents a convincing argument that the Rosicrucian manifestos are neither Lutheran nor esoteric at heart but rather "revolutionary mission statements" (de Vries 2021).

As we have seen, Holy Roman Emperor Rudolf II, with his artistic and occult obsessions and his declaration of freedom of religion, made Prague and the surrounding areas, already known for such pursuits, an irresistible destination for those with similar interests. Alchemists and astrologers participated in experiments that would evolve into the sciences of chemistry and astronomy. Mystics, occultists, kabbalists, and philosophers influenced one another's visions of divine creativity. But when Rudolf died, the area fell back into the hands of an oppressive ruler.

When two volatile chemicals are mixed and added to a third, an explosive reaction can occur. The arrival of Frederick and Elizabeth in Prague had the inevitability of such a reaction. We have no evidence that the king and queen of Bohemia explicitly supported Rosicrucians. Yet they were viewed as the alchemical royal couple, divine rulers sent to liberate the world. The hopes of radicals were amplified when their reign began. Their defeat and exile unleashed the full fury of the Thirty Years' War, as great powers maneuvered for their own gain. Yet the Rosicrucian ideals fostered by that brief euphoria continued to influence poets, political leaders, philosophers, artists, and the explorers and colonizers of what would become America, where the freedom of religion that Rudolf and Frederick tried but failed to guarantee is enshrined in the First Amendment of the Constitution: "Congress shall make no law respecting an establishment of religion."

Understanding the political context of the Rosicrucian dawn shows us that it was no anomaly. The manifestos were very much a product of their time. But we cannot yet and perhaps may never achieve clarity about even so simple a question as what is a Rosicrucian? Nevertheless, *The Da Vinci Code*, a *New York Times* bestseller published in 2003 described Paracelsus, Böhme, and Fludd as Rosicrucians. As we know, the Rosicrucians were students of the works of Paracelsus, but we have no proof that he was one of them. We've seen that Fludd signed an oath declaring that he was not a Rosicrucian.

Rumors persist that the majestic mystic Jakob Böhme accused the Catholic Church of turning the Holy Bible into a whore, exchanged letters with a Rosicrucian. Often included on speculative lists of Rosicrucians, his German surname Böhme means Bohemian. As we have seen, he was in Prague for the arrival of Frederick and Elizabeth. Böhme read Rosicrucian books and must have known other Germans inspired by the Rosicrucians. They shared similar Neoplatonic and Paracelsian influences. He seems to have adopted his idea of the "new reformation" from the Rosicrucian universal reformation. We don't have evidence that he met the authors or authors of the three little books, but we have no evidence that he didn't. His work in turn influenced Rosicrucian-inspired mystical communities in early colonial America and beyond. *Secret Symbols of the Rosicrucians*, published in the 1780s, includes among its enigmatic color illustrations one called *How within this World three Worlds in each other*, which was inspired by Jakob Böhme's work. It's easy to find connections between Böhme and Rosicrucianism, but that doesn't make Böhme a Rosicrucian.

So on the one hand, we have the problem of identifying even one actual and undeniable early Rosicrucian. On the other, we have the challenge of esoteric authors like Bulwer-Lytton who blur the border between fiction and nonfiction. Perhaps the most influential of these was Helena Blavatsky.

Blavatsky's first public statement about her connection to her esoteric masters was published as "A Few Questions to Hiraf" in the July 1875 issue of the *Spiritual Scientist*. In it Blavatsky (1875) wrote:

> The origin of the Brotherhood can be ascertained by any earnest, genuine student of Occultism, who happens to travel in Asia Minor, if he chooses to fall in with some of the Brotherhood, and if he is willing to devote himself to the head-tiring work of deciphering a Rosicrucian manuscript—the hardest thing in the world—for it is carefully preserved in the archives of the very Lodge which was founded by the first Kabbalist of that name, but which now goes by another name. . . . The Rosicrucians strove to combine together the most various branches of Occultism, and they soon became renowned for the extreme purity of their lives and their extraordinary powers, as well as for their thorough knowledge of the secret of secrets.

Four months later she became a founding member of the Theosophical Society.

Blavatsky's friend and editor Alexander Wilder wrote that "Christian Rosenkreuz had been a traveller in the East, where he had received instruction into the profoundest lore—magian, rabbinic, theurgic and alchemic. Among other acquirements, were the knowledge of the philosopher's stone, the art of transmuting metals, and the elixir of life. Returning to Germany, he established a little fraternity of eight disciples, obligating them to keep the doctrine secret for the space of one hundred and twenty years after his death" (Wilder 1880).

Curiously, Wilder insisted that the Rosicrucians would never take action against the authorities who ruled the world. But then he hedges his statement by adding, except in the case of abuse of power. A leader who uses his divinely ordained position to cause harm, who does not live up to the dignity of his office, even a pope or king, the Rosicrucians would fight. But that was not their mission. They devoted themselves to relieving suffering by advancing medicine and education. They dedicated their lives to science, universal reformation, and divine love. Following the undependable expert on Rosicrucianism Hargrave Jennings, Wilder explained: "The Rosicrucian Brotherhood possessed a heritage of all the arcane systems and religions of the earlier world. . . . The Hermetic philosophy of Egypt, the fire-theosophy of Persia, Druidworship, Gnosticism, the Kabala, the Ancient Mysteries and Orders of Knighthood, Magic, Alchemy, Hindu beliefs, etc." (Wilder 1880).

Wilder may have been drawing from Albert Pike's *Morals and Dogma of the Ancient and Accepted Scottish Rite of Freemasonry* (1871). Pike, a former Confederate general, led a troop of Native American soldiers. As a Confederate Indian commissioner he was a genuine advocate for indigenous rights, but he considered slavery a "necessary evil." He didn't believe slaves could handle the jobs white people did. He insisted that most masters were kind. Pike admitted he had an enslaved person himself to handle work that would take time away from writing *Morals and Dogma*.

Morals and Dogma wove together Christianity, the Kabbalah, Pythagoras, Plato, and the Christian occultism of Éliphas Lévi. Pike wrote that Freemasonry is the continuation and new form of the mystery schools of the ancient world. The Templars, he claimed, were the founders of Freemasonry, and Freemasonry went back beyond late medieval Europe and back to the wisdom of ancient Egypt, by which Pike may have meant the *Hermetica*.

In *Morals and Dogma* Pike wrote of the Rosicrucians: "The Rose-Croix adepts respected the dominate, hierarchical, and revealed religion. Consequently, they could no more be the enemies of the Papacy than of legitimate Monarchy; and if they conspired against popes and Kings it was because they considered them personally apostates from duty, and supreme favorers of anarchy" (Pike 1871, 822). On this Pike and Wilder agreed: the Rosicrucians weren't fighting the institutions of the church and the monarchy, only individual popes or kings. But the author or authors of the manifestos clearly wanted the papacy to end.

A generation later Rudolf Steiner was greatly inspired by Rosicrucianism. He's considered by some among his followers to be a Rosicrucian, or at least a representative of the order. Perhaps Steiner was thinking of Bulwer-Lytton and Blavatsky when he commented that for most of the nineteenth century Rosicrucian wisdom had become obscure. He added that the plan had been for Rosicrucian influence to quietly develop, but treachery ruined the mission. For that reason, CRC, who had always been present in the physical world by reincarnating in successive bodies like the Dalai Lama, had to withdraw. However, Steiner assures us, in the late nineteenth century the Rosicrucian current was restored.

In the first half of the twentieth century, H. Spencer Lewis (1883–1939), the founder of the Ancient Mystical Order Rosae Crucis, wrote: "The first Rosicrucians to come to America and bring their wisdom to this new country were those who journeyed to the Pacific Coast early in the seventeenth century and deposited there the 'foundation stone' and documents of the last C.R.C. of Europe." (quoted in Schultz 2007, 12).

Referring to Carmel and Monterey in California in his book *Lemuria: The Lost Continent of the Pacific*, Lewis (writing under the pseudonym Wishar S. Cervé) wrote: "The Carmelites who came here and established a monastery were acquainted with this particular locality long before Vizcaíno made his expeditions and brought scientists, padres, and some Rosicrucian mystics to this region to unite their efforts in further forwarding the settlement and civilization of the Carmel and Santa Clara valleys" (Cervé 1931; quoted in Schultz 2007, 12–13). This was supposed to have occurred about a decade before the release of the Rosicrucian manifestos. We are led to believe that the Invisible Order had already infiltrated the Catholic Church. While we have evidence of individual Catholics, even priests and higher members of the church hierarchy, who were interested in Rosicrucian ideas, researchers have not yet found evidence of a secret organization of Rosicrucians before the word became popular by way of the manifestos.

The evidence Lewis offers is circumstantial. In May 1918, during his explorations of ruins near the Carmel Mission in California, Lewis claims to have found crosses decorated with roses made of coral. He was certain these were Rosicrucian remnants, but of course roses have decorated many crosses that have nothing to do with Rosicrucianism, since both Jesus and his mother, Mary, are called the Rose of Sharon.

In facing this kind of confusion, Ludwig Wittgenstein's perspective comes to mind. Words lose meaning when stretched too far. What then is the term *Rosicrucian* referring to exactly? Is it a metaphor describing similar influences and beliefs shared by a group of otherwise unconnected people? Was Paracelsus a Rosicrucian because his beliefs were similar to theirs? Is Rosicrucian more adjective than proper noun? Is it a term that anyone can choose to apply to themselves or anyone else? Are Rosicrucians a literal secret society of adepts existing throughout time, perhaps even outside the laws of nature? Or were they a group of outsider intellectuals with both spiritual and political motivations?

The alchemist laboring for the philosopher's stone makes his life an experiment. The great alchemical writers tell him that how he lives is as important as his dedication to research and experimentation. If his devotion is pure and he succeeds he can have as much gold as he wants if he still wants it. He need no longer fear disease, for he has attained the power to heal. Most importantly, he has achieved the highest level of consciousness possible to a human being, a communion with divine love and wisdom.

These daring explorers attempted to be practical idealists while chasing the will o' the wisps of young sciences. They could have gone the way of most of their peers, into the confessional or the pew, content to be told what to do for a chance at heaven, buying water by the river. But all these Rosicrucian types engaged with the world as if it was a mystery play, or a language to be learned. They were certain harmony and wisdom could be found in the arrangement of events and of all things. They followed their dangerous pursuits during times when punishment for such activities and beliefs could mean execution. They took the terrible risk of publishing their experiences and theories to inspire later generations, so that others could carry on the great work.

There is another important question to consider: Why are we learning about the Rosicrucians? To achieve a feeling of certainty about exactly what has gone on in the world? Then we may be disappointed. Rosicrucianism is like a Zen koan: the deeper we go, the more it defeats the desire of the rational mind to know what actually happened. If we go deep enough, perhaps we can be comfortable with never being certain. After all, Father CRC followed Socrates, admitting that he knew he did not know. And what if we could be certain about these allegedly historical events? What do we get from this certainty? What if we got all the pieces exactly in place? Will this knowledge help us or others to deal with the challenges of life? Will it comfort us or become hollow and distant in times of grief? Will it heal sickness, feed the hungry, or protect the weak?

As we take the long view of history, we can see how small groups of dedicated people with innovative ideas have put into motion events that changed the world. What Allen Ginsberg's *Howl* and Jack Kerouac's *On the Road* were for midcentury America, a call to awaken from denial, the Rosicrucian manifestos were for their time: the tearing of a veil, the full bloom of insight, the announcement of a radical rejection of a stagnant and oppressive status quo, the discovery that others believe as we do. Books so evolutionary that reading them changed not just the lives of individuals but the trajectory of generations. The recurrence of this social dynamic can be symbolized by the legendary phoenix, as if each of these countercultures served as nests for the miraculous bird of light that symbolizes individual and collective rebirth.

When the elusive facts and elaborate conspiracy theories surrounding Rosicrucianism beguile us, we may remember the wise advice Japanese haiku poet Basho attributed to Kūkai, a Buddhist master of high attainment: "Do not seek to follow in the footsteps of the masters of old, seek what they sought."

The Rosicrucians read Paracelsus, revered Giordano Bruno, and respected the wisdom of the Bible and of the ancient pagans, but the mysterious author or authors of the manifestos were also devoted to direct and personal revelation attained by exploration and experimentation. New England Transcendentalist Ralph Waldo Emerson expressed a similar sentiment when he wrote: "The foregoing generations beheld God and nature face to face; we, through their eyes. Why should not we also enjoy an original relation to the universe? Why should not we have a poetry and philosophy of insight and not of tradition, and a religion by revelation to us, and not the history of theirs?" (1836). This personal revelation is at the epicenter of counterculture. The transmission of that revelation through writing, art, or music can liberate a generation.

Abraham Lincoln may not have been a Rosicrucian but he did leave us a definition of the essential motivation at the heart of the Rosicrucian counterculture and of all countercultures: "The dogmas of the quiet past, are inadequate to the stormy present. The occasion is piled high with difficulty, and we must rise with the occasion. As our case is new, so we must think anew, and act anew."

The universal reformation is not a monoculture; it contains all reactions and responses, changing lives as direct inspiration, but also as a contradiction to be fought in the passionate search for truth. Because individuality is key to counterculture, when countercultures succeed they lose their magic. The glamour of fame replaces the aura of underground charisma. Inspiration shared among friends becomes the dogma of the masses, thus assuring that a new counterculture will be born.

We find ourselves in a unique position today as the artifacts of almost all historically known countercultures can be found online. Thanks to the Getty Museum you can see the very same copy of Bacstrom's Rosicrucian Diploma that I did in the vault of the Philosophical Research Society Library. You can leaf through the earliest editions of the Rosicrucian manifestos or A. E. Waite's *The Brotherhood of the Rosy Cross* with a click of your mouse, thanks to Internet Archive. All the required materials for building the nest of the phoenix can be obtained more easily than ever before in history. We need only reach out to find the inspiration we seek, the revelation that is ours.

Bibliography

Adams, Cox, ed. 2011. *Diplomacy and Early Modern Culture (Early Modern Literature in History)*. New York: Palgrave.

Adamson, Henry. 1774. *The Muses Threnodie; or Mirthful Mournings on the Death of Mr. Gall*. Perth, Scotland: George Johnston.

Åkerman, Susanna. 1998. *Rose Cross over the Baltic: The Spread of Rosicrucianism in Northern Europe*. Leiden, Netherlands: Brill.

Akkerman, Nadine. 2011. *The Correspondence of Elizabeth Stuart, Queen of Bohemia Vol. 2*. Oxford, UK: Oxford University Press.

———. 2015. *The Correspondence of Elizabeth Stuart, Queen of Bohemia Vol. 1*. Oxford, UK: Oxford University Press.

———. 2021. *Elizabeth Stuart: Queen of Hearts*. Oxford, UK: Oxford University Press.

Ambelain, Robert. 1955. *Templiers et Rose-Croix*. Paris: Editions Adyar.

Ammann, Peter. 1967. "The Musical Theory and Philosophy of Robert Fludd." *Journal of the Warburg and Courtauld Institutes* 30, no. 1.

Andreae, J. V. 1991. *The Chemical Wedding of Christian Rosenkreuz*. Translated by Joscelyn Godwin. Grand Rapids: Phanes Press.

Armstrong, Riki. (n.d.) "Francois and the Philosopher's Stone." Bryan Discovers World website.

Ashmole, Elias. 1966. *Elias Ashmole: His Autobiographical and Historical Notes, His Correspondence, and Other Contemporary Sources Relating to His Life and Work*. Edited by C. H. Josten. Oxford, UK: Clarendon Press.

Astington, John H. 1985. "Descent Machinery in the Playhouses." *Medieval & Renaissance Drama in England* 2: 119–33.

Bacon, Francis. 1915. *New Atlantis*. Edited by Alfred B. Gough. Oxford: Oxford University Press.

Baier, Karl. 2018. "Yoga within Viennese Occultism: Carl Kellner and Co." In

Yoga in Transformation: Historical and Contemporary Perspectives. Edited by Karl Baier, Philipp A. Maas, and Karin Preisendanz. Vienna, Austria: Vienna University Press.

Bebergal, Peter. 2016. "Reimagining a Shadowy Medieval Brotherhood That Probably Didn't Exist." *New Yorker*, October 26.

Bembridge, Paul. 1999. "The Rosicrucian Resurgence at the Court of Cromwell." In *The Rosicrucian Enlightenment Revisited*, 219–46. Edited by Ralph White. Great Barrington, MA: Lindisfarne Books.

Benger, Miss. 1825. *Memoirs of Elizabeth Stuart, Queen of Bohemia*. 2 vols. London: Longman, Hurst, Rees, Orme, Brown and Green.

Blavatsky, H. P. 1875. "A Few Questions to Hiraf." *Spiritual Scientist* (July 15, 22): 217–18, 224, 236–7.

Bleiler, Everett. 2008. "Johann Valentin Andreae, Fantasist and Utopist." *Science Fiction Studies* 35, no. 1 (March): 1–30.

Blissett, Luther. 1995. "The Situationists as Rosicrucians." *Here and Now: Guy Debord Supplement* 16/17.

Boner, Patrick. 2021. *Kepler's New Star (1604)*. Leiden, Netherlands: Brill.

Borges, Jorge Luis. 1962. *Labyrinths*. New York: New Directions.

Boulting, William. 1914. *Giordano Bruno: His Life, Thought, and Martyrdom*. London: Kegan Paul, Trench Trübner and Company.

Bulwer-Lytton, Edward. 1842. *Zanoni*. New York: Harper & Brothers.

Burns, Teresa. 2010. "A Golden Storm: Attempting to Recreate the Context of John Dee and Edward Kelley's Angelic Material." *Journal of the Western Mystery Tradition* 19, no. 2 (autumn): 1–25.

Burton, Robert. 1927. *The Anatomy of Melancholy*. New York: Tudor.

Butler, Samuel. 1854, *The Poetical Works of Samuel Butler*. Edinburgh: James Nichol.

Case, Paul Foster. 1989. *The True and Invisible Rosicrucian Order: An Interpretation of the Rosicrucian Allegory and an Explanation of the Ten Rosicrucian Grades*. York Beach, ME: Weiser.

Cervé, Wishar S. (H. Spencer Lewis). 1931. *Lemuria: The Lost Continent of the Pacific*. Philadelphia: AMORC.

Chaitow, Sasha. 2018. "Return from Oblivion: Joséphin Péladan's Literary Estericism." In *The Occult in Modernist Art, Literature, and Cinema*, 113–36. Edited by Tessel M. Bauduin and Henrik Johnsson. New York: Palgrave Macmillan.

———. 2020. *Atalanta Unveiled. Alchemical Initiation in the Emblems of the Atalanta Fugiens*. Research Triangle, NC: Lulu.

Christensen, Thomas, ed. 2002. *The Cambridge History of Western Music Theory*. Cambridge, UK: Cambridge University Press.

Churton, Tobias. 2010. *The Invisible History of the Rosicrucians: The World's Most Mysterious Secret Society*. Rochester, VT: Inner Traditions.

Clapham, J. J. 1940. "Charles Louis, Elector Palatine, 1617–1680: An Early Experiment in Liberalism." *Economica New Series* 7, no. 28 (November).

Comenius, John Amos. 1901. *The Labyrinth of the World and the Paradise of the Heart*. New York: E.P Dutton and Co.

Codrington, Robert. 1664. *Prophecies of Christopher Kotterus, Christiana Poniatovia, Nicholas Drabicius: Three Famous German Prophets*. London: Pawlet.

Cramer, Florian. 1998. "From Fama to Information Society: Of Prophets, Gods and the Nettime Server Demon." Nettime mailing list archives, posted by Pit Schultz, September 25.

Crisos, Tony. 2018. "The Orphic Tradition and the Rosicrucian Manifestos." *2018 Lecture Series*, Chancellor Robert R. Livingston Masonic Library, New York, NY, April 26. Posted July 9, 2020, by the Chancellor Robert R. Livingston Masonic Library. YouTube, 1:04:14.

Culianu, Ioan P. 1987. *Eros and Magic in the Renaissance*. Chicago: University of Chicago Press.

Cumming, Laura. 2012. "The Lost Prince: The Life and Death of Henry Stuart" (review). *Guardian* (Manchester, UK), October 20.

Dantinne, Emile (Sar Hieronymus). 1951. "On the Islamic Origin of the Rose-Croix." *Inconnus*.

Dawkins, Peter. 2015. "Elias the Artist." Rev. May 2020. Francis Bacon Research Trust.

Debus, Allen G. 1977. *The Chemical Philosophy: Paracelsian Science and Medicine in the Sixteenth and Seventeenth Centuries*. Mineola, NY: Dover.

———. 2006. *The Chemical Promise: Experiment and Mysticism in the Chemical Philosophy, 1550–1800: Selected Essays of Allen G. Debus*. New York: Science History.

De Quincey, Thomas. 1824. "Historico-Critical Inquiry into the Origin of the Rosicrucians and Free-Masons." In *The London Magazine*, January 1824.

De Vries, Lyke. 2021. *Reformation, Revolution, Renovation: The Roots and Reception of the Rosicrucian Call for General Reform*. Leiden, Netherlands: Brill.

Dickson, Donald R. 1996. "Johann Valentin Andreae's Utopian Brotherhoods." *Renaissance Quarterly* 49, no. 4: 760–802.

———. 1996. "Johannes Saubert, Johann Valentin Andreæ and the *Unio Christiana*." *German Life and Letters* 49: 18–31.

———. 1998. *The Tessera of Antilia: Utopian Brotherhoods and Secret Societies in the Early Seventeenth Century*. Leiden, Netherlands: Brill.

Donne, John. 1896. *Poems of John Donne*. Vol. 1. London: Lawrence and Bullen.

Edighoffer, Roland. 1967. *Rose-Croix et Société Idéale selon Johann Valentin Andreae*. 2 vols. Paris: Arma Artis.

———. 1981. "Johann Valentin Andreae. Vom Rosenkreutz zur Pantopie." *Daphnis: Zeitschrift für mittlere deutsche Literatur* 10: 211–39.

———. 2005. "Andreæ, Johan Valentin." In *Dictionary of Gnosis and Western Esotericism 1:* 72–75. Edited by Wouter J. Hanegraaff. Leiden, Netherlands: Brill.

Ellis, James. 2015. "Shadows in the Shadows: The Rosicrucians, A Fake Secret Society, Had a Real Impact on the World." *Newsweek*, April 19.

Emerson, Ralph Waldo. 1836. *Nature*. Boston: James Monroe and Company. First published anonymously.

Evans, R. J. W. 1973. *Rudolf II and His World: A Study in Intellectual History 1576–1612*. New York: Oxford University Press.

Fludd, Robert. 1979. *Robert Fludd and His Philosophicall Key; Being a Transcription of the Manuscript at Trinity College, Cambridge*. Edited and with a biographical essay by Allen G. Debus. Primary Sources from the Scientific Revolution series. New York: Science History Publications.

Figala, Karin, and Ulrich Neumann. 1990. "Michael Maier (1569–1622): New Bio-Bibliographical Material." In *Alchemy Revisited: Proceedings of the International Conference on the History of Alchemy at the University of Groningen 17–19 April 1989*, 34–50. Edited by Z. R. W. M. von Martels. Leiden, Netherlands: Brill.

Forshaw, Peter J. 2025. *Epilogue: Reception (from Rosicrucians to Modern Occulture) & Bibliography*. The Mage's Images: Heinrich Khunrath in His Oratory and Laboratory, vol. 4. Leiden, Netherlands: Brill.

Fox, Robert, ed. 2000. *Thomas Harriot: An Elizabethan Man of Science*. Farnham, UK: Ashgate.

Geyroud, Pierre. 1939. *Les religions nouvelles de Paris*. Paris: Editions Emile-Paul Frères.

Gilbert, R. A., and John Hamil, ed. 2009. *The Rosicrucian Seer: Magical Writings of Frederick Hockley*. Chicago: Teitan Press.

Giles, Roseen H. 2016. "The Inaudible Music of the Renaissance: From Marsilio Ficino to Robert Fludd." *Rennaissance and Reformation* 39, no. 2 (Spring): 129–66.

Gilly, Carlos. 1998. "'Theophrastia sancta'—Paracelsianism as Religion in Conflict with the Established Churches." In *The Transformation of Paracelsianism 1500–1800: Alchemy, Chemistry and Medicine*, 151–85. Glasgow Symposium, September 15–19, 1993. Leiden, Netherlands: Brill.

———. 2000. "The 'Midnight Lion', the 'Eagle' and the 'Antichrist': Political, Religious, and Chiliastic Propaganda in the Pamphlets, Illustrated Broadsheets, and Ballads of the Thirty Years War." *Dutch Review of Church History* 80, no. 1: 46–77.

———. 2002. *Magic, Alchemy and Science: 15th–18th Centuries.* 2 vols. Florence, Italy: Centro Di.

Gilly, Carlos, and Sebastiano Gentile. 1999. *Marsilio Ficino e il ritorno di Ermete Trismegisto.* Amsterdam, Netherlands: Bibliotheca Philosophica Hermetica.

Gladwin, Ian H. 2022. "Illuminating the Rosicrucian Altar of the *Fama Fraternitatis*." Published by Pansophic Press on Academia.edu.

Godfrey, Elizabeth. 1909. *A Sister of Prince Rupert: Elizabeth Princess Palatine and Abbess of Herford.* London: Bodley Head.

Godwin, Joscelyn. 1973. "Robert Fludd on the Lute and Pandora." *Lute Society Journal* 15.

———. 1979. Robert Fludd, *Hermetic Philosopher and Surveyor of Two Worlds*, Thames & Hudson Ltd.

———. 1983. "The Rosicrucian Event in Perspective." *Journal of Rosicrucian Studies* 1.

———. 1991. "Hargrave Jennings." *The Hermetic Journal*, 49–77.

———. 1994. *The Theosophical Enlightenment.* Albany: State University of New York Press.

———. 2007. *The Golden Thread: The Ageless Wisdom of the Western Mystery Traditions.* Wheaton, IL: Quest Books.

———. 2019. *The Greater and Lesser Worlds of Robert Fludd: Macrocosm, Microcosm, and Medicine.* Rochester, VT: Inner Traditions.

Godwin, Joscelyn, Christopher McIntosh, and Donate Pahnke McIntosh, trans. 2016. *Rosicrucian Trilogy: Modern Translations of the Three Founding Documents.* Newburyport, MA: Weiser Books.

Gorst-Williams, Jessica. 1977. *Elizabeth, the Winter Queen.* London: Abelard.

Green, Mary Anna Everett. 1857. *Lives of the Princesses of England, from the Norman Conquest.* London: Longman, Brown, Green, Longman, and Roberts.

Grell, Ole Peter, ed. 1998. *Paracelsus: The Man and His Reputation; His Ideas and Their Transformation.* Leiden, Netherlands: Brill.

Guariento, Luca. 2016. "Life, Friends, and Associations of Robert Fludd: A Revised Account." *Journal of Early Modern Studies* 5, no. 1 (Spring).

Hamilton-Jones, J. W. 1960. *Bactrom's Alchemical Anthology*. London: John M. Watkins.

Hauge, Peter. 2008. "Robert Fludd (1574–1637)—A Musical Charlatan?" *International Review of the Aesthetics and Sociology of Music* 39, no. 1 (June).

———. 2011. *'The Temple of Music' by Robert Fludd*. Music Theory in Britain, 1500–1700: Critical Editions, edited by Jessie Ann Owens. Farnham, UK: Ashgate.

Hall, Manly P. 2009. *The Secret Teachings of All Ages*. South Orange, NJ: A&D Books.

Hall, Manly P., and A. Russell Slagle. 1986. *The Rosicrucians and Magister Christoph Schlegel: Hermetic Roots of America*. Los Angeles: Philosophical Research Society.

Hanegraaff, Wouter J. 2001. "Beyond the Yates Paradigm: The Study of Western Esotericism between Counterculture and New Complexity." *Aries: Journal for the Study of Western Esotericism.*

———. 2012. *Esotericism and the Academy: Rejected Knowledge in Western Culture*. Cambridge University Press.

Harkness, Deborah E. 1997. "Managing an Experimental Household: The Dees of Mortlake and the Practice of Natural Philosophy." *Isis* 88, no. 2.

Hart, Vaughn. 1994. *Art and Magic in the Court of the Stuarts*. Oxfordshire, UK: Routledge.

Hay, Marie. 1910. *The Winter Queen: Being the Unhappy History of Elizabeth Stuart, Electress Palatine, Queen of Bohemia; A Romance*. New York: Houghton, Mifflin.

Heisler, Ron. 1989. "Michael Maier and England." In *The Hermetic Journal*. Edinburgh: Megalithic Research Publications.

———. 1989. "Robert Fludd: A Picture in Need of Expansion." In *The Hermetic Journal*. Edinburgh: Megalithic Research Publications.

———. 1990. "Two Worlds that Converged: Shakespeare and the Ethos of the Rosicrucians," In *The Hermetic Journal*. Edinburgh: Megalithic Research Publications.

Heninger, S. K. 1974. *Touches of Sweet Harmony: Pythagorean Cosmology and Renaissance Poetics*. San Marino, CA: Huntington Library Press.

Hessayon, Ariel. 2020. "'Teutonicus': Knowledge of Boehme among English Speakers before the English Civil War." *Daphnis* 48: 247–69.

Higgins, Godfrey. 1874. *Anacalypsis: An Attempt to Draw Aside the Veil of the Saitic Isis*. London: J. Burns.

Hogart, Ron Charles (Gilbert, Bennett). 1986. *Alchemy: A Comprehensive*

Bibliography of the Manly P. Hall Collection of Books and Manuscripts. Los Angeles: Philosophical Research Society.

Holtberg, Anthony. 2011. "Enochian Angel Magic: From John Dee to the Hermetic Order of the Golden Dawn." PhD dissertation, University of Exeter, UK.

Huffman, William. 1988. *Robert Fludd and the End of the Renaissance.* Oxfordshire, UK: Routledge.

———. 2001. *Robert Fludd: Essential Readings.* Berkeley, CA: North Atlantic Books.

Kamen, Henry. 1999. *Philip of Spain.* New Haven, CT: Yale University Press.

Kaminsky, Greg. 2010. "Esotericism in Early Pennsylvania: A Comparative Study of Rosicrucian Tendencies within Johannes Kelpius' Woman in the Wilderness Community and Johann Conrad Beissel's Ephrata Cloister." Academia.edu website.

———. 2011. "The Influence of Alchemy in Seventeenth-Century New England: A Historical Analysis of Alchemy in the Puritan Society of Massachusetts and Connecticut." Academia.edu website.

Keatinge, M. W. 1910. *The Great Didactic of John Amos Comenius.* New York: Russell & Russell.

Ketzan, Erik. 2019. "Borges and the Name of the Rose." Shipwreck Library website, September 4.

Kim, Younkyung. 2007. "Remembering Cynthia: The Legacy of Elizabeth I in the Poetry of Aemilia Lanyer and Diana Primrose." *Medieval and Early Modern English Studies* 15 (February).

Kronick, David. 2001. "The Commerce of Letters: Networks and 'Invisible Colleges' in Seventeenth- and Eighteenth-Century Europe." *The Library Quarterly* 71, no. 1.

Kupperman, Karen. 2000. *Indians and English: Facing Off in Early America.* Ithaca, NY: Cornell University Press.

Lambert, Nick. 2010. "Technology, Statecraft and the Soul: Themes emerging in Francis Bacon's The New Atlantis." Available on Academia.edu (website).

Lévi, Éliphas. 1913. *The History of Magic.* London: Rider.

Louv, Jason. 2018. *John Dee and the Empire of Angels: Enochian Magick and the Occult Roots of the Modern World.* Rochester, VT: Inner Traditions.

MacLeod, Catharine. 2012. The Lost Prince: The Life and Death of Henry Stuart. London: National Portrait Gallery.

Maier, Michael. 1617. *Symbola aureæ mensæ duodecim nationum.* Available on Internet Archive (website).

Marshall, Peter. 2006. *The Magic Circle of Rudolf II: Alchemy and Astrology in Renaissance Prague.* London: Walker Books.

McClean, Adam, and Daniel MacClean. 1979. "Bacstrom's Rosicrucian Society." In *The Hermetic Journal* No 6.

———, n.d. "Speculum sphicum rhodostauroticum: The 'Mirror of Wisdom' of Theophilus Schweighardt." Levity.com.

McIntosh, Christopher. 1972. *Eliphas Lévi and the French Occult Revival*. New York: Weiser.

———. 1998. *The Rosicrucians: The History, Mythology, and Rituals of an Esoteric Order*. York Beach, ME: Weiser Books.

———. 2021. "The Rosicrucian Diaspora in the Seventeenth Century." In *Innovation in Esotericism from the Renaissance to the Present*, 135–54. Edited by Georgiana D. Hedesan and Tim Rudbøog. Palgrave Studies in New Religions and Alternative Spiritualities, edited by James R. Lewis and Henrik Bogdan. New York: Palgrave Macmillan.

McKenna, Terence. 1996. "The Winter King, Fredrich V Elector Palatine." Lecture at Stoffwechsel, Mannheim, Kurpfalz, Germany, recorded during the filming of the *Coincidencia Oppositorum: A Union of Opposites* documentary.

Mitchell, Kenneth. 1994. "Musical Conceptions in the Hermetic Philosophy of Robert Fludd" 130–131. PhD dissertation, Washington University.

Montgomery, John Warwicke. 1973. *Cross and Crucible: Johann Valentin Andreae (1586–1654), Phoenix of the Theologians*. New York: Springer.

Moran, Bruce T. 1991. *The Alchemical World of the German Court: Occult Philosophy and Chemical Medicine in the Circle of Moritz of Hessen*. Stuttgart, Germany: Franz Steiner.

Morgan, Luke. 2007. *Nature as Model: Salomon de Caus and Early Seventeenth-Century Landscape Design*. Philadelphia: University of Pennsylvania Press.

Mosheim, Johann Lorenz. 1832. *Institutes of Ecclesiastical History: Ancient and Modern*. 4 vols. Translated by James Murdock. New York: Harper and Brothers.

———. 1842. *An Ecclesiastical History*. Translated by Archibald MacLaine. London: Thomas Tegg.

Nummedal, Tara. 2007. *Alchemy and Authority in the Holy Roman Empire*. Chicago: University of Chicago Press.

Oman, Carola. 1938. *The Winter Queen: Elizabeth of Bohemia*. London: Hodder.

Paglia, Camille. 2019. *Provocations: Collected Essays on Art, Feminism, Politics, Sex, and Education*. New York: Knopf Doubleday.

Parker, Geoffrey. 1997. *The Thirty Years' War*. Oxfordshire, UK: Routledge.

Pauli, W. 1955. "The Influence of Archetypal Ideas on the Scientific Theories of Kepler." In *The Interpretation of Nature and the Psyche: The Work of Carl*

Jung and Wolfgang Pauli, 147–212. Edited by Roderick Main. New York: Routledge & Kegan Paul.

Pelling, Nick. n.d. "The Secret History of the Rosicrucians." Cipher Mysteries website.

Penman, Leigh T. I. 2009. "The *Batavia* Legacy: Implications of the *Batavia* Shipwreck (1629)" in History and Imaginary." In *Imagined Australia: Reflections around the Reciprocal Construction of Identity between Australia and Europe.* Edited by Renata Summo-O'Connell. Bern, Switzerland: Peter Lang.

———. 2009. "'Sophistical Fancies and Mear Chimaeras'? Traiano Boccalini's 'Ragguagli Di Parnaso' and the Rosicrucian Enigma." *Bruniana & Campanelliana* 15, no. 1: 101–20.

Philalathes, Eugenius (Thomas Vaughan) translates Johann Valentin Andre. 1652. *The Fame and Confession of R: C: Commonly of the Rosie Cross with A Praeface Annexed Thereto and a Short Declaration of their Physicall Work.* London: Printed by J. M. for Giles Calvert.

Pike, Albert. 1871. *Morals and Dogma of the Ancient and Accepted Scottish Rite of Freemasonry.* Charleston, SC.

Purs, Ivo, and Vladimir Karpenko. 2016. *Alchemy and Rudolf ll: Exploring the Secrets of Nature in Central Europe in the 16th and 17th Centuries.* Prague: Artefactum.

Pursell, Brennan C. 2003. *The Winter King: Frederick V of the Palatinate and the Coming of the Thirty Years' War.* Farnham, UK: Ashgate.

Raleigh, Sir Walter. 1628. *The History of the World.* London: H. Lownes, G. Lathum, and R. Young. First published 1614.

Rait, Robert S., ed. 1902. *Five Stuart Princesses: Margaret of Scotland, Elizabeth of Bohemia, Mary of Orange, Henrietta of Orleans, Sophia of Hanover.* London: Constable.

Robinson, Samuel. 2011. *The Rosicrucian Tradition of the Golden Dawn.* Research Triangle, NC: Lulu.

———. 2021. *Alois Mailander: A Rosicrucian Remembered.* Lisle, IL: Pansophic Press.

Rochlin, Sheldon, and Morgan Harris, directors. 2008. *The Alchemical Dream: Rebirth of the Great Work* (film). Performed by Terence McKenna. Merrillville, IN: Mystic Fire Productions.

Ross, Josephine. 1979. *The Winter Queen: The Story of Elizabeth Stuart.* New York: St. Martin's Press.

Roth, Remo F. 2021. "Wolfgang Pauli: 'I Carry both Kepler and Fludd within Myself.'" Academia.edu website.

Rowse, A. L. (1977). *Homosexuals in History: Ambivalence in Society, Literature and the Arts*. New York: MacMillan.

Sabol, Andrew, ed. 1978. *Four Hundred Songs and Dances from the Stuart Masque: With a Supplement of Sixteen Additional Pieces*. Providence, RI: Brown University Press.

Salvadori, Stefania. 2014. "From Spiritual Regeneration to Collective Reformation in the Writings of Christoph Besold and Johann Valentin Andreae." *Aries* 14 (1).

Sanderson, William. 1658. *A Compleat History of the Life and Raigne of King Charles From His Cradle to His Grave*. Available on Internet Archive (website).

Savinainen, Antti. 2025. *Journey through the Visible and Invisible Cosmos: Perspectives from Rosicrucian Theosophy*. Ruusu-Ristin Kirjallisuusseura Ry.

Schick, Hans. 1942. *Das Ältere Rosenkreuzertum*. Berlin: Nordland-Verlag.

Schmidt-Biggemann, Wilhelm. 2007. "Robert Fludd's Kabbalistic Cosmos." In *Platonism at the Origins of Modernity*, edited by D. Hedley and S. Hutton. *International Archives of the History of Ideas*, vol. 196. Dordrecht: Springer.

Schuchard, Marsha Keith. 2023. "Dr. Sigismond Bacstrom and Alexander Tilloch: Scientific Explorers of the Twilight Zone between Rosicrucianism and Freemasonry." *Heredom* 31.

Schultz, Richard A. 2007. "The Essene Lineage in California: Carmelites and Rosicrucians at Carmel in 1602." *Rosicrucian Digest* 85, no. 2: 12–20.

Scott, Eva. 1900. *Rupert Prince Palatine*. New York: Putnam.

Scott, Walter. 1811. *Secret History of the Court of James the First*. Edinburgh, Scotland: Ballantyne.

Sédir, Paul. 1910. *Histoire des Rose-Croix*. Paris: Collection des Hérmetistes.

Selman, Ruth. 2018. "Royal Weddings in History: A Stuart Valentine." National Archives, United Kingdom.

Shapiro, Lisa, ed. 2007. *The Correspondence between Princess Elisabeth of Bohemia and René Descartes*. Chicago: University of Chicago Press.

Spoto, Stephanie. 2011. "John Dee's Conversations with Spirits and Problems with Practical Occultism." Daimonic Imagination: Uncanny Intelligence conference. University of Kent, Canterbury, Kent, UK, May 6–7.

Steiner, Rudolf. 2006. *Rosicrucianism Renewed: The Unity of Art, Science & Religion: The Theosophical Congress of Whitsun 1907*. SteinerBooks.

Stoyle, Mark. 2011. *The Black Legend of Prince Rupert's Dog: Witchcraft and Propaganda during the English Civil War*. Liverpool, UK: Liverpool University Press.

Student of Occultism (Anonymous). 1887. *An Adventure among the Rosicrucians.* Boston: Occult Publishing.

Szonyi, Gyorgy E. 2004. *John Dee's Occultism: Magical Exaltation through Powerful Signs.* Albany: State University of New York Press.

Szulakowska, Urszula. 2000. *The Alchemy of Light: Geometry and Optics in Late Renaissance Alchemical Illustration.* Leiden, Netherlands: Brill.

Takehara, Issei. 2012. "Sympathetic Magic, the Weapon Salve and the Powder of Sympathy in the 17th Century Europe." Isseicreekphilosophy (blog April 28).

Taylor, Charles. 2018. *A Secular Age.* Cambridge, MA: Belknap Press.

Thomas, Keith. 1973. *Religion and the Decline of Magic.* Harmondsworth, UK: Penguin.

Thompson, C. J. S. 1932. *The Lure and Romance of Alchemy.* London: George G. Harrap.

Tilton, Hereward. 2002. "Regni Christi Frater: Count Michael Maier and the Fraternity R.C." in *Aries* 2, no. 1.

———. 2003. *The Quest for the Phoenix: Spiritual Alchemy and Rosicrucianism in the Work of Count Michael Maier (1569–1622).* Berlin, Germany: De Gruyter.

———. 2014. "The Rosicrucian Manifestos and Early Rosicrucianism." In *The Occult World.* Oxfordshire, UK: Routledge.

Trevor-Roper, Hugh. 1960. "Three Foreigners and the Philosophy of the English Revolution" in *Encounter*, 14: 3–20.

Vaughan, Thomas. 1919. *The Works of Thomas Vaughan: Eugenius Philalethes.* Edited by Arthur Edward Waite. London: Theosophical Publishing House.

Vurm, Robert B. 1997. *Rudolph II and His Prague: Mysteries and Curiosities of Rudolfine Prague, 1550–1650.* Independently published.

Wachsmann, K. P. 1970. "A Drum from Seventeenth Century Africa." *Galpin Society Journal* 23: 97–103.

Waite, A. E. 1887. *The Real History of the Rosicrucians.* London: George Redway.

———. 1924. *The Brotherhood of the Rosy Cross.* London: William Rider & Son.

Wedgwood, C. V. 1982. *The Thirty Years War.* Oxfordshire, UK: Routledge Kegan & Paul.

Weeks, Andrew. 1991. *Boehme: An Intellectual Biography of the Seventeenth Century Philosopher and Mystic.* Albany: State University of New York Press.

Weichenhan, Michael. 2010. Review of "Robert Fludd. Der Versuch einer hermetischen Alternative zur neuzeitlichen Naturwissenschaft." *Early Science and Medicine* 15, no. 3: 305–6.

Westcott, Dr. W. Wynn, Supreme Magus, IX°. 1915. *The Rosicrucians Past and Present, at Home and Abroad.* Yorkshire: Societas Rosicruciana in Anglia

White, Ralph, ed. 1999. *The Rosicrucian Enlightenment Revisited*. Great Barrington, MA: Lindisfarne Books.

Wilder, Alexander. 1880. "The Brethren of the Rosy Cross." *Theosophist* 1, no. 5 (February): 108–11.

Willard, Thomas. 1983. "The Rosicrucian Manifestos in Britain." *Papers of the Bibliographical Society of America* 77, no. 4.

——. 2013. "The Strange Journey of Christian Rosencreutz." In *East Meets West in the Middle Ages and Early Modern Times: Transcultural Experiences in the Premodern World*, edited by Albrecht Classen. Berlin, Boston: De Gruyter.

——. 2017. "Dreams and Symbols in the Chemical Wedding." In *Lux in Tenebris: The Visual and the Symbolic in Western Esotericism*, 130–51. Edited by Peter J. Forshaw. Leiden, Netherlands: Brill.

——. 2022. *Thomas Vaughan and the Rosicrucian Revival in Britain: 1648–1666*. Leiden, Netherlands: Brill.

Wilson, Peter. 2009. *The Thirty Years War: Europe's Tragedy*. Cambridge, MA: Harvard University Press.

Wither, George. 1633. *Epithalamia or Nuptiall Poems Upon the most blessed and happy marriage between the High and Mightie Prince Frederick the Fifth, Count Palatine of the Rhein, Duke of Bauier, etc. and the most Virtuous, Gracious, and thrice-Excellent Princess Elizabeth, sole daughter to our dread sovereign James, By the Grace of God, King of Great Britain*. London: R. Badger for R. Allot.

Wyatt, Matthew. 1856. *Notices of Sculpture in Ivory: Consisting of a Lecture on the History, Methods, and Chief Productions of the Art*. London: Office of the Arundel Society.

Yates, Frances. 1975a. *The Rosicrucian Enlightenment*. Oxfordshire, UK: Routledge.

——. 1975b. *Shakespeare's Last Plays: A New Approach*. Oxfordshire, UK: Routledge.

Yoder, Russell. 2005. *Light Dawning: Gichtel, Boehme, Ephrata, and the Origin of Rosicrucian Mysticism in the New World*. Sequim, WA: Holmes.

——. trans. 2024. *Sisters of the Rosy Cross; or, Short Discovery of these Ladies, and what Religion, Knowledge of Divine and Natural Things, Trades and Arts, Medicines, &c., may be found therein*. Nonthaburi, Thailand: Radiant Ra. First published 1620.

Zika, Charles. 2003. *Exorcising Our Demons: Magic, Witchcraft, and Visual Culture in Early Modern Europe*. Studies in Medieval and Reformation Traditions. Leiden, Netherlands: Brill.

Zuber, Mike A. 2021. *Spiritual Alchemy: From Jacob Boehme to Mary Anne Atwood*. New York: Oxford University Press.

Index